PENGUIN ACA

Sociology as a Life or Death Issue

ROBERT J. BRYM

University of Toronto

Toronto

Library and Archives Canada Cataloguing in Publication

Brym, Robert J., 1951–
   Sociology as a life or death issue / Robert J. Brym.

Includes bibliographical references and index.

ISBN-13: 978-0-205-50376-6
ISBN-10: 0-205-50376-4

   1. Sociology. I. Title.

HM585.B79 2008   301   C2006-905714-1

ISBN-13: 978-0-205-50376-6
ISBN-10: 0-205-50376-4

Editor-in-Chief, Vice-President of Sales: Kelly Shaw
Acquisitions Editor: Ky Pruesse
Executive Marketing Manager: Judith Allen
Developmental Editor: Patti Altridge
Production Editors: Valerie Adams and Laura Neves
Copy Editor: Valerie Adams
Proofreader: Susan Broadhurst
Production Coordinators: Sharlene Ross and Christine Kwan
Composition: Laserwords
Photo & Permissions Research: Sandy Cooke
Art Director: Julia Hall
Cover Design: Chris Tsintziras
Interior Design: Chris Tsintziras
Cover Image: Corbis

1 2 3 4 5   12 11 10 09 08
Printed and bound in Canada.

In memory of my mother
Sophie Brym (1912–2004)

שפרה מרים ברים, אשת-חיל

ז״ל

Contents

List of Figures and Tables

Figures

Tables

Preface

Sociology at its best speaks to the big issues of the day and the big issues of life but it often fails to speak plainly enough to reach a broad audience. My aim in writing this little book is to speak plainly about the urgent need to think sociologically. Sociological understanding, I argue, is a life or death issue.

I don't make that claim for dramatic effect. I mean it literally. By helping us understand the social causes of death, sociology can help us figure out how to live better. Hence the urgency of sociological knowledge.

I develop my argument in five linked essays. In the title essay I argue that it is useful to keep in mind the inevitability of death because doing so compels us to focus on how best to live in our remaining time. I then outline how higher education in general and the sociological perspective in particular can contribute to that goal.

The next three chapters add substance to the assertions of the opening essay. I examine death due to violence and death due to supposedly natural disasters and find that in both cases powerful social forces help to determine who lives and who dies. To make my case, I enter three worlds that figure prominently in popular culture and the evening news—those of American hip hop, Palestinian suicide bombers, and the victims of hurricanes in the Caribbean region and the coast of the Gulf of Mexico.

Many undergraduates want to know what sociology is and what they can do with a sociology degree. In the concluding essay, I draw on material from the preceding chapters to sketch the broad outlines of the discipline and offer career advice to undergraduates. I argue that my analyses of the social causes of death illustrate the fundamental aim of sociology at its best: to help people enjoy longer and happier lives.

Acknowledgments

Authors often say that they alone bear responsibility for their work. For two reasons, I make no such claim here.

First, I am a sociologist, and I therefore delight in acknowledging that I am embedded in intellectual and publishing networks whose members have helped to shape my work. I gladly share with them a full measure of responsibility for this book's strengths and weaknesses. Among the co-owners of this volume are colleagues who read and offered critical comments on all or part of the manuscript and provided useful bibliographic assistance: Bader Araj (University of Toronto), Shyon Baumann (University of Toronto), John Kirk (Dalhousie University), Rodney Kueneman (University of Manitoba), Rhonda Lenton (York University), Malcolm Mackinnon (University of Toronto), Adie Nelson (University of Waterloo), Susan Robertson (University of Saskatchewan), Carmen James Schifellite (Ryerson University), and Jack Veugelers (University of Toronto). Also culpable are the members of the editorial, marketing, and production team at Pearson Canada, who saw the value of my initial proposal and offered much encouragement and useful critical advice: Valerie Adams, Judith Allen, Patti Altridge, Sally Aspinall, Laura Neves, Ky Pruesse, Patty Riediger, and Michael Young. I hope you all feel that the final product justifies your deeply appreciated efforts.

A journalist once asked the great Jewish poet Chaim Nachman Bialik (1873–1934) whether he preferred speaking Hebrew or Yiddish. Bialik answered in Yiddish: *"Hebraish ret man, ober Yiddish ret sikh alein"* ("Hebrew one speaks, but Yiddish speaks by itself"). I understand what he meant. Like all authors, I have struggled mightily on many occasions to get things right. This time, however, the job was almost effortless. That is the second reason I don't claim sole responsibility for this book: it practically wrote itself.

Robert J. Brym

Toronto

Instructor Supplements

Instructors will be able to make use of the online **Test Item File and PowerPoint Presentation** for *Sociology as a Life or Death Issue,* Canadian Edition. These supplements can be downloaded by instructors from a password-protected location on Pearson Education Canada's online catalogue (vig.pearsoned.ca). Simply search for the text, and then click on "Instructor" under "Resources" in the left-hand menu. Contact your local sales representative for further information.

About the Author

Robert J. Brym (www.chass.utoronto.ca/brym) is Professor of Sociology at the University of Toronto. He has published widely on politics and society in Russia and Canada, and has recently shifted his attention to the Middle East. He is currently conducting research with Israeli and Palestinian sociologists on collective violence during the second *intifada* (2000–2005). Brym's popular introductory sociology textbook, *Sociology: Your Compass for a New World* (with John Lie), has been published in American, Canadian, and Brazilian editions, with Australian, Japanese, and Turkish editions planned. He began teaching introductory sociology immediately after graduate school and can't stop.

Professor Brym is the 2007 winner of the Northrop Frye Award, given by the University of Toronto to recognize faculty members who have set themselves apart through innovation in teaching and commitment to conveying the excitement and importance of research to students.

Source: Alex Colville, *Pacific*, 1967, acrylic on hardboard, Copyright A.C. Fine Art Inc.

1

Sociology as a Life or Death Issue¹

A Detour

To inspire you, I will take the unusual course of talking about death. I apologize in advance if this makes you uncomfortable. I know it is customary when addressing university students to remind them that they are young, have accomplished much, and are now in a position to make important decisions that will shape the rest of their lives. I will eventually get around to that too. But to arrive at the optimistic and uplifting part, I feel I must take a detour through the valley of the shadow of death.

When I was seven years old, I lived across the street from a park where I engaged in all the usual childhood games with my friends. We played tag, hide-and-seek, baseball, and cops-and-robbers. We also invented a game that we awkwardly called "See Who Drops Dead the Best." We would line ourselves up on a park bench and choose one boy to shoot the rest of us in turn, using a tree branch as a machine gun. Once shot, we did our best to scream, fall to the ground, writhe, convulse, and expire. The shooter would choose the most convincing victim—the boy who dropped

---

¹ This is an expanded version of a commencement address delivered in May 2005 to graduates of the "Steps to University" Program, University of Toronto. "Steps to University" identifies promising senior high school students who might otherwise not complete school or attend college or university because of their economic and social situation and offers them selected university courses to encourage them to pursue post-secondary education.

dead the best—to play shooter in the next round. The game would occupy us for ten minutes or so, after which we'd pick ourselves up and move on to baseball. At the age of seven, death was entertaining.

I didn't live in a war zone and there were no deaths in my family, so I really didn't begin to take death personally until I was 15. Then, one Sunday evening, it quite suddenly dawned on me that someday I would really die, losing consciousness forever. The moment this realization hit, I ran to my parents in panic. I rudely switched off the TV and asked them to tell me immediately why we were living if we were going to die anyway. My parents looked at each other, stunned, and then smiled nervously, perhaps thinking their son had taken leave of his senses. They were not especially religious people and they had only a few years of elementary schooling between them. They had no idea how to address questions about the meaning of life. Eventually, my father confessed he didn't know the answer to my question, whereupon I ran to my bedroom, shouting that my parents were fools to have lived half a century without even knowing why they were alive. From that moment and for the next three decades, death became a source of anxiety for me.

Denial

And so it is for most adolescents and adults. We all know that we might die at any moment. This knowledge makes most of us anxious. Typically, we react to our anxiety by denying death. To a degree, denying death helps us to calm ourselves.

The denial of death takes many forms. One is religious. Religion offers us immortality, the promise of better times to come, and the security of benevolent spirits who look over us. It provides meaning and purpose in a world that might otherwise seem cruel and senseless (James, 1976: 123, 139).

In one of its extreme forms, religion becomes what philosophers call **determinism**—the belief that everything happens the way it does because it was destined to happen in just that way. From the determinist's viewpoint, we can't really choose how to live because forces larger than us control life. Even religions that say we can choose between good and evil are somewhat deterministic because they guarantee eternal life only if we choose to do good; and that requires submitting to the will of God as defined by some authority, not us. Many people worry less about death because they believe that the reward for submitting to the will of God is eternal life in heaven.[2]

A second way in which we calm our anxiety about death involves trying to stay young. Consider the cosmetic surgery craze. Every week, millions of North Americans watch *Nip/Tuck*, *The Swan*, *Extreme Makeover*, and other popular TV series about cosmetic surgery. Every year, millions of North Americans undergo cosmetic surgical procedures (including dermabrasion and Botox injections). In 2005 alone, 10.5 million plastic surgeries were performed in North America, up nearly 2500 percent since 1992, when statistics were first collected (American Society of Plastic Surgeons, 2006). And that's not all we do to stay young. We diet. We exercise. We take vitamin supplements. We wear makeup. We dye our hair. We strive for stylishness in our dress. We celebrate youthfulness and vitality in movies, music, and advertising. We even devalue the elderly and keep them segregated in nursing homes and hospitals, in part so we won't be constantly reminded of our own mortality.

The search for eternal youth is a form of what philosophers call **voluntarism**, the belief that we alone control our destiny. From the voluntarist's point of view, we can overcome forces larger than us and thereby make whatever we want of our lives. Thus, many people worry less about death because they delude themselves into thinking they can cheat it.

A Trap

Ladies and gentlemen, I have good news and bad news for you, and I'm going to deliver the bad news first. The bad news is that the denial of death is a trap. Denying death makes it more difficult to figure out how to live well and thus be happy.

Let's say, for example, that a religion promises you eternal life in exchange for obeying certain rules. One rule says you can marry people only of your own religion. Another says that once you marry, you can't divorce. A third severely limits the steps you can take to

---

[2] Secular versions of determinism also exist. Various forms of nationalism and communism promise a heavenly future for certain nations or classes. Paradoxically, however, they require that individuals submit to a higher party or state authority and act in prescribed ways if they hope to achieve what is supposedly historically inevitable (Berlin, 2002a).

control the number of children you have. A fourth says you have to marry someone of the opposite sex. Many people live comfortably under the guidance of these rules but the rules happen to make others miserable. That, however, is the price they must pay for the religion's promise of eternal life. In general, by denying people the opportunity to figure out and do what is best for them as individuals, the deterministic denial of death can make some people deeply unhappy.

So can the voluntaristic denial of death. In the TV series *Nip/Tuck*, plastic surgeons Christian Troy and Sean McNamara begin each consultation with these words: "Tell me what you don't like about yourself." Notice they don't ask prospective patients what they dislike about their bodies. They ask them what they dislike about their selves. They assume that your body faithfully represents your self—that your weight, proportions, colour, scars, and hairiness say something fundamentally important about your character, about who you are. If, however, we believe our happiness depends on our physical perfection and youthfulness, we are bound to be unhappy because nobody can be perfect and because we will inevitably grow old and die. And in the meantime, pursuing youthfulness in the belief that you are no more than your appearance distracts you from probing deeply and finding out who you really are and what you need from life to make you happy. I conclude that denying death for whatever reason prevents you from figuring out how to live in the way that is best for you.[3]

Higher Education

Finally, some good news: You don't have to deny death and thus become distracted from figuring out what you need to do to live a happy life. Instead, you can try to remain aware that you will die and that you could die at any moment. That awareness will inevitably cause you to focus on how best to achieve a meaningful life in your remaining time: the kind of career you need to pursue to make you happiest, the kind of person you need to develop a long-term intimate relationship with, the way you can best contribute to the welfare of

---

[3] Some scientists believe we will conquer death before this century is over by developing the ability to upload our minds to robots (Kurzweil, 1999). If that happens, I may have plenty of time to revise my argument accordingly.

others, the political principles you should follow, and so forth. As an old saying goes, the gallows in the morning focuses the mind wonderfully (Frankl, 1959).

I have more good news. People are well equipped to figure out how best to live. That is because we are meaning-creating machines. Faced with ambiguity in any social setting, we instantly start investing imaginative energy to define the situation and figure out what is expected of us and others. We abhor uncertainty, so we always strive to make social reality meaningful (Berger and Luckmann, 1966). And since there is nothing more uncertain or ambiguous than death, when we face awareness of our own mortality we almost instinctively want to create a durable purpose for our lives (Becker, 1971; 1973). In fact, we are so devoted to making life meaningful that we have created an institution especially devoted to helping us discover what the good life is for each of us: the system of higher education.

I imagine your parents and teachers have told you to stay in school as long as you can because a degree is a ticket to a good job. They are right, at least in part. A stack of studies shows that each additional year of education will increase your annual income for the rest of your life. Moreover, the economic value of education increases year after year (Appleby, Fougère, and Rouleau, 2004). But the view that colleges and universities are just places for job training is a half-truth. Above all, the system of higher education was developed as a place devoted to the discovery, by rational means, of truth, beauty, and the good life. Said differently, if you treat higher education not just as job training but as a voyage of self-discovery, you will increase your chance of finding out what you value in life, what you can achieve, and how you can achieve it.

Colleges and universities are divided into different departments, centres, schools, and faculties, each with a different approach to improving the welfare of humanity. The physician heals; the instructor in physical education teaches how to improve strength, stamina, and vigour; and the philosopher demonstrates the value of living an examined life. A good undergraduate education will expose you to many different approaches to improving your welfare and that of humanity as a whole and will give you a chance to discover which of them suits you.

What does the sociological approach offer?

Sociology

The sociological approach to improving human welfare is based on the idea that the relations we have with other people create opportunities for us to think and act but also set limits on our thoughts and actions. Accordingly, we can better understand what we are and what we can become by studying the social relations that help shape us.

A classic illustration of the sociological approach to understanding the world and improving human welfare is Émile Durkheim's late-nineteenth-century study of suicide in France (Durkheim, 1951 [1897]; Hamlin and Brym, 2006). Most people think that suicide is the most nonsocial and antisocial action imaginable, a result of deep psychological distress that is typically committed in private and involves a rejection of society and everything it stands for. Yet Durkheim showed that high rates of psychological distress often do not result in a high suicide rate, while low rates of psychological distress sometimes do. He also argued that the rate and type of suicide that predominates in a society tells us something fundamentally important about the state of the society as a whole.[4]

According to Durkheim, the probability that your state of mind will lead you to suicide is influenced by the social relations in which you are embedded—in particular, the frequency with which you interact with others and the degree to which you share their beliefs, values, and moral standards. Durkheim referred to the frequency of interaction and the degree of sharing of beliefs, values, and morals in a group as its level of **social solidarity**. Figure 1.1 illustrates Durkheim's theory.

Simplifying for brevity's sake, Durkheim analyzed the effects of three levels of social solidarity on suicide rates (for more details, see the note accompanying Figure 1.1):

- *Low solidarity.* According to Durkheim, groups and societies characterized by a low level of social solidarity typically have a high

---

[4] Dividing the number of times an event occurs (e.g., the number of suicides in a certain place and period) by the total number of people to whom the event could occur in principle (e.g., the number of people in that place and period) and then calculating how many times it would occur in a population of standard size (e.g., 100 000) will give you the **rate** at which an event occurs. Rates let you compare groups of different size. For instance, if 2 suicides occur in a town of 10 000 people and 4 suicides occur in a city of 100 000 people, the suicide rate is 20 per 100 000 in the town and 4 per 100 000 in the city.

Figure 1.1 *Durkheim's Theory of Suicide*

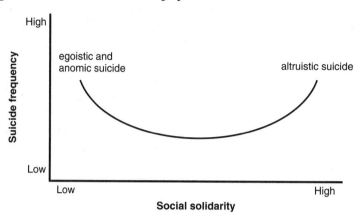

Note: Durkheim argued that as the level of social solidarity increases, the suicide rate declines. Then, beyond a certain point, it starts to rise. Hence, the U-shaped curve in this graph. Durkheim called suicides that occur in high-solidarity settings **altruistic**. In contrast, suicide that occurs in low-solidarity settings is egoistic or anomic. **Egoistic suicide** results from a lack of integration of the individual into society because of weak social ties to others. **Anomic suicide** occurs when norms governing behaviour become vaguely defined.

suicide rate. Interacting infrequently and sharing few beliefs, values, and moral standards, people in low-solidarity settings lack emotional support and cultural guidelines for behaviour. They are therefore more prone to commit suicide if they experience distress. Accordingly, Durkheim found that married adults were half as likely as unmarried adults to commit suicide because marriage typically created social ties and a moral cement that bound individuals to society. He found that women were only a third as likely as men to commit suicide because they were generally more involved in the intimate social relations of family life. Jews were less likely to commit suicide than Christians because centuries of persecution had turned them into a group that was more defensive and tightly knit. Elderly people were more prone than young and middle-aged people to take their own lives when faced with misfortune because they were most likely to live alone, to have lost a spouse, and to lack a job and a wide network of friends. On a broader, historical canvas, Durkheim viewed rising suicide rates as a symptom of the state of modern society. In general, social ties are weakening, he argued, and people share fewer beliefs, values, and moral standards than they used to.

- *Intermediate solidarity.* It follows that if we want suicide rates to decline, we must figure out ways of increasing the strength of social ties and shared culture in modern society. For example, if North Americans created a system of high-quality, universally accessible daycare, then more children would be better supervised, enjoy more interaction with peers and adults, and be exposed to similar socializing influences. At the same time, more adults (particularly single mothers) would be able to work in the paid labour force and form new social ties with their workmates. By thus raising the level of social solidarity, we would expect the suicide rate to drop.

- *High solidarity.* Despite a *general* decline in social solidarity, some groups are characterized by exceptionally high levels of social solidarity. When members of such a group perceive that the group is threatened, they are likely to be willing to sacrifice their lives to protect it. For instance, a soldier who is a member of a close-knit military unit may throw himself on a grenade that is about to explode to protect his buddies. Similarly, some suicide bombers see the existence of their group threatened by a foreign power occupying their homeland. They are willing to give up their lives to coerce the occupying power into leaving (Pape, 2005). The increased rate of suicide bombing in the world since the early 1980s is in part a symptom of increasing threats posed to high-solidarity groups by foreign occupying forces. It follows that if we want fewer suicide bombings, one thing we can do is to figure out ways of ensuring that high-solidarity groups feel less threatened.

Much of the best sociological research today follows Durkheim's example. Sociologists frequently strive to identify (1) a type of behaviour that for personal, political, or intellectual reasons they regard as interesting or important, (2) the specifically social forces—the patterns of social relations among people—that influence that behaviour, and

(3) the larger institutional, political, or other changes that might effectively improve human welfare with respect to the behaviour of interest. By conducting research that identifies these three elements, sociologists help people understand what they are and what they can become in particular social and historical contexts (Mills, 1959).

Winning the Game

You have accomplished much and you are now in a position to make important decisions that will shape the rest of your life. At this threshold, I challenge you not to be seduced by popular ways of denying death. I challenge you to remain aware that life is short and that by getting a higher education you will have the opportunity to figure out how to live in a way that will make you happiest. I personally hope you find sociology enlightening in this regard. But more importantly, you should know that higher education in general ought to encourage you to play the game of "See Who Lives Life the Best." You will be declared a winner if you play the game seriously. Socrates once said to his pupils that "What we're engaged in here isn't a chance conversation but a dialogue about the way we ought to live our lives." Accept nothing less from your professors.

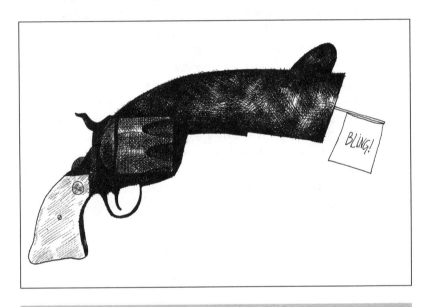

Source: Drawing © Copyright 2006 Jonathan Twingley.

2

Hip Hop from Caps to Bling[1]

Strolling Down the Avenue

In January 2006, my wife and I were attending a conference in New York. One afternoon we decided to take a break and walk over to Central Park. The weather was unusually pleasant for the time of year, and we enjoyed people-watching and window-shopping until we reached the pricey stores on Fifth Avenue. There, a barricade manned by two of New York's finest stopped our progress. About 10 metres farther down the street, a second barricade blocked pedestrian traffic flowing in the opposite direction. The barricades cleared a space in front of Salvatore Ferragamo's flagship store, famous for its thousand-dollar shoes, stylish handbags, and other must-have accessories for the well-to-do.

Two black Lincoln Navigators were parked in front of the store. A high-tech garden of antennas and satellite dishes sprouted from the roof of one of them. Its tinted windows were shut. The windows of the second Navigator were wide open, and we could clearly see the driver and three other men inside, all clad in black. The passengers held AK-47 assault rifles upright. They wanted us to notice them. Two tall, athletic-looking men in suits, white shirts, ties, and well-tailored overcoats stood on

[1] Part of this chapter first appeared online as "Hip Hop from Dissent to Commodity" at http://www.societyinquestion4e.nelson.com/article1.html. © Robert Brym.

either side of the store's front doors, their eyes roaming the crowd. Each had his right hand inside his overcoat, presumably gripping a firearm. About half a dozen police vans and cruisers were blocking vehicular traffic. Police officers stood outside their cruisers. Whatever emergency was in progress, an intimidating company of about two dozen well-armed men was positioned to deal with it.

"Hey!" I said to one of the men in blue. "Did you guys catch Osama or something?"

The police officer suppressed a smile. "Not yet," he replied.

"So what's up?" I persisted.

"Can't say."

"Aw, come on. You can't stop all these taxpayers from enjoying the nice weather without an explanation. What's the occasion?"

"I guess Puffy needs a new tie."

"You mean Diddy, the hip hop artist?"

"Whatever."

In hip hop slang, "caps" are bullets and "bling" is flashy jewellery, as in "You don' hand over dat bling, I'ma bust a cap in yo' ass." Caps are the means, bling is the goal, as in the title of 50 Cent's movie *Get Rich or Die Tryin'*. There was no slaughter on Fifth Avenue that fine January day, but I have to admit that, like the rest of the crowd, my wife and I were captivated by the staged threat of violence and the spectacle of material excess offered by Diddy's shopping excursion. We knew the show was contrived for publicity—Diddy is not the president of the United States and Fifth Avenue is not the inner city—but we were still excited to be close to the biggest revolution in youth culture since rock and roll, a revolution that unites death and wealth in a troubled marriage.

1.8 Million Black Men Are Missing

Nobody should be surprised that a popular subculture rooted in the lives of African-American men focuses so tightly on violence and death. About a third of African-American households enjoy annual incomes of US$50 000 a year or more, but for the roughly one-quarter of African Americans who live in poverty, violence and death are a big part of everyday life.

One indicator of the disproportionate amount of violence faced by African-American men is the **sex ratio**, the number of men per 100 women in a population. In most of the world, the sex ratio is about 96. There are about 96 white American men for every 100 white American women, for example. More men than women work in dangerous jobs and engage in high-risk behaviour such as smoking and excessive alcohol consumption. Besides, women are the hardier sex, biologically speaking. That's why there are fewer men than women in most populations.[2]

Among African Americans, however, the sex ratio is less than 87, an extraordinarily low figure. Assuming that a sex ratio of 96 is normal, we can conclude that 9 black men are missing for every 100 black women (since 96 minus 87 equals 9). Given 19.3 million black women in the United States in 2004, that works out to about 1.8 million missing black men. In 2004 there were 16.7 million black men in the United States but there should have been 18.5 million (calculated from U.S. Census Bureau, 2006).

Many missing black men died violently. The **homicide rate** is the number of murders per 100 000 people in a population. The black male homicide rate in the United States was nearly 39 in 2003, but reached about 60 in Illinois, Louisiana, and Pennsylvania. In contrast, the homicide rate was 5.7 for the United States as a whole and 1.7 for Canada. Figure 2.1 plots the homicide rate for black men against the black sex ratio for each U.S. state. It shows that in states where few black men are murdered, there are more black men than black women. But in states where many black men are murdered, there are many fewer black men than black women.[3]

In 2003, nearly 6000 more black men than black women were murdered in the United States. But homicide is not the only cause of excess deaths among black men. In addition, about 4000 more black men than black women died accidentally, mainly due to car accidents and drug overdoses. About 2500 more black men than black women died of AIDS, and about 1000 more black men than black women committed

---

[2] There are important exceptions. In Asia and North Africa, women suffer markedly poorer access to food and health services than men. Moreover, in China, India, Singapore, Taiwan, and South Korea, ultrasound tests are widely used to determine the sex of babies before birth, and abortion of female fetuses is common. In such countries, the ratio of men to women is unusually high—about 106 (Brym and Lie, 2007: 588; Sen, 1990; 2001).

[3] In Figure 2.1 and several other graphs in the book I include a "trend line" that summarizes the relationship between the two variables in the graph. Technically, the trend line is known as the **least-squares regression line**. It is a straight line in a two-dimensional graph that is drawn so as to minimize the sum of the squared perpendicular distances between each data point and the line itself.

Figure 2.1 *Male Homicide and the Sex Ratio, African Americans, 2003*

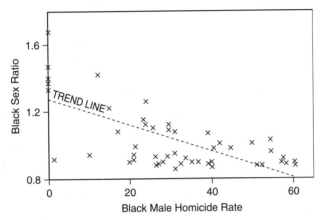

Sources: National Center for Injury Prevention and Control, 2006. "WISQARS Leading Causes of Death Reports, 1999–2003," on the World Wide Web at http://webappa.cdc.govsasweb/ncipc/leadcaus10.htm (accessed 15 April 2006); U.S. Census Bureau, 2006. "Entire Data Set." On the World Wide Web at http://www.census.gov/popest/datasets.html (accessed 15 April 2006).

Note: The black male homicide rate is the number of black men murdered per 100 000 black men in each state. The black male/female sex ratio is the number of black men divided by the number of black women in each state. Montana and Wyoming have been omitted because they are outliers and accounted for just 4 black homicides out of 7083 in the United States in 2003.

suicide (calculated from National Center for Injury Prevention and Control, 2006; see Kubrin, Wadsworth, and DiPietro, 2006). These figures oblige us to conclude that the destruction of the lives of poor African-American men by violence and high-risk behaviour is horrifyingly routine. It is therefore to be expected that violence and death would form central themes in their cultural expression.

Social Origins of Hip Hop

The situation of the African-American community as a whole has improved since the 1960s. The civil rights movement created new educational, housing, and job opportunities for African Americans and resulted in the creation of a substantial black middle class. The United States became a more tolerant and less discriminatory society. Yet in the midst of overall improvement, the situation of the roughly one-quarter of African Americans who live in poverty became bleaker.

After World War II, and especially in the 1960s, millions of southern blacks migrated to northern and western cities. Many were unable to find jobs. In some census tracts in Detroit, Chicago, Baltimore, and Los Angeles, black unemployment ranged from 26 to 41 percent in 1960. Many of the migrants were single women under the age of 25. Many had children but lacked a husband and a high school diploma.

The race riots of the 1960s helped to persuade the government to launch a "war on poverty" that increased the welfare rolls. In 1973, the American poverty rate fell to 11.1 percent, its lowest point ever. After 1973, however, everything went downhill. Manufacturing industries left the inner city for suburban or foreign locales, where land values were lower and labour was less expensive. In the three decades following 1973, the proportion of the American labour force employed in industry fell from about one-third to one-fifth. Unemployment among African-American youth rose to more than 40 percent. Middle-class blacks left the inner city for the suburbs. The migration robbed the remaining young people of successful role models. It also eroded the taxing capacity of municipal governments, leading to a decline in public services. Meanwhile, the American public elected conservative governments at the state and federal levels. They cut school and welfare budgets, thus deepening the destitution of ghetto life (Piven and Cloward, 1977: 264–361; 1993; Wilson, 1987).

With few legitimate prospects for advancement, poor African Americans turned increasingly to crime and, in particular, the drug trade. In the late 1970s, cocaine was expensive and demand for the drug was flat. So in the early 1980s, Colombia's Medellin drug cartel introduced a less expensive form of cocaine called "rock" or "crack." Crack was not only inexpensive—it also offered a quick and intense high, and it was highly addictive. Crack cocaine offered many people a temporary escape from hopelessness and soon became wildly popular in the inner city. Turf wars spread as gangs tried to outgun each other for control of the local traffic. The sale and use of crack became so widespread it corroded much of what was left of the inner-city African-American community (Davis, 1990).

The shocking conditions described above gave rise to a shocking musical form: hip hop. Stridently at odds with the values and tastes of both whites and middle-class African Americans, hip hop described and glorified the mean streets of the inner city while holding the police, the mass media, and other pillars of society in utter contempt. Furthermore, hip hop tried to offend middle-class sensibilities, black and white, by using highly offensive language.

In 1988, more than a decade after its first stirrings, hip hop reached its political high point with the release of the album *It Takes a Nation to Hold Us Back* by Chuck D and Public Enemy. In "Don't Believe the Hype," Chuck D (Carlton Douglas Ridenhour) accused the mass media of maliciously distributing lies. In "Black Steel in the Hour of Chaos," he charged the FBI and the CIA with assassinating the two great leaders of the African-American community in the 1960s, Martin Luther King and Malcolm X. In "Party for Your Right to Fight," he blamed the U.S. government for organizing the fall of the Black Panthers, the radical black nationalist party of the 1960s. Here, it seemed, was an angry expression of subcultural revolt that could not be mollified.

Hip Hop Transformed

However, there were elements in hip hop that soon transformed it (Bayles, 1994: 341–62; Neal, 1999: 144–8). For one thing, early, radical hip hop was not written as dance music. It therefore cut itself off from a large audience. Moreover, hip hop entered a self-destructive phase with the emergence of gangster rap, which extolled criminal lifestyles, denigrated women, and replaced politics with drugs, guns, and machismo. The release of "Cop Killer" by Ice T (Tracy Marrow) in 1992 provoked strong political opposition from Republicans and Democrats, white church groups, and black middle-class associations. "Cop Killer" was not hip hop, but it fuelled a reaction against all anti-establishment music. Time/Warner was forced to withdraw the song from circulation. The sense that hip hop had reached a dead end, or at least a turning point, grew in 1996, when rapper Tupac Shakur (Parish Crooks) was murdered in the culmination of a feud between two hip hop record labels, Death Row in Los Angeles and Bad Boy in New York (Springhall, 1998: 149–51).

If these events made it seem that hip hop was self-destructing, the police and insurance industries helped to speed up its demise. In 1988, a group called Niggas with Attitude released "Fuck the Police," a critique of police violence against black youth. Law enforcement officials in several cities dared the group to perform the song in public, threatening to detain the performers or shut down their shows.

Increasingly thereafter, ticket holders at hip hop concerts were searched for drugs and weapons, and security was tightened. Insurance companies, afraid of violence, substantially raised insurance rates for hip hop concerts, making them a financial risk. Soon, the number of venues willing to sponsor hip hop concerts dwindled.

While the developments noted above did much to mute the political force of hip hop, the seduction of big money did more. As early as 1982, with the release of Grandmaster Flash and the Furious Five's "The Message," hip hop began to win acclaim from mainstream rock music critics. With the success of Run-D.M.C. and Public Enemy in the late 1980s, it became clear there was a big audience for hip hop. Significantly, much of that audience was composed of white youths. As one music critic wrote, they "relished ... the subversive 'otherness' that the music and its purveyors represented" (Neal, 1999: 144). Sensing the opportunity for profit, major media corporations, such as Time/Warner, Sony, CBS/Columbia, and BMG Entertainment, signed distribution deals with the small independent recording labels that had formerly been the exclusive distributors of hip hop CDs. In 1988, *Yo! MTV Raps* debuted. The program brought hip hop to middle America.

Most hip hop recording artists proved they were eager to forego political relevancy for commerce. For instance, WU-Tang Clan started a line of clothing called WU Wear, and, with the help of major hip hop recording artists, companies as diverse as Tommy Hilfiger, Timberland, Starter, and Versace began to market clothing influenced by ghetto styles. Independent labels, such as Phat Farm and FUBU, also prospered. The members of Run-D.M.C. once said that they "don't want nobody's name on my behind" but those days were long past. By the early 1990s, hip hop was no longer just a musical form but a commodity with spin-offs. Rebellion had been turned into mass consumption.

Diddy

No rapper has done a better job of turning rebellion into a commodity than Sean John Combs, better known as Puff Daddy, later as P. Diddy, and, as of 2005, Diddy. Diddy was born into a middle-class family in a New York suburb, became an avid Boy Scout, attended private school, played high school football, and then enrolled in Washington D.C.'s

Howard University, the leading black university in the United States. Yet, despite his background, he seems to promote rebellion. For example, the liner notes for his 1999 CD, *Forever*, advertise his magazine, *Notorious*, as follows: "*Notorious* magazine presents provocative profiles of rebels, rulebreakers and mavericks—Notorious people who are changing the world with their unique brand of individuality.... In essence, *Notorious* is for everyone who wants to live a sexy, daring life— a life that makes a difference" (Combs, 1999). Thus, although he says he's committed to changing the world, Diddy encourages only individual acts of rebellion, not radical, collective, political solutions. Diddy is in fact so politically mainstream that he became a prominent activist in the "get out the vote" campaign for the 2004 presidential election. Diddy's brand of dissent thus appeals to a broad audience, much of it white and middle class. As his video director, Martin Weitz, observed in an interview for *Elle* magazine, Diddy's market is not the inner city: "No ghetto kid from Harlem is going to buy Puffy. They think he sold out. It's more like the 16-year-old white girls in the Hamptons, baby!" (quoted in Everett-Green, 1999).

It is also important to note that Diddy encourages individual acts of rebellion only to the degree they enrich him and the media conglomerate he works for.[4] And rich he has become. Diddy lives in a multimillion-dollar mansion on Park Avenue in Manhattan and a multimillion-dollar house in the Hamptons. In 2005, *Forbes* magazine ranked him the 20th most important celebrity in the United States and the third biggest money earner among musicians, with an annual income of US$36 million ("The Celebrity 100," 2005). Diddy is entirely forthright about his self-enriching aims. In his 1997 song, "I Got the Power," Diddy referred to himself as "that nigga with the getting-money game plan" (Combs and the Lox, 1997). And in *Forever*, he reminds us: "Nigga get money, that's simply the plan." From this point of view, Diddy has more in common with Martha Stewart than with Chuck D and Public Enemy (Everett-Green, 1999).

---

[4] *Notorious* is marketed, manufactured, and distributed by a unit of BMG Entertainment, the multibillion-dollar entertainment division of Germany's Bertelsmann AG, the sixth largest media conglomerate in the world.

Bling

Some hip hop artists come from the inner city, have criminal backgrounds, served time in prison, and glorify the gangster lifestyle. As of this writing, Curtis "50 Cent" Jackson is probably the best known among them. Some hip hop artists remain true to their political birthright. For example, Chuck D's mother was a Black Panther activist, and to this day he is engaged in raising black political consciousness as a writer, publisher, and producer. It seems, however, that a large number of prominent hip hop artists emulate the gangster lifestyle neither because it reflects their origins nor because they regard it as a political statement but simply because it is stylish and profitable to do so. Their backgrounds have nothing in common with drug suppliers, pimps, and gang leaders, and their politics is mainstream or nonexistent. Even in the early years of hip hop, a gap between the biographies of many hip hop artists and their public personae was evident for those who took the time to do a background check. Three examples:

- D.M.C. (Darryl McDaniels) was part of the legendary Run-D.M.C., the first hip hop group that looked like it ran with a gang and had just come off the street corner. Run-D.M.C. was credited with bringing hip hop into the mainstream in the 1980s. Yet D.M.C. was born into a solidly middle-class, suburban family. His parents were college-educated. He was described by rock critic Bill Adler as a good Catholic school kid, a mama's boy (Samuels, 2004: 149).
- Another infamous figure was Ice T. He is often credited with starting the gangster rap movement with his single, "6'n the Morning." He released "Cop Killer" in 1992, causing a national scandal. Yet Ice T completed high school and served in the Army as a ranger in the 25th Infantry. He now continues serving the forces of good by playing a detective in the TV show *Law and Order: Special Victims Unit*.
- Flavor Flav (William Jonathan Drayton, Jr.) was a member of the notorious Chuck D and Public Enemy. Yet he graduated high school and attended Adelphi, an old, respected college in Long Island, New York. He trained as a classical pianist. After a stint on the reality TV show *The Surreal Life*, he made a living co-starring in another reality TV show, *Strange Love*, with Brigitte Nielsen, a Danish actress once married to Sylvester Stallone. His latest TV venture is *The Flavor of*

Table 2.1 **Brand Names in Top 20 Songs, 2005**

Brand	Number of Mentions
Mercedes-Benz automobile	100
Nike sports shoes	63
Cadillac automobile	62
Bentley automobile	51
Rolls-Royce automobile	46
Hennessy cognac	44
Chevrolet automobile	40
Louis Vuitton luggage	35
Cristal champagne	35
AK-47 assault rifle	33
Total	509
Average mentions/song	25.5

Source: Adapted from Agenda Inc. (2005): 4–7. Courtesy of Agenda Inc., http://agendainc.com.

Love, in which 20 single women who profess to adore him move into a "phat crib" in Los Angeles and compete for his affections.

My contention that the "getting-money game plan" drives many hip hop artists is supported by the near-worship of luxury commodities in much of their music. Consider Tables 2.1 and 2.2, based on the top 20 songs of 2005 on the Billboard charts, almost all of which were in the hip hop genre. Table 2.1 shows how many times the ten most frequently mentioned brands were referred to in the top 20 songs. Table 2.2 lists the eight recording artists who referred to brands most frequently. The numbers tell a fascinating story. Each of the top 20 songs of 2005 mentioned brands 25.5 times on average. Assuming the average song is two-and-a-half minutes long, that works out to a brand mentioned every six seconds. From this point of view, hip hop is a lot like one of those soap commercials that rely mainly on brand-name repetition to ensure that consumers keep the product in mind when they go grocery shopping. Only in the world of hip hop, the good life is strongly associated not with laundry detergent but with

Table 2.2 **Top Brand Name–Dropping Artists, 2005**

Artist	Number of Brands
50 Cent	20 brands in 7 songs
Ludacris	13 brands in 6 songs
The Game	13 brands in 2 songs
Ciara	10 brands in 4 songs
Jamie Foxx	6 brands in 1 song
Kanye West	6 brands in 1 song
Lil' Jon	6 brands in 2 songs
Trick Daddy	6 brands in 2 songs
Total	80 brands in 25 songs
Average brands/song	3.2

Source: Adapted from Agenda Inc. (2005): 4–7. Courtesy of Agenda Inc., http://agendainc.com.

driving a Mercedes, wearing Nikes, drinking Hennessy cognac, and packing an AK-47.

Street Cred

The runaway financial success of some hip hop artists can rob them of what they call "street cred." One's claim to be a pimp or a cop killer can lose credibility when one shops at Salvatore Ferragamo and lives in the suburbs.

Successful hip hop artists have responded to the problem of street cred in three ways. First, some decide to give up any pretence of street cred by using their money to insulate themselves from the inner city. A Diddy or a Will Smith (formerly the Fresh Prince) makes no bones about catering to a largely white, suburban, culturally and politically mainstream, middle-class audience. They never lived in the inner city and apparently have no plans to visit anytime soon.

Successful hip hop artists whose audience appeal derives from their self-characterization as street toughs often take a more dangerous tack. They may live in the wealthy suburbs but they still frequent the inner city, where some of them were born. Many of them are undoubtedly nostalgic about inner-city life, but they seem also to be motivated to visit the clubs and street corners of their old 'hood to show that they have not sold out. The trouble is that permanent residents often envy their wealth and fame, and this resentment can easily boil over into lethal violence. Famous hip hop artists who were shot and killed visiting their old neighbourhoods after striking it rich include Scott La Rock (Scott Sterling) in 1987 (the first high-profile hip hop slaying), Run-D.M.C.'s Jam Master Jay (Jason Mizell) in 2002, and Proof (DeShaun Holton), Eminem's right-hand man and member of D-12, in 2006 (Dawsey, 2006).

A compromise between rejecting the inner city and visiting it as a rich tourist involves staging gun battles for public consumption. For example, in March 2005, a sidewalk gunfight broke out near hip hop radio station WQHT in New York City between the entourages of hip hop star The Game and his former mentor, 50 Cent. The Game had hinted that he might record with one of 50 Cent's rivals, so 50 Cent expelled The Game from his inner circle. The gunfight followed. Four years earlier, on the same street corner, a similar incident occurred between followers of Lil' Kim, one of the few female hip hop stars, and rival Capone after Capone's group had referred to Lil' Kim as "lame" in their appropriately titled song "Bang, Bang." In both gunfights, the hip hop stars' followers discharged many rounds of ammunition at close range but damage was minor. Total casualties in the 2001 and 2005 gun battles combined: one man shot in the leg in 2005.

It seems plausible that the gunfights were actually for show. They help to reinforce the violent image and street cred of the hip hop stars involved. Hip hop stars are multimillionaire members of the music elite but the gunfights confer "the illusion of their authenticity as desperate outlaws" (Hajdu, 2005). In that light, shootouts are low-risk investments by savvy businesspeople. Lil' Kim's shootout certainly paid off handsomely. She claimed in front of a Grand Jury that two of her associates were not present at the 2001 gunfight. But witnesses contradicted her testimony and WQHT's security tape showed her holding a door open for one of the men. She was subsequently sentenced to a year and a day in prison for perjury. The two weeks preceding her imprisonment on 19 September 2005 were videotaped for a reality show on Black Entertainment Television. The first episode of *Lil' Kim: Countdown to Lockdown* was the most watched series debut in the network's 25-year history. It has not been disclosed how much Lil' Kim earned for her efforts (Associated Press, 2005; Strong, 2006).

The Three Promises of Hip Hop
Identity

[M]an ain't like a dog ... because ... he know about death.... [W]e ain't gonna get no move on in this world, lyin' around in the sun, lickin' our ass all day ..., [S]o with this said, you tell me what it is you wanna do with your life.

—*DJay (Terrence Howard), a pimp, to Nola (Taryn Manning), one of his prostitutes, in* Hustle and Flow *(2005)*

People create, share, and socially transmit languages, beliefs, symbols, values, material objects, routine practices, and art forms to help them survive and prosper. Sociologists call the sum total of these responses to real-life problems **culture**. Medicine, Christianity, the Russian language, and the pulley help people cope, respectively, with ill health, questions about the meaning of life, the desire to communicate, and the need to raise heavy objects. Hip hop is no different. It is also a response to real-life problems.

For example, the 2005 box-office hit *Hustle and Flow* tells the story of how DJay responds culturally to his life problems. Knowing that we will die, we must choose how to live meaningfully or be reduced to an existence little better than that of a dog, says DJay. He finds that he can achieve self-fulfillment by giving up his life as a pimp and giving voice to the joys and frustrations of the life he knows in the largely black, poor, violent, downtown core of Memphis, Tennessee. He becomes a hip hop artist. Artistic self-expression renders his life meaningful and rewarding. It gives him a sense of identity.

To operate in the world, all people must develop a sense of who they are and what they can do (and who they aren't and what they can't do). The construction of identity is a lifelong task; people may alter their occupational, religious, national, ethnic, and even sexual identity as they mature and their circumstances change. But adolescence is the stage of life when most people lay the foundation for future development. It is typically a turbulent period, full of tentative experiments, exuberant strivings, the emulation of heroes, self-doubt, false starts, and confrontation with stubborn authority. By means of these experiments, strivings, and so forth, adolescents form a baseline identity. Particular styles of popular music—unique patterns of rhythm, melody, and lyrics—express adolescent struggles in particular social contexts and give them form. That is why popular music is so meaningful and important to most adolescents (and most nostalgic adults) (Gracyk, 2001).

Minor currents in hip hop oppose violence, crime, drugs, and the mistreatment of women, but the dominant identity promoted by the genre is that of proud, arrogant, violent, criminal, misogynistic, black hypermasculinity. The identity is largely a response to the degrading effects of racism on the self-esteem of black men in the American inner city. Take persistent poverty and bad schools, remove social services and industrial jobs, introduce crack and gang wars, and you soon get hip hop (Dyson, 2006). Nelson George, the genre's leading historian, writes that hip hop is "a system of survival" and "an invigorating source of self-empowerment" (George, 1998: 50). It negates middle-class sensibilities because many black men believe that middle-class sensibilities have tried to negate them.

Upward Mobility

George is correct to note that "hip hop didn't start as a career move but as a way of announcing one's existence in the world" (George, 1998: 14). Nonetheless, a career move it soon became. If hip hop's first promise was to provide a sense of black male identity in the context of the American inner city in the 1970s and 1980s, its second promise was to serve as a path of upward social mobility out of that context. (**Upward mobility** refers to movement up a system of inequality.)

Yet hip hop's lure resembles the largely false hope offered by professional sports. In 2004, the National Basketball Association, the National Football League, and Major League Baseball employed 3911 players of whom 1650 were black (see Table 2.3). That's 1650 out of roughly 5 million black men between the ages of 18 and 40. The odds of an African-American man in the 18-to-40 age cohort being a top professional athlete are 3030 to 1. If he lives to the age of 80, he has a better chance (3000 to 1) of getting struck by lightning in his lifetime (estimated from "Facts about Lightning," 2006; U.S. Census Bureau, 2002b). Although statistics on the subject are not available, it is evident that the odds of an African-American man becoming a hip hop star are considerably worse than his odds of becoming a top professional athlete; the black men who become well-known hip hop artists even at the regional level, let alone nationally or internationally, number in the low hundreds, not the low thousands.

The poor black youth who regard professional athletes and hip hop artists as role and mobility models have little chance of realizing their dreams, all the more so because their unrealistic aspirations often deflect their attention from a much safer bet—staying in school, studying hard, and pursuing an ordinary career (Doberman, 1997). The odds of an

Table 2.3 **African-American Men in Professional Sports, 2004**

Sport	Players	Black players	Blacks as percent of total
National Football League	1842	1228	67
National Basketball Association	478	311	65
Major League Baseball	1591	111	7
Total	3911	1650	42

Note: The disproportionately large number of black players in the NBA and the NFL is sometimes used to defend the view that blacks are *genetically* superior athletes (Entine, 2000). However, no genetic evidence of black athletic superiority exists. Besides, non-blacks dominate many sports, including hockey (Canadians and Russians), swimming (Australians), gymnastics (East Europeans and Chinese), and soccer (West Europeans and South Americans). Superiority of particular racial, ethnic, and national groups in certain sports is the result of unique combinations of climate, geography, history, culture, and government and private-sector sponsorship, not genes.
Source: *Adapted from Lapchick (2004: 15, 26, 35). 2004 Racial and Gender Report Card Orlando, FL: University of Central Florida. On the World Wide Web at http://www.bus.ucf.edu/sport/public/downloads/2004-Racial_Gender_Report_Card.pdf (accessed 29 April 2006) pp.15, 26, 35.*

African-American man in the 18-to-40 age cohort being a physician are roughly seven times better than the odds of his being a professional athlete or a well-known hip hop artist, and the odds of his being a lawyer are roughly 14 times better (estimated from Holmes, 2005; King and Bendel, 1995; U.S. Census Bureau, 2002a). Yet because so many young African-American men seek to follow the career paths and emulate the lifestyles (including the criminality) of a 50 Cent or an Allen Iverson, too few of them sing the praises of Dr. James McCune Smith, the first African-American doctor, or seek to emulate the uncool but respectable accomplishments of TV's Dr. Heathcliff Huxtable. In 2005, the number of black law students in the United States fell to a 12-year low despite a growing black population (Holmes, 2005).

An important lesson about the nature of culture lies embedded in this story. Culture is created to solve human problems, as we have seen. But not all elements of culture solve problems equally well. Some elements of culture even create new problems. After all, the creators of culture are only human. In the case at hand, it seems that by promoting unrealistic hopes for upward mobility and encouraging a lifestyle that draws young African-American men away from school, hard work, and the pursuit of an ordinary career, hip hop culture badly short-changes them.

Power

Like hip hop's promise of upward mobility, its assurance of power has proven largely an illusion.

We saw that hip hop emerged among African-American inner-city youth as a counsel of despair with strong political overtones. Many commentators believed that by reflecting the traditions, frustrations, and ambitions of the community that created it, hip hop would help the otherwise isolated voices of poor black youth sing in unison, shape a collective identity, and engage in concerted political action to improve the conditions of all African Americans (cf. Mattern, 1998).

There are still radical political currents in hip hop. For the most part, however, it has become an apolitical commodity that increasingly appeals to a heterogeneous but mainly white, middle-class audience. As one of hip hop's leading analysts and academic sympathizers writes, "the discourse of ghetto reality or 'hood authenticity remains largely devoid of political insight or progressive intent" (Forman, 2001: 121).

Hip hop substantially lost its politics for three reasons. First, as one industry insider notes, "Mainstream media outlets and executive decision-makers ... fail to encourage or support overt political content and militant ideologies because ... 'it upsets the public'" (KRS-One cited in Forman, 2001: 122). The recording industry got excited about hip hop precisely when executives saw the possibility of "crossover," that is, selling the new black genre in the much larger white community. For them, hip hop was an opportunity little different from that offered by Motown in the 1960s. They apparently understood well, however, that to turn hip hop into an appealing mass-marketed commodity it had to be tamed and de-clawed of its political content so as not to offend its large potential audience. If they needed to be sensitized to the need to tone down the rhetoric, the political opposition to hip hop that was stimulated by gangster rap and songs like "Cop Killer" in the early 1990s certainly helped. That opposition was the second reason hip hop lost its politics. Third, hip hop artists themselves contributed to the de-politicization of their music. For the most part untutored in politics, history, and the social sciences, they are unequipped to think clearly about the public policies that are needed to help the black underclass and the specific forms of political action that are needed to get the black underclass to help itself. At most, they offer the flavour of rebelliousness, the illusion of dissent, giving members of their audience the feeling of being daring and notorious rule breakers and revolutionaries but offering nothing in the way of concrete ideas, let alone leadership.

Vladimir Lenin, leader of the Russian Revolution of 1917, once said that capitalists are so eager to earn profits they will sell the rope from which they themselves will hang. But he underestimated his opponents. Savvy executives and willing recording artists have taken the edge off hip hop to make it more appealing to a mass market, thus turning dissent into a commodity (Frank and Weiland, 1997). Young consumers are fooled into thinking they are buying rope to hang owners of big business, political authorities, and cultural conservatives. Really, they're just buying rope to constrain themselves.

Culture and Social Structure

Social structures are relatively stable patterns of social relations that constrain and create opportunities for thought and action. For example, in a social structure composed of just two people, both individuals must be engaged for the structure to persist. If one person fails to participate and contribute to the satisfaction of the other, the relationship will soon dissolve. In contrast, three-person social structures are generally more stable because one person may mediate conflict between the other two. In addition, three-person structures allow one person to exploit rivalry between the other two in order to achieve dominance. Thus, the introduction of a third person makes possible a new set of social dynamics that are impossible in a two-person structure (Simmel, 1950). What is true for two- and three-person relationships holds for social structures composed of millions of people that are organized into institutions, racial groups, social classes, and entire societies; they constrain and create a host of opportunities for the people who comprise them.

Sociologists have long debated whether social structure gives rise to culture or vice-versa. At first glance, this may seem to be a chicken-and-egg problem. For instance, in this chapter I have argued that the social structure of the American inner city gave rise to the cultural phenomenon of hip hop. But I have also argued that the culture of hip hop, insofar as it encourages violence and diverts attention from more realistic avenues of social mobility, encourages the persistence of the social structure of the American inner city. Chicken or egg?

Research on Media Violence

Since the 1960s, social scientists have employed a wide range of sociological methods to investigate the effects of mass media violence on real-world behaviour. This body of research can help us achieve a more precise understanding of the relationship between hip hop culture and inner-city social structure.

Some of the research is based on **experiments**, carefully controlled artificial situations that allow researchers to isolate presumed causes and measure their effects precisely. In a typical experiment, a group of children is randomly divided into "experimental" and "control" groups. The experimental group alone is shown a violent TV program. The level of aggressiveness of both groups at play is measured before and after the showing. If, after the showing, members of the experimental group play significantly more aggressively than they did before the showing, and significantly more aggressively than members of the control group, the researchers conclude that TV violence affects real-world behaviour.

Scores of such experiments show that exposure to media violence has a short-term effect on violent behaviour in young children, especially boys. Results are mixed when it comes to assessing longer-term effects, especially on older children and teenagers (Anderson and Bushman, 2002; Browne and Hamilton-Giachritsis, 2005; Freedman, 2002).

Sociologists have also used **surveys** to measure the effect of media violence on behaviour. In a survey, randomly selected people are asked questions about their knowledge, attitudes, or behaviour. Researchers aim to study part of a group (a "sample") to learn about the whole group of interest (the "population"). The results of most surveys show a significant relationship between exposure to violent mass media and violent behaviour, albeit a weaker relationship than experiments show. Some surveys find no relationship between exposure to violent mass media and violent behaviour (Anderson and Bushman, 2002; Huesmann, Moise-Titus, Podolski, and Eron, 2003; Johnson, Cohen, Smailes, Kasen, and Brook, 2002).

Field research—systematically observing people in their natural social settings—has also been employed to help us understand how media violence may influence behaviour. For example, sociologists have spent time in schools where shooting rampages have taken place. They have developed a deep appreciation of the context of school shootings by living in the neighbourhoods where they occur, interviewing students, teachers, neighbourhood residents, and shooters' family members, and studying police and psychological reports, the shooters' own writings, and other relevant materials (Harding, Fox, and Mehta, 2002; Sullivan, 2002). They have tentatively concluded that only a small number of young people—those who are weakly connected to family, school, community, and peers—are susceptible to translating media violence into violent behaviour. Lack of social support allows their personal problems to become greatly magnified, and if guns are readily available, they are prone to using violent media messages as models for their own behaviour. In contrast, for the overwhelming majority of young people, violence in the mass media is just a source of entertainment and a fantasy outlet for emotional issues, not a template for action (Anderson, 2003).

Finally, **official statistics** (numerical data originally compiled by state organizations for purposes other than sociological research) have been analyzed to put the effect of media violence on real-world behaviour into broader perspective. For example, researchers have discovered big differences in violent behaviour between Canada and the United States. The homicide rate (the number of murders per 100 000 people) has historically been about three to four times higher in the United States. Yet TV programming, movies, and video games are nearly identical in the two countries, so exposure to media violence can't account for the difference. Most researchers attribute the difference in homicide rates to the higher level of economic and social inequality and the wider availability of handguns in the United States (Government of Canada, 2002; Lenton, 1989; National Rifle Association, 2005).

My literature review leads me to unscramble this particular chicken-and-egg debate as follows. Media violence in general, and hip hop culture in particular, probably do stimulate real-world violence among a minority of young people, although to a considerably lesser degree than some alarmists would have us believe (McWhorter, 2005: 315–51). The effects are strongest among male adolescents who lack strong ties to family and other institutions that, by example, instruction, and discipline, typically socialize young people to refrain from violence. The effects are especially exaggerated in settings where economic and social inequality is high and where handguns are readily available. These findings imply that, although hip hop culture reinforces the violent social structure of the inner city, social reformers interested in lowering levels of violence could achieve more by figuring out ways of limiting the availability of handguns and shoring up or providing alternatives to faltering social institutions (especially schools and families) than by bashing hip hop culture.

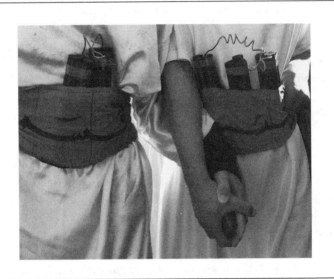

Source: Photo by Ahmed Jadallah, Corbis #UT0058971 (RM).
© Reuters/CORBIS.

3

Explaining Suicide Bombers[1]

From Karbala to Mekhola

"Ya Karbala! Ya Hussein! Ya Khomeini!" That was the cry of waves of Iranian children and youths armed with Kalashnikovs and hand grenades as they attacked Iraqi positions during the early years of the Iran–Iraq war (1980–88). Entrenched machine guns and helicopter gun ships mowed them down but new waves kept on coming. By 1982, the Iranians had recovered all of the territory they had lost and stood on Iraqi soil. They fought for Karbala, the town where, in 680 CE,[2] a battle took place between factions that disagreed over how they should choose the successor to the prophet Muhammad; the Sunni wanted the successor to be elected from a certain tribe, while the Shiites wanted him to be Muhammad's direct descendant. The youthful suicide attackers in the Iran–Iraq war also fought in the name of Hussein, the prophet Muhammad's grandson, who led the vastly outnumbered Shiites in their suicidal battle against the attacking Sunni at Karbala. Finally, they fought for Khomeini, the spiritual and political leader of Shiite Iran in the early 1980s. Lacking weapons and a well-organized army, Khomeini proclaimed it an honour to die in holy battle and instructed recruiters to find human cannon fodder in Iran's schools. In this way, suicide attacks were institutionalized as a technique of collective violence in the modern Islamic world.

---

[1] Part of this chapter is based on Brym and Araj (2006; 2007).
[2] "CE" stands for "common era" and is now preferred over the ethnocentric "AD," which stands for *anno Domini* (Latin for "the year of our Lord").

Suicide attacks were moulded into a precision instrument shortly afterwards, when Iranian militants arrived in southern Lebanon to support the anti-Western and anti-Israel Hizballah movement (see Figure 3.1). The first suicide bombing against Western interests in the Middle East took place in Beirut, Lebanon, in October 1983, when Shiite militants attacked the military barracks of American and French peacekeepers, killing nearly 300 people. Four months later, Western troops fled the country, teaching the attackers not only that suicide bombings could be inexpensively organized, accurately directed, and precisely controlled, but that under some circumstances they could yield quick and substantial payoffs.

Israel had invaded Lebanon in the summer of 1982 in an attempt to crush the Palestine Liberation Organization (PLO), which sought to recapture territory won by Israel in earlier wars (Brym, 1983; see Figure 3.2). The Israelis succeeded in forcing the PLO leadership out of Lebanon. However, the Iranian-backed Hizballah and several copy-cat groups used the presence of Israeli troops in Lebanon as an opportunity to launch more suicide attacks.

In 1985, Israel partially withdrew from Lebanon. It now sought to weaken the PLO in the West Bank and the Gaza Strip, territories it had occupied since its 1967 war with its Arab neighbours. To that end, Israel permitted the establishment of a conservative Islamic organization—the Islamic Resistance Movement, or Hamas. It judged that the new organization would serve as a moderate political counterweight to the PLO. Israel let Hamas accept funding from Saudi Arabia, turned a blind eye as its supporters stormed cinemas and set fire to restaurants selling alcohol, and allowed the creation of the Islamic University of Gaza. Ironically, the university later became a recruiting ground for suicide bombers (Reuter, 2004: 98).

Hamas, in fact, became the leading proponent of suicide bombings inside Israel and its occupied territories. In April 1993, the first such attack took place in the rural Israeli settlement of Mekhola. Nineteen similar attacks were staged over the next four years in Israel, the West Bank, and Gaza. Between 1993 and 1997 suicide bombers were responsible for the death of 175 people (including 21 suicide bombers) and the injury of 928 others (Johnston, 2003). A second and more lethal wave of suicide bombings began on 26 October 2000. By 18 April 2006, suicide bombers were responsible for the death of an additional 685 people (including 153 suicide bombers) and the injury of 3849 others

Figure 3.1 *The Middle East*

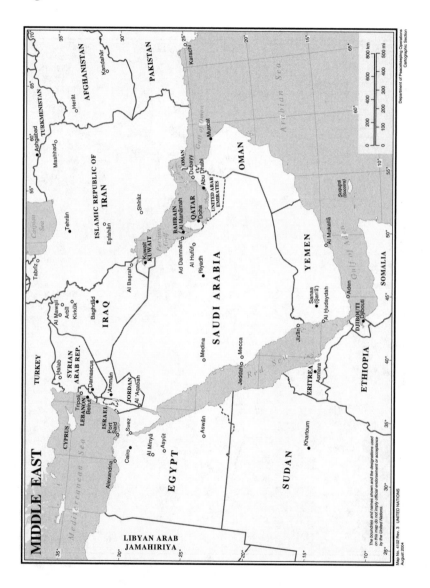

Source: United Nations (2006). United Nations Cartographic Section.

Figure 3.2 Israel, the West Bank, and Gaza

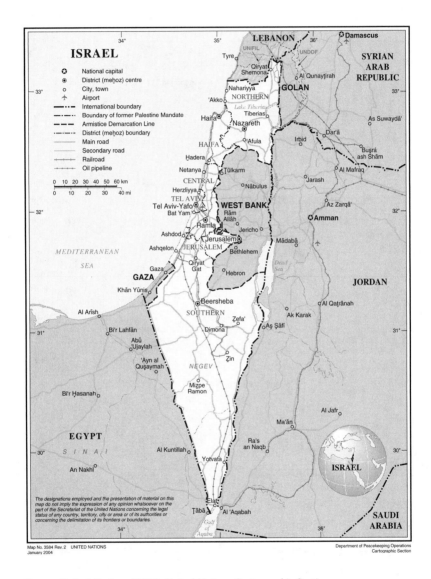

Source: United Nations (2006). United Nations Cartographic Section.

(*al-Quds*, 2000–05; *al-Quds al-'Arabi*, 2000–05; International Policy Institute for Counter-Terrorism, 2004; Israeli Ministry of Foreign Affairs, 2004; *New York Times*, 2000–06). In the early years of the twenty-first century, Israel, the West Bank, and Gaza became the region of the world with the highest frequency of, and the highest per capita death toll due to, suicide bombing.

Explanations

Explanations for the rise in suicide bombing since the early 1980s focus on three sets of factors:

- the characteristics of the suicide bombers;
- the occupation, by perceived foreigners, of territory claimed by the suicide bombers and their organizations; and
- the interaction between perpetrators of suicide attacks and occupiers.

Let us examine each of these explanations in turn.

Focus on the Perpetrators

Psychopathology

Lance Corporal Eddie DiFranco is the only survivor of the 1983 suicide attack on the U.S. Marine barracks in Beirut who saw the face of the bomber. DiFranco was on watch when he noticed the attacker speeding his truck full of explosives towards the main building on the marine base. "He looked right at me [and] smiled," DiFranco recalls (quoted in Reuter, 2004: 53).

Many Western observers quickly passed a verdict: People willing to blow themselves up to kill others must be abnormal, and if they die happily they must surely be deranged. Characteristically, several psychologists characterized the Beirut bombers as "unstable individuals with a death wish" although they lacked any evidence of the bombers' state of mind (Perina, 2002). Similarly, following the 11 September 2001 suicide attacks on the United States, U.S. government and media interpretations underscored the supposed irrationality and even outright insanity of the bombers, again without the benefit of supporting data (Atran, 2003: 1535–6).

Despite such claims, interviews with prospective suicide bombers and reconstructions of the biographies of successful suicide bombers do not suggest a higher rate of psychopathology than in the general population (Davis, 2003; Reuter, 2004; Stern, 2003; Victor, 2003). A recent study of all 462 suicide bombers who attacked targets worldwide between 1980 and 2003 found not a single case of depression, psychosis, past suicide attempts, and so forth, and only one case of probable mental retardation (Pape, 2005: 210). Evidence collected by other experts suggests that "recruits who display signs of pathological behaviour are automatically weeded out for reasons of organizational security" (Taarnby, 2003: 18). It seems reasonable to conclude that individualistic explanations based on psychopathology are of no value in helping us understand the rising incidence of suicide bombing in the world.

Deprivation

A second explanation of suicide bombing that focuses on the characteristics of perpetrators is the deprivation argument. In this view, suicide bombers act because they suffer extreme deprivation, either absolute or relative. **Absolute deprivation** refers to longstanding poverty and unemployment, **relative deprivation** to the growth of an intolerable gap between what people expect and what they get out of life (Gurr, 1970). Presumably, deprivation of one sort or the other frustrates some categories of people until they are driven to commit self-destructive acts of aggression against the perceived source of their suffering.

Evidence does not support the deprivation theory. One researcher found education and income data on about 30 percent of Arab suicide bombers between 1980 and 2003. He reported that they were much better educated than the populations from which they were recruited. They were typically from the working and middle classes and were seldom unemployed or poor (Pape, 2005: 213–5). Another scholar discovered that suicide bombers from Egypt and Saudi Arabia have come mainly from middle- or upper-middle-class families (Laqueur, 2004: 16). The perpetrators of the 11 September 2001 attacks on the United States were well-educated, middle-class men. Such evidence lends no credence to the notion that suicide bombers are especially deprived in any absolute sense.

Arguments about relative deprivation are purely speculative. To date, no researcher has measured the degree to which suicide bombers are relatively deprived and compared their level of relative deprivation with that of non–suicide bombers. The consensus in the literature today is that suicide bombers do not experience extraordinarily high levels of deprivation, either relative or absolute (Stern, 2003: 50–2; Taarnby, 2003: 10–12; Victor, 2003).

Culture

Explanations for suicide bombing that focus on the individual characteristics of the attackers began to fray in the late 1980s, partly because the evidence collected by researchers did not support them. Consequently, many analysts now shifted their focus to the *collective* characteristics of suicide bombers and, in particular, their culture.

Some social scientists attributed much of the collective violence in the world to a "clash of civilizations" between Islam and the West (Huntington, 1996).[3] From their point of view, Islamic culture inclines Muslims to fanatic hatred of the West, violence, and, in the extreme case, suicide attacks. For example, the martyrdom of Hussein at the battle of Karbala in 680 CE was a signal event in Islamic history and it is often said to have reinforced the readiness of Muslims, especially Shiites, to sacrifice their lives for the collective good in the face of overwhelming odds (Reuter, 2004: 37–9).

While such cultural resources likely increase the chance that some groups will engage in suicide attacks, one must be careful not to exaggerate their significance. One difficulty with the clash-of-civilizations thesis is that public opinion polls show that Arabs in the Middle East hold strongly favourable attitudes toward American science and technology, freedom and democracy, education, movies and television, and largely favourable attitudes toward the American people. They hold strongly negative attitudes only toward American Middle East policy (Zogby, 2002). This is less evidence of a clash of civilizations than a deep political disagreement.

Nor is the notion that an affinity exists between Islam and suicide bombing supported by most Western students of Islam. Thus, according to one such expert, "much of the so-called Islamic behaviour that the West terms terrorism is outside the norms that Islam holds for political violence" (Silverman, 2002: 91).

---

[3] For an excellent critique of the clash-of-civilizations thesis, see Hunter (1998).

One must also bear in mind that secular Muslim groups in the Middle East and non-Muslim groups outside the Middle East have employed suicide bombing as a tactic. Among the 83 percent of suicide attackers between 1980 and 2003 for whom background data are available, only 43 percent were religious (Pape, 2005: 210). In Lebanon, Israel, the West Bank, and Gaza between 1981 and 2003, fewer than half of suicide missions were conducted by religious individuals (Ricolfi, 2005). This hardly increases confidence in the view that Islamic fundamentalism is the source of suicide bombing.

A final difficulty with cultural interpretations is that suicide attacks are by no means a constant in Islamic history. They appear in eleventh century northern Persia, in the eighteenth century in parts of India, Indonesia, and the Philippines, and in the late twentieth century in various parts of the Muslim world. The episodic nature of suicide attacks suggests that certain social and political circumstances may be decisive in determining which cultural resources are drawn upon at a given time to formulate tactics for collective violence. For example, in the eighteenth century, suicide attacks were chosen as a tactic because little else proved effective against vastly militarily superior European and American colonial powers (Dale, 1988). Similarly, militant Islamic groups in the late twentieth and early twenty-first centuries adopted suicide bombing only after other tactics were tried and failed. Suicide bombing, it seems, is a weapon of last resort. All of this points to the difficulty of trying to explain political variables with cultural constants.

Focus on the Occupiers

Although cultural explanations of suicide bombing still have their supporters, a shift of focus occurred in the late 1990s. Scholars now began to analyze suicide attacks as strategically rational political actions (Sprinzak, 2000). With the publication of Robert Pape's study of all 462 suicide bombers who attacked targets worldwide between 1980 and 2003, this school of thought was given a strong empirical basis of support (Pape, 2005).

According to Pape, every group mounting a suicide campaign since the early 1980s has shared one objective: to coerce a foreign state to remove its military forces from territory that group members view as their homeland (Pape, 2005: 21). Pape makes his case by first quoting the leaders of organizations that have mounted suicide attacks. They stated plainly and forcefully that their chief aim is to liberate territory from what they regarded as foreign occupation or control (Pape, 2005: 29–33). To support his contention that suicide bombing is a fundamentally rational strategy, Pape then notes that suicide attacks are not randomly distributed but occur in clusters as part of a campaign by an organized group to achieve a political goal. He identifies 18 suicide bombing campaigns that have taken place since the early 1980s, five of them ongoing (Pape, 2005: 40). Finally, Pape argues that the strategic rationality of suicide bombing is evident in the correlation between the increasing use of suicide bombing campaigns and their relative success in achieving their goals. He finds that suicide bombing has a roughly 50 percent success rate and regards that as high, since, by comparison, international military and economic coercion achieves its goals less than a third of the time (Pape, 2005: 65). In short, Pape claims that strategic rationality is evident in the *timing, objectives,* and *results* of suicide bombing campaigns.

Pape's research has convinced analysts that many instances of suicide bombing are not devoid of strategic logic. I contend, however, that it oversimplifies matters considerably to think that suicide bombing campaigns are launched only to liberate territory, that they are typically timed to maximize their impact in that regard, and that they often meet with success.

In the remainder of this chapter I analyze one of the three most protracted and destructive series of suicide bombings in the past quarter of a century—those of the second Palestinian *intifada* ("shaking off," or uprising) in Israel, the West Bank, and Gaza between 2000 and 2005. My analysis leads me to three conclusions:

1. First, with respect to *objectives*: Suicide bombing is an action that typically involves mixed motives and mixed organizational rationales. Strategic thinking is only one element that may combine with others in the creation of a suicide bomber. It predominates less frequently than Pape leads us to believe.

2. Second, with respect to *timing*: Because the individual motivations and organizational rationales of suicide bombings are often mixed, suicide bombing campaigns are not always or even often timed to maximize the strategic advantages of insurgents. The timing of suicide bombings may be detached from strategic considerations because they take place for nonstrategic reasons such as revenge or

retaliation or simply when opportunities for attack happen to emerge. As a result, their timing may not maximize the strategic gains of the attackers and on occasion may even minimize such gains.

3. Third, with respect to _results_: Suicide bombing campaigns sometimes encourage targets to make minor concessions, but they often fail to achieve their main objectives. Sometimes they have consequences that are the opposite of those intended by suicide attackers and their organizations. If suicide bombing pays, as Pape claims, its net returns are often meagre and sometimes negative.

Suicide Bombing during the Second Intifada

One of my PhD students and I collected information on all 138 suicide bombings that took place in Israel, the West Bank, and Gaza from 26 October 2000 to 12 July 2005 (Brym and Araj, 2006). Our sources included the online database of the International Policy Institute for Counter-Terrorism (ICT) in Israel; the website of Israel's Ministry of Foreign Affairs; the East Coast evening edition of the *New York Times*; and two authoritative Arabic newspapers—*al-Quds*, published in Jerusalem, and *al-Quds al-'Arabi*, published in London. I was especially interested in three issues: (1) the reasons suicide bombers gave for their actions in public statements they made prior to attacking (i.e., the bombers' *motives*); (2) the reasons that representatives of organizations claiming responsibility for suicide attacks gave for their actions (i.e., the organizations' *rationales*); and (3) the specific preceding events that affected the timing of suicide bombings according to representatives of organizations claiming responsibility for the attacks (i.e., the attacks' *precipitants*).

I classified the three causal mechanisms—bomber motives, organizational rationales, and event precipitants—as either "proactive" or "reactive." *Reactive* causes are Israeli actions that elicited a Palestinian reaction in the form of a suicide attack. Such Israeli actions include the assassination of organizational leaders and members, the killing of Palestinians other than organizational leaders and members, and other actions not involving killing, such as the demolition of houses owned by the families of people involved in anti-Israel activities. *Proactive* causes are political, religious, or ideological events that elicited a suicide attack without provocation by specific Israeli actions. In such cases, organizations used symbolically significant anniversaries, elections, or peace negotiations as opportunities to further their goals by means of suicide attacks.

I found that the great majority of suicide attacks during the second *intifada* were reactive, that is, provoked by specific Israeli actions (see Table 3.1). This finding has enormous implications for our understanding of the objectives, timing, and results of suicide bombing campaigns. Let us consider each of these issues in turn.

Table 3.1 **Suicide Bombing and the Second *Intifada:* Causal Mechanisms (in percent)**

Cause	Type		
	Reactive	Proactive	Total
Bomber motive (with implications for objectives)	71	30	101*
Organizational rationale (with implications for results)	59	41	100
Event precipitant (with implications for timing)	82	18	100

Note: * Does not equal 100 because of rounding.
Source: *Adapted from Brym and Araj (2006).*

Objectives

Revenge and retaliation figured prominently in the bombers' stated reasons for planning suicide attacks. For the most part, they gave up their lives not as part of some grand rational strategy, but to avenge the killing of a close relative, as retribution for specific attacks against the Palestinian people, or as payback for perceived attacks against Islam. This finding supports the educated but impressionistic conclusion that Israeli political philosopher Avishai Margalit reached:

> Having talked to many Israelis and Palestinians who know something about the bombers, and having read and watched many of the bombers' statements, my distinct impression is that the main motive of many of the suicide bombers is revenge for acts committed by Israelis, a revenge that will be known and celebrated in the Islamic world (Margalit, 2003).

Timing

The great majority of suicide attacks were precipitated by specific Israeli actions. Their timing was in that sense not of the Palestinians' choosing, and therefore not rationally planned to maximize strategic gains. To be sure, Israel's response to suicide bombings influenced the ease with which subsequent attacks could be mounted. Especially after the extraordinarily frequent and lethal suicide missions of March 2002, Israel's stepped-up counterterrorist activities significantly decreased the number of suicide bombings and increased the time between precipitant and reactive attack. But I found little evidence to support Pape's contention that suicide attacks are timed to maximize the achievement of strategic or tactical goals. My analysis of precipitants leads me to conclude that most suicide bombings were revenge or retaliatory attacks and were advertised as such by insurgents.

Results

Pape's claim that suicide bombing achieves a relatively high rate of success in terms of achieving strategic goals is also questionable. Pape defines success as the withdrawal of occupying forces. The second *intifada* witnessed just one such withdrawal—Israel's August/ September 2005 pullout from Gaza. Can the pullout be construed as a consequence of Palestinian suicide attacks?

Two facts argue against such an interpretation. First, when I examined the geographical locations of suicide bombings and the geographical origins of the bombers themselves, I found that Gaza was the site of a disproportionately small number of suicide attacks and the recruiting ground for a disproportionately small number of suicide bombers. If suicide attacks were a decisive factor in leading to territorial concessions, one would expect those concessions to have been made not in Gaza but in the West Bank, where the great majority of bombers were recruited and from which the great majority of suicide attacks were launched.

Second, to the degree that militant Palestinian organizations mount suicide attacks to coerce Israel to abandon territory, the results of such attacks seem to be the opposite of what was intended. Rather than pushing the Israeli public to become more open to the idea of territorial concessions, suicide bombings have had the opposite effect. Israeli polls thus show that suicide attacks helped hardliner Ariel Sharon win the February 2001 election and, in general, drove Israeli public opinion to the right throughout the second *intifada* (Arian, 2001; 2002; Elran, 2006).

Suicide bombings also encouraged Israel to reoccupy Palestinian population centres in the West Bank and Gaza. Israel had withdrawn from those population centres in 1995–97 as a result of peace talks. But in March 2002, 135 Israeli civilians were killed in suicide attacks, the most infamous of which was the so-called Passover massacre at the Park Hotel in Netanya, in which 30 Israelis lost their lives. Within 24 hours, Israel launched Operation Defensive Shield. Twenty thousand reservists were called up in the biggest mobilization since the 1982 invasion of Lebanon and the biggest military operation in the West Bank and Gaza since the 1967 war. The West Bank and Gaza were almost completely reoccupied by April. Even if the strategic aim of the suicide bombings in March was purely to coerce Israel to withdraw from the occupied territories, the result of those attacks was just the opposite. On a broader canvas, substantial West Bank territory has been incorporated on the Israeli side of the wall that Israel is building to make it harder to launch suicide attacks. Therefore, in the long run, too, suicide bombings will have made it more difficult for the Palestinians to gain territorial concessions from Israel. Many Palestinians themselves recognize that suicide bombing is a problematic strategy that rarely achieves strategic territorial goals and often has unintended, negative consequences from the Palestinian point of view. Among them is Palestinian President Mahmoud Abbas, who typically declares each suicide bombing "a crime against our people" ("al-Ra'is ....," 2005).

Focus on the Interaction

I and the public know
What all schoolchildren learn,
Those to whom evil is done
Do evil in return.

—W. H. Auden (1940: 98)[4]

How can we explain the rise of suicide bombing since the early 1980s? There seems little advantage in focusing on the characteristics of suicide bombers themselves. On close inspection, neither their mental state nor their supposed deprivation nor their alleged cultural background adequately accounts for their actions.

---

[4] "September 1, 1939," cpoyright 1940 and renewed 1968 by W.H. Auden from COLLECTED POEMS by W.H. Auden. Used by permission of Random House, Inc.

Focusing on the occupier—seeing suicide bombing as a rational, strategic response to the perception that a foreign power has taken control of one's homeland—is a step forward, analytically speaking. The desire to regain control over territory does motivate some suicide bombers, accounts for the timing of some of their attacks, and sometimes results in concessions on the part of occupying forces. For example, my impression is that rational, strategic considerations linked to the desire to regain territory were more evident in the suicide bombings that took place in Israel, the West Bank, and Gaza between 1993 and 1997, and have been more évident in Iraq between 2003 and the present, than they were during the second *intifada*.

My analysis of suicide bombing during the second *intifada* shows, however, that focusing on occupation as the sole or even the most important reason for suicide bombings can be an oversimplification of a complex social process. In most of the 138 cases I examined, rational, strategic considerations linked to the desire to regain control of territory did not account for observable patterns in the objectives, timing, and results of suicide attacks.

It seems most fruitful to base explanations for patterns of suicide bombing on the *interaction* between occupied people and occupying forces. When other tactics fail to bring about strongly desired results, an occupied people may engage in suicide attacks out of desperation. But a resolute occupier has the will and the means to retaliate, often violently. Israel, for example, has responded to suicide attacks by engaging in the widespread assassination of Palestinian activists. Israel's actions have provoked more suicide attacks and other forms of collective violence on the part of the Palestinians, who are just as resolute as the Israelis; and renewed Palestinian violence has typically resulted in still more Israeli repression. I conclude that patterns of collective violence, including suicide bombings, are not shaped by one side or the other in the conflict. They are governed by a deadly interaction—a lethal and escalating dialogue—between conflicting parties. Interpreting that dialogue is the sociologist's job.

An Escalating Dialogue

Stephen Spielberg's 2005 film *Munich* recounts the events surrounding the massacre of 11 Israeli athletes at the 1972 Olympics by Palestinian militants. A squad of Israeli secret service agents is quickly given the green light to track down and assassinate the Palestinians who master-minded the massacre. After the squad's first few hits, a letter bomb sent to the Israeli embassy in London kills an Israeli official. Other letter bombs are found at Israeli embassies in Argentina, Austria, Belgium, Canada, the Congo, and France. "They're talking to us," one Israeli agent says to another in *Munich* when he learns about the letter bombs. "We are in dialogue now."

The violent dialogue to which the secret agent refers has been going on for 125 years as of this writing—ever since the first Eastern European Jews arrived in Palestine with the hope of establishing a Jewish homeland and Arabs objected to their presence. Periodically, each side in the conflict comes to the conclusion that an escalation in violence will finally silence the other side, but it never turns out that way. Instead, after a lull, renewed and more intense violence erupts.

The importance of each side's resolve cannot be underestimated in the perpetuation of the conflict. American and French troops aban-doned Lebanon in 1983 after one suicide attack on each of their barracks. Spanish troops exited Iraq immediately after the Madrid train bombings in 2004. In these cases, relatively low resolve on the part of the perceived occupiers resulted in their making quick concessions to the attackers. In contrast, in the Israeli and Palestinian cases, the prob-ability of serious concessions is low because the resolve on both sides is so high.

In the most recent phase of their battle over territory that both sides claim as their historical and religious birthright, one side was too weak to imagine a balance of power, so instead it concocted a scheme to achieve a balance of horror, justified by the idea that "a nation whose sons vie with each other for the sake of martyrdom does not know defeat" (quoted in Oliver and Steinberg, 2005: 61). The power-ful side responded to martyrdom operations (as suicide bombings are called by Palestinian militants) in the way that most of its enraged population demanded—by teaching the other side a series of lessons it wouldn't soon forget. The weak side obliged by remembering well and avenging its losses with all the fury it could muster. Some of the thinkers in Israel's strategic planning offices undoubtedly recognized that murderous retribution is often counterproductive. They had to answer to their political bosses, however, who were in turn obliged to respond to public outrage by getting tough. Some of the Palestinian strategic thinkers in the warrens of Gaza City undoubtedly knew that Israel would not capitulate in response to suicide bombing. But they had to answer to their publics too, and so they often forsook the strict calculation of costs and benefits for political expediency and a culture of mutual destruction.

To call the deadly interaction between Palestinians and Israelis "rational" distorts the meaning of the word. There is nothing rational about suicide bombing provoking assassination and assassination provoking more suicide bombing; the interaction pushes both sides farther from their ultimate objectives of peace and security and threatens both sides with more horrible forms of violence in the future.

The irrationality of the interaction between Palestinians and Israelis was driven home to me at the New York conference I mentioned at the beginning of Chapter 2. It was a conference on human rights. One of the speakers was Dr. Yoram Dinstein, former president of the University of Tel Aviv and Israel's foremost expert on human rights law. Dr. Dinstein took part in a spirited debate on the legality of the Israeli policy of assassinating Palestinian militants. He reminded his audience that Israel is at war with a terrorist enemy, and Duchess of Queensberry rules therefore don't apply. He also suggested that Israel's assassination policy lowers the danger of violent acts against Israel by defusing human "ticking bombs."

I spoke to Dr. Dinstein after his lecture. "Legal issues aside," I asked, "do you really think that Israel's policy of targeted killings is rational?" I proceeded to tell him about my research suggesting that the assassination of Palestinian militants provokes more suicide attacks. I also argued that assassinations help to radicalize Palestinians, making it easier to recruit a new, larger, more determined and more ruthless generation of militants. Finally, I mentioned the collaborator problem. Assassinations require real-time information on the whereabouts of targets. A large network of Palestinian collaborators feeds this information to the Israeli security services. The existence of this network causes mistrust, conflict, and internal violence among Palestinians in the West Bank and Gaza. Such social chaos undermines the unity and stability of Palestinian society that is required if one wants a negotiating partner who can make binding, authoritative decisions (Gross, 2003). Maintaining a wide network of Palestinian collaborators helps the Israeli security services locate targets in real time, but it also helps to undermine whatever slight chance for peace remains in the region. I concluded that, regardless of their legal status, targeted killings are politically irrational; they are intended to stop violence but have the effect of perpetuating hostility. Dr. Dinstein dismissed my claims with a wave of the hand. "So," I suggested, "you conclude that the Palestinians understand only power?" To which he replied, "Even that they don't understand." And he was right. If the Palestinians understood power, they would have capitulated long ago. Instead, the exercise of repressive power by Israel only deepens their resolve. Which raises an obvious question that the legions of legal and counterterrorist experts have been unable to answer: If the Palestinians don't respond to the use of repressive power like "reasonable" people ought to, what is the good of using it? And if Israelis don't make concessions like Robert Pape says they should, what is the good of launching suicide attacks against them?

Social Interaction

Max Weber, one of the founding fathers of sociology, defined **social action** as human behaviour that is meaningful in the sense that it takes into account the behaviour of others. From his point of view, one person may intervene in a situation, a second may deliberately refrain from intervention, and a third may passively acquiesce in the situation. But all three act socially if their behaviour results from taking into account what others are likely to do. Tripping on a rock is not a social action but failing to speak up for fear of punishment is (Weber, 1947: 88).

Social interaction is a dynamic sequence of social actions in which people (or entire categories of people) creatively react to each other. Social interaction is of such fundamental importance that, without it, individuals would not be able to develop a sense of identity, an idea of who they are. Nor would mere social categories (such as the residents of a particular street) be able to crystallize into self-conscious social groups (such as a true neighbourhood).

Individual and group identity formation is possible only because humans enjoy a highly developed capacity to empathize or "take the role of the other" (Mead, 1934). We develop a sense of who we are by interpreting the actions of others and imagining how they see us. All social interaction sharpens a person's identity, including interaction that involves conflict. In fact, nothing makes people feel more a part of their nation than a good war (Coser, 1956: 87–103).

The capacity to take the role of the other is especially valuable in conflict situations because it increases the likelihood of conflict resolution. This is well illustrated by *The Fog of War*, which won the 2003 Oscar for best documentary film. The film surveys the life of Robert McNamara, U.S. Secretary of Defense during the Kennedy and Johnson administrations and architect of the Vietnam War. In the film, McNamara outlines 11 lessons that he learned over his years of public service. His lesson number one: empathize with your enemy.

McNamara was present in October 1962, when President Kennedy was ready to start a nuclear war with the Soviets if they didn't remove their missiles from Cuba. Kennedy believed that Khrushchev, the Soviet leader, would never negotiate a removal. But Tommy Thompson, former U.S. ambassador to Moscow, disagreed. Thompson knew Khrushchev personally and understood that he would back down from his belligerent position if presented with an option that would allow him to remove the missiles and still say to his hard-line generals that he had won the confrontation with the United States. "The important thing for Khrushchev," Thompson argued, "is to be able to say, 'I saved Cuba; I stopped the invasion.'" Thompson convinced Kennedy. Negotiations began and nuclear war was averted. "That's what I call empathy," McNamara observes. "We must try to put ourselves inside [the enemy's] skin and look at us through their eyes." Note that being empathic does not mean having warm and fuzzy feelings about an enemy but understanding things from the enemy's perspective so a resolution can be designed that will enable the greatest gains and the fewest losses.

The great tragedy of the Israeli–Palestinian conflict is that it has been so bitter and protracted that the capacity of each side to empathize with the other has been deeply eroded. An increasingly large number of Israelis believe that the Palestinians want to destroy Israel as a Jewish state, and an increasingly large number of Palestinians believe that the Israelis want to prevent the creation of a viable Palestinian state. Increasingly, Palestinians fail to appreciate the legitimate security needs of Israel and Israelis fail to appreciate the legitimate national ambitions of the Palestinians. No Nelson Mandela–like figure who can peacefully reconcile the warring parties has risen above the fray, and the United States has not recently shown any willingness to drag both sides to the negotiating table and use its political and economic might to compel them to hammer out a resolution. It is therefore unclear whether the impasse can be broken anytime soon.

Source: AP Photo/Dave Martin.
A makeshift grave near New Orleans after Hurricane Katrina, September 2005.

4

Hurricane Katrina and the Myth of Natural Disasters

A Racist President or an Act of God?

On 2 September 2005, the NBC television network broadcast a telethon in support of American Red Cross disaster relief efforts along the coast of the Gulf of Mexico. Hurricane Katrina, one of the largest hurricanes of its strength ever to reach the United States, had made landfall about 80 hours earlier. Large swaths of Louisiana, Mississippi, and Alabama lay flooded and in ruins. After Harry Connick, Jr., sang "Do You Know What It Means to Miss New Orleans?" Canadian comedian Mike Myers and rapper Kanye West took the floor. Myers faithfully followed the teleprompter and described the wretched state of New Orleans and its people. But West veered wildly off script. He damned the mass media for their portrayal of black people as looters, criticized the government for taking so long to arrive with aid, and concluded with the memorable sentence: "George Bush doesn't care about black people." Myers then asked viewers to "Please call ..." but didn't get to finish his sentence. Someone in the NBC control room apparently figured out where West was headed and ordered the camera to turn away and cut to comedian Chris Tucker (Dyson, 2006: 26–7).

Two months later, hip hop star 50 Cent was interviewed by Contactmusic.com. "I don't know where that came from," he said, referring to Kanye West's televised outburst. "The New Orleans disaster was meant to happen. It was an act of God" ("50 Cent ...," 2005).

The comments by Kanye West and 50 Cent received a lot of attention and provoked much debate over whether the disaster was the result of one man's alleged racism or nature's wrath. From a sociological point of view, however, neither rap star came close to understanding how it came about that a storm in the world's richest and most powerful country could kill 2300 people, cause more than US$100 billion in damage, seriously disrupt the supply of oil and natural gas to the nation, and force the eventual evacuation of 80 percent of New Orleans' population.[1] After all, the danger of such a storm was widely and precisely known years earlier. The Federal Emergency Management Agency (FEMA) issued a report in early 2001 saying that a hurricane striking New Orleans was one of the three most likely disasters to hit the United States (the others were a terrorist attack on New York City and a major earthquake in San Francisco). Since 2001, long, detailed and, as Hurricane Katrina later proved, shockingly accurate articles had appeared in *Scientific American*, *Time*, *National Geographic Magazine*, *Popular Mechanics*, the *New York Times*, and the New Orleans *Times-Picayune* that made the results of research on the effect of a powerful hurricane hitting New Orleans available to the broad public and its political representatives (see, for example, "Washing Away ...," 2002). Yet almost nothing was done to prepare for the inevitable.

Explaining this sociological mystery is the chief aim of this chapter. My explanation consists of two main parts. First, for centuries powerful and well-to-do people made economic and political decisions that placed New Orleans, and especially its poor black citizens, at high risk of hurricane-related death. Second, for an equally long period, powerful and well-to-do people resisted charging the American government with responsibility for ensuring the welfare of the citizenry as a whole. As a result, relatively inexpensive measures that prevent hurricane-related deaths in other countries have not

---

[1] In June 2005, the Gulf of Mexico was responsible for nearly 30 percent of U.S. oil production and 20 percent of U.S. natural gas production (Energy Information Administration, 2005). In addition to 1836 confirmed deaths due to Katrina as of mid-May 2006, experts estimate that roughly 500 Louisiana residents were swept away and will never be found or identified (Krupa, 2006).

been implemented in the United States. Neither God nor one man should be held responsible for the decisions and neglect of entire social classes.[2]

The Development of New Orleans

In 1840, New Orleans was the fourth most populous city in the United States, and until the 1920s it was the world centre of jazz. On the eve of Hurricane Katrina, it was still an important port and tourist town with a metropolitan population of more than 1.3 million. And, of course, it had a reputation. Tennessee Williams's *A Streetcar Named Desire* branded New Orleans sensual and decaying. John Kennedy Toole's *A Confederacy of Dunces* rendered it a magnet for loose screwballs. Anne Rice added to its mystery in *Interview with the Vampire*. Everyone knew it as a party town, home of the Mardi Gras, a place that gave the world gumbo and jambalaya, and the only city in North America with a major street named after a 90-proof liquor.

New Orleans is situated on the coast of the Gulf of Mexico (see Figure 4.1). Most of it lies below sea level—in places, as much as 2.5 metres (8 feet) below. To the south, the Mississippi River flows past the city, through wetlands, and into the Gulf. To the north lies Lake Pontchartrain, the second-biggest salt-water lake in the United States and the largest lake in Louisiana (see Figure 4.2). Imagine half a dozen exuberant eight-year-olds splashing in a swimming pool on a hot summer afternoon. New Orleans is like a plastic soup bowl floating in the pool.

About 1.5 metres (5 feet) of rain falls on New Orleans annually—more than twice the annual rainfall in Toronto and nearly 40 percent more than that in New York. Every spring, the Mississippi tries to flood, and it often succeeded even after people started building dykes (or levees as they are called locally) to block the overflow. In the twentieth century, city residents achieved a measure of control over flooding by constructing a series of canals that allow 900 million cubic metres (24 billion gallons) of water to be collected and pumped into Lake Pontchartrain and other nearby bodies of water every day. Still, every summer and fall, tropical storms and hurricanes assault the Gulf coast.

---

[2] **Social class** is perhaps the single most important concept in sociology and much controversy surrounds its definition. For my purposes it is sufficient to define social class as a position occupied by people in a hierarchy that is shaped by economic criteria including wealth.

Figure 4.1 *The Caribbean Basin and Gulf Coast*

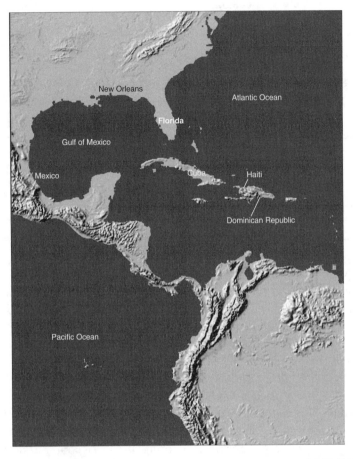

Source: Adapted from U.S. Geological Survey, Department of the Interior/USGS (2006).

Figure 4.2 *Hurricane Katrina Disaster Areas*

Hurricane Katrina Disaster Areas
Louisiana, Mississippi, and Alabama Region
(September 14, 2005)

• Places with a population
  of 40,000 or more
— Interstate
— State boundary
— County/Parish boundary

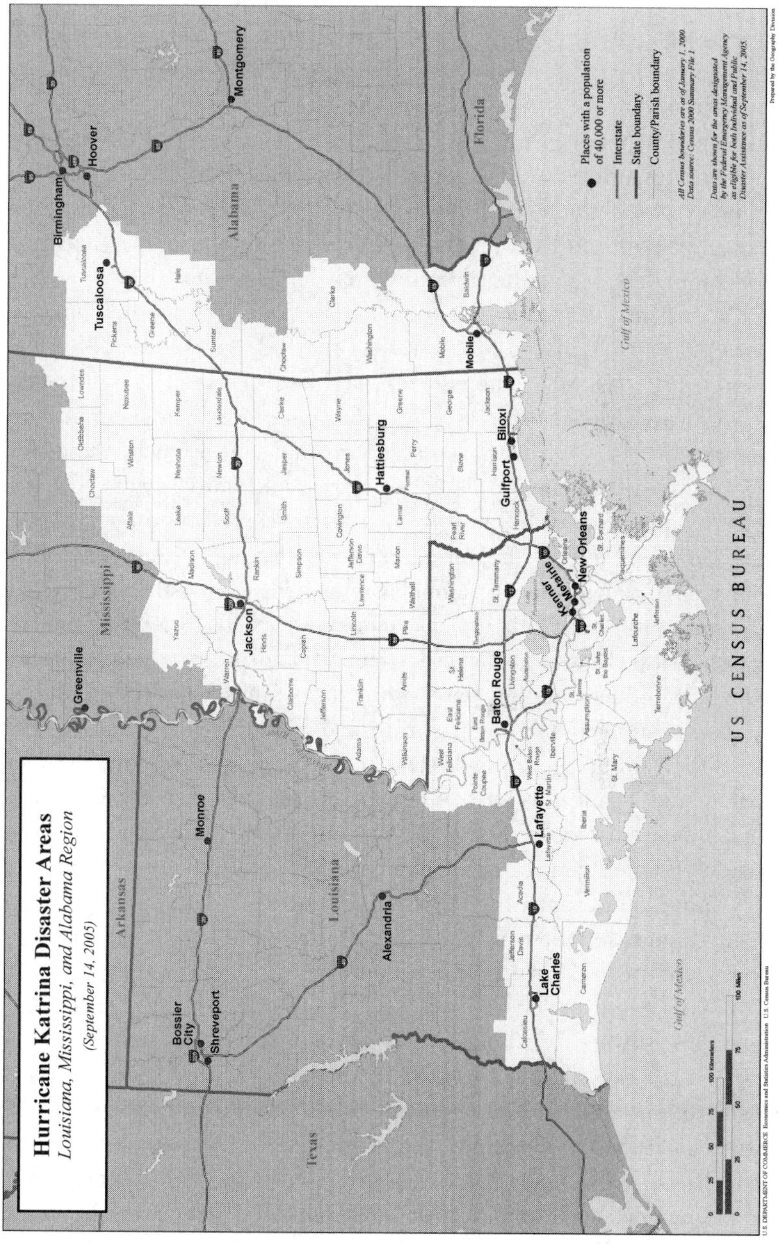

Source: U.S. Census Bureau (2005).

Sometimes, great waves of seawater surge into New Orleans. Levees were built to protect the city from storm surge too (see Figure 4.3). Yet there is enough threatening water in the area to make a reasonable person ask why the French ever settled New Orleans in the first place.

They did so as part of their strategy for continental control. The Mississippi leads deep into the North American interior, links to other rivers that empty into the Great Lakes, and thus offers access to Canada, which the French had founded in 1608 (calling it "New France"; Sexton and Delehanty, 1993). The swampy and treacherous Mississippi delta was difficult for the French to negotiate, so they settled 200 kilometres (125 miles) upstream from the river mouth. Thus was New Orleans born in 1718. It served as one end of a continental bridge between French land holdings, a bridge that also served as a barrier to the westward drift of British settlers, who were already moving into the disputed Ohio River valley. Soon, several thousand French, Canadian, and German colonists, West African slaves, and natives were living in New Orleans. Mainly because women were scarce, intermarriage was common, resulting in the formation of a distinct ethnic group, the Louisiana Creole, a social jambalaya that was unusually open to all races and cultures. With typical colour and exaggeration, yet with a grain of truth, Louisiana Governor Huey Long said two centuries later that you could feed all the "pure" white people in New Orleans with half a cup of beans and half a cup of rice, and still have food left over.

In the middle of the eighteenth century, war broke out between Britain and France. France lost Canada and its grip on Louisiana weakened. Spain took control of Louisiana for 38 years, and when the French resumed control they sold Louisiana to the United States for US$15 million (about US$400 billion in today's dollars), in one stroke raising money for their next war with Britain and helping to reinforce a power that could rival France's chief enemy.

White American settlers now flocked to New Orleans. Census data show that between 1810 and 1860, the population grew tenfold as the city became the country's second largest port. Tobacco, lumber, rice, sugar, cotton, and grain were shipped out. Manufactured goods, slaves, luxury goods, and coffee flowed in. In that half century, the number of New Orleanians of European origin increased from 37 to 85 percent of the population, while those of African origin fell from 63 to 15 percent (Logsdon and Bell, 1992: 206). A distinct, modern American neighbourhood was built uptown, its inhabitants separated from the Creole

Figure 4.5 The New Orleans Levee System

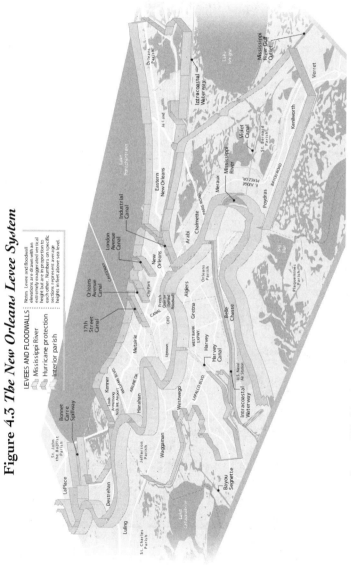

Source: "Washing Away ..." (2002). The Times Picayune.

residents of the old French city by broad Canal Street and the Americans' sense of social, moral, and economic superiority.

The Growth of Black–White Inequality

New Orleans before the Louisiana Purchase was not a city without racial inequality. Black slaves were brought there from the beginning. Still, the colour line was less rigid in New Orleans than in other cities of the United States. Racial intermarriage was relatively common. Many freed slaves lived in New Orleans, and they were often employed not as menial workers but as skilled tradespeople. French ideas about equality found eager supporters in the city. As a result, no sharp line separated blacks from whites. Social contact flourished among all categories of New Orleanians, fostered by musicians, live-in lovers, the Catholic clergy, grocers, and saloonkeepers. Class, culture, and complexion elevated many black residents to a status that most Americans of African descent could envy but not reach (Logsdon and Bell, 1992).

Once Americans started settling in the city, the situation of the black population deteriorated. In the 1840s and 1850s, an influx of white American workers displaced many freed slaves who worked on the docks and in skilled trades. Racism increased as job competition mounted; some freed slaves left for Haiti to escape it. Louisiana's fight to protect slavery during the Civil War (1861–65) hardened the colour line. Then, from 1890 to 1952, a series of laws institutionalized racial segregation. Blacks and whites now had to be kept apart in trains, schools, streetcars, bars, prisons, homes for elderly people, and even in circus audiences. They could not marry or cohabit, nor could they adopt a child of a different race. They could not dance or engage in athletic competition together. Blacks could not receive permits to build houses in white neighbourhoods, and whites could not receive permits to build houses in black neighbourhoods ("Jim Crow Laws ...," 2006). A comparison of the situation before and after the Louisiana Purchase illustrates the fact that **races** are defined not so much by biological differences as by social forces. Specifically, racial distinctions are typically made and reinforced by advantaged people for the purpose of creating and maintaining a system of inequality.

In the 1920s, new levee construction permitted the shoreline of Lake Pontchartrain to be heightened and extended, creating desirable real estate north of the city for white residents (Hirsch and Logsdon,

1992). After World War II, new highways accelerated suburban growth.

As a result of "white flight" to the suburbs, African Americans became a majority in the city of New Orleans proper after 1980, a position they had not held for 140 years. Just before Katrina hit, the city of New Orleans was 68 percent African American and just 25 percent non-Hispanic white. The poverty rate for African Americans was 35 percent—7.5 percent above the national average for African Americans. Two-thirds of the city's public schools were deemed "academically unacceptable" by the U.S. Department of Education. The city's homicide rate was the highest of any city in the country (Mahoney and Freeman, 2005). And the black population was increasingly concentrated in the city's least desirable, low-lying areas.

Flood Control?

The situation of New Orleanians was especially precarious because flood control measures were inadequate (Blumenthal, 2005; Bourne, 2004; Comfort, 2006; Nordheimer, 2002; Tidwell, 2004). Two big problems existed (and, in fact, persisted a year after Katrina hit):

1. *The disappearance of coastal wetlands.* When waves of seawater from the Gulf of Mexico are whipped up by hurricane-force winds, they pound New Orleans. The first line of defence against this onslaught consists of the marshes and barrier islands of the wetlands between New Orleans and the Gulf. Every 3.2 km (2 miles) of wetland reduces storm surge by 15 cm (6 inches). Before levees were built along the Mississippi, silt from the river's flood-waters used to stop or at least slow down the sinking of coastal wetlands into the Gulf. But the levees divert silt into the Gulf, causing the wetlands to disappear at an alarming rate. The first line of defence against storm surge has thus been weakened.

   In addition to removing much of the physical barrier against storm surge, the disappearance of the wetlands has another negative consequence for flood control. Hurricanes are machines fuelled by heat. They gain strength from the heat that is released as vapour from warm seawater condenses and falls as rain. They weaken as they pass over land, which is cooler and, of course, drier. The disappearance of coastal wetlands has effectively brought the warm waters of the Gulf closer to New Orleans, ensuring that hurricanes have less chance to weaken before they make landfall.

2. *The inadequacy of the levees.* The second big flood control problem is that the levees along Lake Pontchartrain and in other areas around the city were last reinforced with higher walls after Hurricane Betsy struck in 1965, killing more than 70 people. The U.S. Army Corps of Engineers then built up the storm walls to withstand a category 3 storm.[3] Forty years after Betsy, the Lake Pontchartrain and other levees desperately required upgrading, as Hurricane Katrina painfully demonstrated; Katrina made landfall in Louisiana as a category 3 storm, and the surge off the lake smashed the levees, engulfing the city. In all, about half the levee system was damaged (Burdeau, 2006). What is worse, in any given year, New Orleans stands an estimated 1 percent chance of facing a category 5 hurricane. Leaving the levees at less than category 3 readiness was like playing Russian roulette using an atom bomb instead of a bullet.

Aware of the problems just outlined, the federal government acted, but without resolve. It established a task force to help restore lost wetlands around New Orleans in 1990. In 2003, however, the Bush administration effectively ended that effort by allowing largely unrestricted development in the wetlands. Remarkably, in November 2005, two months *after* Katrina, the Bush administration refused to fund a US$14 billion plan to restore the barrier islands and wetlands. (If that seems like a lot of money, bear in mind that it equals just six weeks of spending for the war in Iraq or 7 percent of the estimated cost of restoration following Katrina; Tidwell, 2005.)

---

[3] The Saffir-Simpson scale ranks hurricanes as follows (National Weather Service, 2005):

- Category 1: minimum one-minute sustained winds of 74–95 mph (199-153 km/hr) and above-normal storm surge of 4–5 ft (1.2–1.5 metres)
- Category 2: minimum one-minute sustained winds of 96–110 mph (154–177 km/hr) and above-normal storm surge of 6–8 ft (1.8–2.4 metres)
- Category 3: minimum one-minute sustained winds of 111–130 mph (178–209 km/hr) and above-normal storm surge of 9–12 ft (2.7–3.7 metres)
- Category 4: minimum one-minute sustained winds of 131–155 mph (210–249 km/hr) and above-normal storm surge of 13–18 ft (4.0–5.5 metres)
- Category 5: minimum one-minute sustained winds greater than 155 mph (249 km/hr) and above-normal storm surge greater than 18 ft (5.5 metres)

Less than 17 hours before it made landfall in Louisiana, Katrina had been a category 5 storm.

In addition, Congress authorized a project to improve the pumping of water out of the New Orleans area in 1996. Unfortunately, the project was only half finished when money effectively dried up in 2003. The Corps of Army Engineers received money to improve the levees on Lake Pontchartrain and vicinity. But the Bush administration cut funding for the project by more than 80 percent in 2004 and made additional cuts at the beginning of 2005, ranking other priorities, such as the war in Iraq, higher. Because of budget cuts, the Corps was unable to buttress the 17th Street levee on Lake Pontchartrain, the location of the biggest levee breach during Katrina.

Brewing Storms

New Orleans on the eve of Katrina was unusually poor, black, segregated, unequal, violent, and vulnerable to flooding. As we have seen, there was nothing natural about this state of affairs. Centuries of human effort—in the form of geopolitical rivalry, economic competition, public policy, and social exclusion—were required to create it.

People's actions may have contributed to New Orleans' vulnerability in another way too. I refer to the increasing use of fossil fuels such as gasoline, oil, and coal. Burning fossil fuel releases carbon dioxide into the atmosphere. Carbon dioxide is a heat-trapping gas; it allows more radiation to enter the atmosphere than escape it. The result is global warming. In turn, global warming may increase the intensity of tropical storms.

I say "may" because controversy surrounds the last part of my argument. Hardly any climate scientists doubt the atmosphere is heating up or that the concentration of carbon dioxide and other heat-trapping gases has increased since the Industrial Revolution (Goddard Institute for Space Studies, 2006; Karl and Trenberth, 1999; Quashning, 2003). A large majority of climate scientists believes there is a cause-and-effect relationship at work here, not a coincidence.[4] Thus, in 2001, the Intergovernmental Panel on Climate Change, which is sponsored by the United Nations and includes climate scientists from around the world,

---

[4] More precisely, they believe that there is a cause-and-effect relationship with feedbacks that accelerate disequilibrium. For example, global warming melts permafrost. When permafrost melts, it releases methane, a much more potent heat-trapping gas than carbon dioxide. Global warming also melts the polar ice caps. When white ice is turned into dark ocean water, more solar radiation is absorbed by the earth and less is reflected back into space. Through these positive feedback loops, small temperature changes cause bigger temperature changes (Kolbert, 2006).

concluded that "most of the warming observed over the last 50 years is attributable to human activities" (Intergovernmental Panel on Climate Change, 2001: 5). Leading scientific bodies in the United States, including the National Academy of Sciences, the American Meteorological Society, the American Geophysical Union, and the American Association for the Advancement of Science, agree that the evidence for human impact on climate is compelling. A study of 928 papers on climate change published in scientific journals between 1993 and 2003 found not a single one that disagreed with the consensus view (Oreskes, 2004). True, some scientists dispute the consensus. But their criticism should be taken with a grain of salt because much of their research is funded by the coal and petrochemical industries.

How might global warming affect hurricanes? In brief, global warming causes more water to evaporate. More vapour in the atmosphere does not increase the frequency of hurricanes, but evidence suggests it may ratchet up their intensity and cause the hurricane season to start earlier (Emanuel, 2005; Knutson and Tuleya, 2004; Webster, Holland, and Chang, 2005). Some scientists legitimately question whether enough data have yet been collected to substantiate these early findings on the subject (Schiermeier, 2005a; 2005b). Therefore, the link between global warming and hurricane destructiveness must still be treated as an intriguing possibility rather than a proven fact. One thing can be said with certainty, however. If research substantiates the connection, it will be a global problem with deep local roots. With 4 percent of the world's population, the United States burns a quarter of the world's fossil fuels, more than any other country. And it is one of the very few countries in the world that has not committed itself to substantially reducing their use.

A Comparative Perspective

The strongest argument that deaths due to hurricanes are more a social than a natural disaster comes not from climate science but from sociology. It is an argument in three parts:

1. The populations of some countries are more exposed to the threat of hurricanes than the populations of other countries.
2. *At the same level of exposure*, some countries experience relatively few deaths due to hurricanes while others experience relatively many such deaths.

3. Countries that experience relatively few deaths take extensive precautions to avoid the catastrophic effects of hurricanes. Countries that experience relatively many deaths take few such precautions.

Figure 4.4 adds weight to this argument. The graph contains data from 34 countries that were exposed to hurricanes from 1980 to 2000. It plots the number of people in each country who were exposed to hurricanes (along the horizontal axis) against the average number of deaths due to hurricanes each year (along the vertical axis). In the period 1980–2000, the number of people exposed to hurricanes ranged from just over 18 000 in the small West African country of Cape Verde to more than 579 million in China. Average annual deaths due to hurricanes ranged from less than 0.5 in New Zealand to more than 7400 in Bangladesh.

Figure 4.4 *Relative Vulnerability to Hurricanes, 1980–2000*

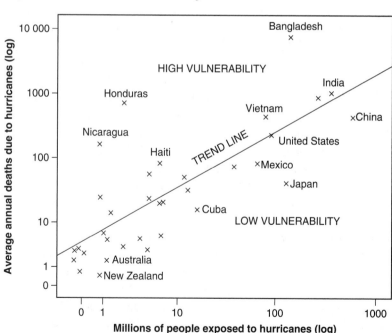

Note: Some values are negative because the variables are logged.
Source: Compiled from data in United Nations (2004b: 38, 146). A Global Report Reducing Disaster Risk: A Challenge for Development. United Nations Development Programme. Bureau for Crisis Prevention and Recovery, www.undp.org/bcpr.

In general, countries with large exposed populations experienced more annual hurricane-related deaths than those with small exposed populations. That tendency is illustrated by the upward-sloping trend line in Figure 4.4. The line shows the number of deaths one would expect in an exposed population of a given size. Countries lying above the line were more vulnerable to hurricane-related deaths than one would expect given the size of their exposed population. Countries lying below the line were less vulnerable than one would expect given the size of their exposed population.

This is where the graph starts to get interesting. The exposed populations of Bangladesh and Japan were approximately the same size (126 million in Japan, 135 million in Bangladesh). Based on the size of their exposed populations, one would expect both countries to have experienced an average of about 250 hurricane-related deaths per year. Yet Japan experienced an average of only 39 hurricane-related deaths per year, while Bangladesh experienced more than 7400. That is partly because Japan took far more extensive precautions to guard against such deaths than Bangladesh did.

True, Bangladesh is one of the world's poorest countries while Japan is one of the richest. The Japanese can therefore afford to take precautions that the Bangladeshis can only dream of. But wealth is not the only factor that determines a country's ability to take precautions. After all, the United States is about as wealthy as Japan, and had a considerably smaller exposed population (89 million people), yet it experienced an average of 222 hurricane-related deaths per year compared to Japan's 39. In fact, of the four rich countries represented in Figure 4.4, three of them—Japan, Australia, and New Zealand— experienced considerably fewer hurricane-related deaths than one would expect given the size of their exposed populations. But the fourth rich country—the United States—experienced about as many hurricane-related deaths per year as a relatively poor country with an exposed population of the same size. In the period 1980–2000, Americans were more vulnerable to death by hurricane than Mexicans (with 65 million exposed people and an average of 85 hurricane-related deaths per year) and much more vulnerable than Cubans (with 11 million exposed people and an average of just 3 hurricane-related deaths per year).

Cuba

The Cuban case illustrates well the kinds of precautions a country can take to prevent hurricane-related deaths, even if it is relatively poor (Cohn, 2005; Hamilton, de Valle, and Robles, 2005; Martin, 2005; Reuters News Agency, 2005; United Nations, 2004a). The last time Cuba suffered a large number of casualties because of a hurricane was 1963, when Hurricane Flora killed 1126 people. After Flora, the Cubans took action to prevent a recurrence of the terrible tragedy.

They first implemented an educational program in schools, universities, and workplaces to teach people how to prepare for and cope with natural disasters. The program trains the population from a young age to interpret and heed weather reports, which are broadcast continuously and updated frequently in the event of an impending storm. Every May, an annual two-day training session known as Meteoro is held. It focuses on risk reduction, including exercises that simulate evacuation and rescue in the event of a hurricane. Meteoro also encourages preventative measures, such as trimming tree limbs and checking for weaknesses in dams, and it involves a review and update of all emergency plans in the light of what has been learned in the preceding year.

Cuba has organized its civil defence network to coordinate evacuation and rescue operations at the neighbourhood level in the event of a big storm. Civil defence workers and members of organizations such as the Federation of Cuban Women go door-to-door to ensure that people fill their bathtubs with water, tape their windows, put their cars in the garage, unplug electrical appliances, and have an adequate supply of batteries, transistor radios, candles, matches, drinking water, and food. They create lists of the ill, elderly people, people with disabilities, and single mothers—people who would need help evacuating—and they ensure that help is available if these people are required to leave their homes.

If evacuation is necessary, neighbourhood doctors evacuate together with residents so people who need medication can be properly treated. Refrigerators, TV sets, pets, and other valuable items are evacuated with the people so they won't be reluctant to leave. Evacuation routes, means of transportation, and temporary housing facilities for evacuees (mainly in schools) are set up well in advance, as are stores of emergency water, food, and medicine. The existence and locations of these stores are widely publicized. Buses, trucks, ambulances, vans, helicopters, even horse carts are mobilized to get people to shelter. Regular water supplies are turned off to avoid the spread of disease.

As a result of these precautions, Cuba lost only 22 lives in ten major hurricanes between 1985 and 2004. But the big test for the Cuban system of preventing hurricane-related deaths came between 7 and 9 July 2005, when Hurricane Dennis, the most ferocious storm since Flora, lashed the island. Dennis hit Cuba twice as a category 4 storm (Katrina hit Louisiana once as a category 3 storm). One hundred and twenty thousand houses were badly damaged, 2.5 million people were left without electricity, and 12 000 hectares (30 000 acres) of banana trees were flattened. However, the timely evacuation of 1.5 million people—a remarkable 13 percent of Cuba's entire population—minimized the loss of life. Dennis killed just 16 Cubans. One can very crudely estimate that if precautions similar to those employed in Cuba had been taken in the United States nearly three months later when Katrina hit, the American death toll would have been 128 people rather than 2300.[5]

Cuba is a communist country. Some people might argue that its sterling achievement in preventing hurricane-related deaths has been accomplished only by means of strict political control of its population—control that freedom-loving Americans would never tolerate. But the argument is suspect. Vietnam is also a communist country with strict political control of its population, yet it is highly *vulnerable* to hurricane-related deaths (see Figure 4.4). Japan is a capitalist country *without* strict political control of its population, yet its record of preventing hurricane-related deaths is better than Cuba's. Communism versus capitalism is not the issue here. What is decisive in determining a country's tolerance of hurricane-related deaths is its population's collective will to take responsibility for helping fellow citizens in need, a will that is typically expressed through government policy. Compared to other rich countries, that collective will is weak in the United States.

---

[5] My logic is as follows: The United States is about 8 times more exposed to hurricanes than Cuba (89 million vs. 11 million exposed people). There were 16 Cuban deaths due to Dennis, a storm of very roughly the same magnitude as Katrina. It follows that if the United States had taken precautions similar to Cuba's, Katrina would have killed approximately 128 Americans (since $16 \div 11\ 000\ 000 = 128 \div 89\ 000\ 000$).

Katrina

Here is how it went down.[6] On 25 August 2005, Hurricane Katrina hit Florida as a category 1 storm, killing seven people. It then veered into the Gulf of Mexico, where it was soon upgraded to category 3. Kathleen Blanco, governor of Louisiana, declared a state of emergency on 26 August and President Bush followed suit on the 27th. New Orleans mayor Ray Nagin declared a voluntary evacuation order that night. At 10 a.m. on the 28th, Nagin finally announced a mandatory evacuation order. At that point, Katrina was a category 4 storm about 20 hours from landfall. Seventeen hours later, at 3 a.m. on the 29th, the 17th Street levee on Lake Pontchartrain collapsed. Other major levee breaches occurred at the London Avenue canal and the Industrial canal (see Figure 4.3 on page 59). Eighty percent of New Orleans was soon flooded, in some places to a depth of nearly 5 metres (16 feet).

The response of government to the impending disaster was remarkably restrained, to put it politely. Top officials gravely underestimated the severity of the catastrophe about to befall residents of the Gulf coast. Mayor Nagin hesitated to call a mandatory evacuation order because he was worried that the city would be legally liable for closing hotels, hospitals, and businesses. Consequently, he turned down an offer by Amtrak to evacuate several hundred New Orleanians on the last train out of town and he failed to mobilize the city's 804 operational buses to get people out. The director of the National Hurricane Center had to call the mayor at home during dinner on the evening of the 27th to tell him that the storm was the worst he had ever seen and practically beg the mayor to declare a mandatory evacuation order the next morning.

The White House found out about the 17th Street levee breach at midnight on 29 August but on the morning of the 30th, President Bush, vacationing at his Texas ranch, expressed relief that New Orleans had "dodged the bullet." An e-mail confirming the levee breach had arrived at the Department of Homeland Security two-and-a-half hours before the information reached the White House, but the next morning, Michael Chertoff, Secretary of the Department of Homeland Security, flew to Atlanta for a conference on bird flu.

---

[6] The following account is based mainly on Dyson (2005), U.S. House of Representatives (2005), and reports in the *New York Times*.

The consequences of official inability to appreciate the gravity of the problem were aggravated by woefully inadequate planning. For example, before the hurricane hit, nobody was in charge of overseeing the response and nobody had figured out how to avoid conflict over which agency should be in charge of law enforcement so that people could be evacuated effectively. The Louisiana transportation secretary was legally responsible for evacuating thousands of people from hospitals and nursing homes but had no plan in place to do so. The New Orleans Police Department unit responsible for the rescue effort was equipped with three small boats and no food, water, or extra fuel. For years it was known that 100 000 people lacked transportation out of the city. According to the 2000 census, residents of New Orleans were less likely to own cars than residents of any other city in the United States aside from New York, with its highly developed mass transportation system. Almost all of the New Orleans residents who did not own cars were black, poor, and/or elderly (Berube and Raphael, 2005). Yet an evacuation plan for these people was only 10 percent finished when Katrina struck.

Complicating matters further was the inexperience—many say incompetence—of high-ranking officials in the Federal Emergency Management Agency (FEMA). Five of the eight top people in FEMA, including its head, Michael Brown, joined the agency without any experience in disaster management. Many of the agency's top officials, including Brown, were political appointees whose chief claim to fame was loyal service during President Bush's run for the White House. Lacking professional qualifications and relevant job experience, such people often didn't know what to do and didn't appreciate how urgently they had to act. It hardly helped matters that FEMA had lost its independent status after becoming part of the newly formed Department of Homeland Security in 2001 and then suffered budget cuts as resources were diverted to fighting terrorism. Little wonder that the New Orleans relief and rescue effort was slow, inadequate, and often brutal, leading to many deaths (see this chapter's Appendix on pages 75–78).

Tens of thousands of New Orleanians were trapped in the flooded city after the storm passed. Many of them had to be rescued from rooftops by boat or helicopter. Moreover, the bowl was now overflowing with toxic soup; the waters that engulfed the city contained a witch's brew of industrial and household chemicals, sewage, garbage, and rotting human and animal corpses. People were nonetheless forced to wade through the waters to scrounge for drinking water, food, and medicine, and to get to higher ground. Conditions in the Superdome and the New Orleans Convention Center were especially appalling. Thousands of people sought shelter in those two buildings, where they were stranded for days in stifling heat, with little or no drinking water, food, medicine, or sanitation. Women miscarried, elderly people died, all suffered horribly.

A Smaller, Whiter New Orleans

Some white New Orleans neighbourhoods were extensively damaged by Katrina. Some black districts escaped serious damage. Overall, however, a disproportionate amount of moderate and catastrophic damage took place in poor, black districts. Thus, if all residents returned to lightly damaged neighbourhoods and none returned to moderately and cata-strophically damaged districts, the city would lose 80 percent of its black population and 50 percent of its white population (Logan, 2006). Of course, many people have returned and more may do so. Five months after the storm, the population of the city stood at just under 68 percent of its pre-Katrina level (Katz, Fellowes, and Mabanta, 2006: 5). Private insurance, individual spending, philanthropic contributions, and govern-ment aid have funded and will continue to fund clean-up, reconstruction, and levee repair and improvement. Still, it seems likely that the new New Orleans will be smaller and whiter than the pre-Katrina city.

Indeed, in the uptown district life was starting to return to normal just three weeks after the storm. Along its broad, tree-lined streets, work crews and hired help were restoring the Civil War–era mansions, and well-to-do white families were already living in them. The uptown and other well-off districts (Algiers, the French Quarter, the Central Business District) are on higher ground and they escaped the worst of the flooding. But the poor districts, where most of the city's African Americans lived, tended to be on low ground. There, flooding was typi-cally more severe. Three weeks after Katrina, the poor districts were deserted. Much floodwater remained, stagnant and toxic. Emaciated dogs were running wild. Everything was rotting. A great many of the houses in the poor districts will have to be destroyed (Mahoney and Freeman, 2005).

It is unclear how many African Americans will return to New Orleans, but an indication of what might lie ahead comes from a survey conducted in Houston between 10 and 12 September 2005 among 680 randomly selected Katrina evacuees. Ninety-eight percent of them came from New Orleans, 93 percent were black, and 86 percent had household incomes of less than US$30 000 a year. Just 43 percent of the respondents said they planned to move back to their hometown ("Survey of Hurricane Katrina Evacuees," 2005).

African Americans are less likely to return than whites because they lack the money required to do so and, in any case, have less to return to. In addition, evidence suggests that reconstruction efforts discriminate against the black community. Such efforts have first concentrated on less-damaged, white neighbourhoods, delaying the reconstruction of predominantly black districts. As time passes and people get settled elsewhere, they are less likely to return. Most government grant assistance has gone to white, middle-class storm victims. In white districts, government loans to small business are approved at about seven times the rate of loan approval in poverty-stricken black neighbourhoods. Blacks are less likely than whites to receive insurance settlements that will allow them to reconstruct their houses (Bullard, 2006). As has been the case throughout the history of New Orleans, class and race powerfully shape people's life-chances.

Markets, Citizenship, Power, and Policy

> I think you all know that I've always felt the nine most terrifying words in the English language are, "I'm from the government and I'm here to help."
>
> —*President Ronald Reagan, 1986*

Markets are social relations that regulate the exchange of goods and services. In a market, the prices of goods and services are established by how plentiful they are (supply) and how much they are wanted (demand). For example, if demand for labour increases and the supply of labour stays the same, the price of labour (the hourly wage) rises. Workers spend and save more, and unemployment falls. In contrast, if the supply of labour increases and demand for labour stays the same, wages fall. Workers earn and spend less, and unemployment grows.

Late-eighteenth-century Britain most closely approximated a completely free market for labour. However, the supply of labour exceeded demand to such a degree that starvation became widespread. The threat of social instability forced the government to establish a system of state-run "poor houses" that provided minimal food and shelter for people without means (Polanyi, 1957). Because perfectly free labour markets periodically cause much suffering and death if left unchecked, they must be regulated by governments. For example, North American laws outlaw child labour, stipulate maximum work hours, make certain holidays compulsory, and specify a minimum wage. Like most people, Americans and Canadians know that without such regulations, the whip of the labour market would destroy many of us.

The rights of people to protection under the law are embodied in the concept of **citizenship**. To varying degrees, citizens of different countries have fought for and won civil rights (free speech, freedom of worship, justice under the law), political rights (freedom to vote and run for office), and social rights (freedom to receive a minimum level of economic security and participate fully in social life) (Marshall, 1965). Note the phrase "to varying degrees." In the fight for citizenship rights, the citizens of some countries have been more successful than the citizens of other countries. And note the word "fight." Citizenship rights are rarely granted because of the grace and generosity of people in positions of power. They are typically extracted by subordinates using force. Consequently, success in achieving citizenship rights depends heavily on how powerful different categories of people are. **Power** is the ability to realize one's will, even against the resistance of others (Weber, 1946: 180). Oversimplifying for the sake of brevity, the balance of power between authorities and subordinates in a given society largely determines how extensive and entrenched citizenship rights become. If subordinates are relatively powerful, citizenship rights become extensive and well entrenched. Laws that ensure broad civil, political, and social rights are passed. Among rich countries, societies like Sweden emerge in the extreme case. If authorities are relatively powerful, citizenship rights do not become extensive and well entrenched. Fewer and weaker laws ensuring civil, political, and social rights are passed. Among rich countries, societies like the United States emerge at the other extreme.

On almost every imaginable measure of citizenship rights, the United States lags behind the other 20 or so other rich countries in the world. For example, long after all adult citizens won the right to vote in other rich countries, many African Americans were still unable to vote. It was only in the 1960s that African Americans won such rights. Nor did the United States lead with respect to women's voting rights. It became the 26th country to grant women the right to vote, following the Scandinavian countries, the British dominions, a number of continental European countries, and the Soviet Union. The United States compares unfavourably with other rich countries as far as social rights are concerned too. Thus, the gap between rich and poor is greater in the United States than in any other rich country, and the proportion of the population classified as poor is larger. Americans enjoy no national health-care system, no national system of paid parental leave, no national system of job retraining, and no national child-care system. In recent decades, the government has slashed the number of families receiving welfare benefits and the cash and noncash assistance available to each family. As a result, the plight of America's poor—disproportionately composed of children, single mothers with children, and African Americans—has been worsening steadily (Block, Korteweg, and Woodward, 2006).

According to former Harvard human rights professor Michael Ignatieff (who is now a Canadian Member of Parliament for the Liberal party), the circumstances surrounding Hurricane Katrina demonstrate that the government of the United States has broken its "contract" with its citizens (Ignatieff, 2005). I disagree. The contract never stipulated that the American government would care much for its citizens in the first place. True, there have been periods when American governments were charged with greater responsibility. The Great Depression of the 1930s, with its massive nationwide strikes, and the civil rights era of the 1950s and 1960s, with its marches, demonstrations, sit-ins, and race riots, were times when Democratic administrations took important steps forward in that regard. But the overall tendency, grown stronger since Ronald Reagan first came to power in 1980, has been for government to minimize its involvement in the lives of its citizens, giving the freest possible reign to the forces of the free market. From this point of view, the tragedy of Katrina was ultimately the result of the imbalance of power between upper and lower classes, and between authorities and subordinates, in the United States.

Appendix

Written Testimony for the Record
by Leah Hodges
Evacuee, New Orleans, Louisiana
Select Bipartisan Committee to Investigate the Preparation
for and Response to Hurricane Katrina
U.S. House of Representatives
December 6, 2005

I wish to thank everyone who is listening today for the chance to communicate my story. I come to Congress today representing not just myself, but hundreds, even thousands of other New Orleans residents who experienced the same or similar traumatic experiences and witnessed the same or similar events.

...

Let me begin with a few general points.

1. I don't need to point out the failures of the President, the Governor of Louisiana and the Mayor of New Orleans, as these individuals have already claimed responsibility for everything that happened to us as the result of the hurricane and its aftermath.
2. The people of New Orleans were stranded in a flood and were allowed to die. The military had personnel stationed just 40 miles outside the city, and they could have moved in and gotten people out sooner. People were allowed to die.
3. Animals from the animal shelter and fish from the fish aquarium were evacuated before the people.
4. The President and local officials issued "shoot to kill orders" and people were shot. People who asked for help were threatened with being shot. My niece and her fiancé, they needed gas. Her fiancé asked military [for] help and they told [him] "if you don't get back inside we will shoot you."
5. Bodies are still being found every day in New Orleans. Most people in New Orleans do not believe the official body counts.
6. The devastation that hit New Orleans was foreseeable and avoidable, and because it was not avoided, New Orleans was turned into a mass grave.
7. As a hurricane survivor, I and my family were detained, not rescued.

My family was ordered to evacuate our home. We were directed to evacuation points. Beforehand, I, my mother, my brother and two sisters visited a nursing home where the elderly clients had been abandoned by the owners and staff. There were five elderly persons there; the others had been evacuated earlier, perhaps by family. The day before the flood, the manager had come and told everyone they had to get out. Taking the keys to the bus that the home used to transport the senior citizens, the manager left them stranded. We rescued them. We shared all our food and provisions. When we approached the police and asked for help, the[y] refused to help us. Instead, they threatened to shoot my baby brother.

We were then lured to the so-called evacuation points. This was several days after the hurricane had struck. The city was flooded. Soldiers had showed up with M16s and military weapons. They had declared New Orleans and Jefferson Parish a war zone. They loaded us onto military trucks after they told us they would take us to shelters where our basic needs would be met.

We were dropped off at a site where we were fenced in, and penned in with military vehicles. The armed military personnel brought in dogs. There we were subjected to conditions only comparable to a concentration camp.

We were in a wide open space along the interstate and under the Highway 10 causeway. The overpass provided little shade, however. During the days, we were exposed to the hot sun. August is the hottest month in New Orleans. It was early September and still extremely hot. Our skin blistered. My mother's skin is still not fully healed.

We were just three miles from an airport, but we were detained there for several days. Many of those who were there when we arrived had already been there several days. On any given day there were at least ten thousand people in the camp. On my last day there, I would estimate there were still three thousand detainees. By that time, nearly all the white people had been selected to evacuate first. They were put on buses and shipped out, leaving the remaining population 95 per cent black.

There was muck and trash all over the causeway. Nothing was done to clean it up. At night, we were subject to sleep deprivation as low-flying helicopters were deliberately flown right over us. They would throw up the muck and trash, so that it would get all over us, even the pregnant women, the elderly, the infirm.

The military did not bring anything to help keep any of us alive. Not even a first aid kit. But they had body bags. They were doing nothing for the pregnant women. Some women miscarried. I know that conditions at the Convention Center were much the same. My niece was there. She was pregnant and she was terrified that her unborn baby had died. When she asked the military for help, they told her to wait until she was sure the baby was dead and then talk to them.

When I later spoke of my experience to a state trooper, he told me: "I would have rebelled." They set us up so that we would rebel, so that they could shoot us. At one point they brought in two truckloads of dogs and let the dogs out.

We would circulate through the camp to assist the sick and elderly and pregnant. One day, when I was on my way to get some water, I met a friend. He was a fellow musician. He told me that he wanted to try to get word out to the news media. But he was afraid to leave his family. I told him I would look after his family. But while he was gone I also had to circle back and check on my own family. I found that my brother had come up with an idea. He had persuaded a woman who was pregnant and due for labor to fake as if she were in labor. They told those in charge that she needed medical attention or she could have a miscarriage, and that got her out.

There was an old man from the senior center, he was an amputee. We had to carry him to the bathroom. They would not assist in caring for our people. The heat was unbearable. We got to the point we were so afraid of losing him to a heat stroke. We told them he was in a diabetic coma, that's how we got him out.

Mother is a cardiac patient, born with an enlarged heart. She suffers extreme hypertension. For three days I pleaded with them for care, and they would not do anything. Finally, on the third day, someone came out to check her blood pressure. The sphygmomanometer did not appear to be in working condition. I told the man, who was from the Coast Guard, to take my blood pressure first. The thing fell to pieces in his hands. It never worked.

The camp was so big, and people were scattered. People were deliberately kept apart. One woman was not allowed to see her two children.

At the camp, they lied and told us all the buses were going to the same place. They wouldn't tell us when the buses were coming. Meanwhile, my Mother sat in the blazing hot sun ...

On the last day they refused to give food and water to the ill for 24 hours.

People died in the camp. We saw the bodies lying there.

They were all about detention, as if it were Iraq, like we were foreigners and they were fighting a war. They implemented war-like conditions. They treated us worse than prisoners of war. Even prisoners of war have rights under the Geneva Convention.

Source: U.S. House of Representatives (2005). Reprinted with permission of the Select Bipartisan Committee to Investigate the Preparation for the Response to Hurricane Katrina.

5

Sociology as a Vocation

It's All About the Context

If this book has any value, then the next time you hear about people dying, you won't just ask, "What did they die of?" Instead, like a sociologist, you'll also ask, "What was the context of their death?" Analytically and practically, a world of difference separates the two questions. Consider that the four leading causes of death in North America are heart disease, cancer, stroke, and chronic lung disease. Close to two-thirds of North Americans die of these ailments. But the *context* in which these ailments become leading causes of death is one in which a quarter of the population is addicted to smoking tobacco and most people eat too much unhealthy food, get insufficient exercise, and are exposed to all manner of dangerous pollutants. Any analysis that focuses just on the immediate causes of death is inadequate because it fails to take into account the social context that allows heart disease, cancer, stroke, and chronic lung disease to become leading causes of death in the first place (Mokdad, Marks, Stroup, and Gerberding, 2004).

Focusing on context is important practically, not just analytically. Governments, businesses, charitable organizations, universities, and individuals invest enormous sums to increase life expectancy. Yet far more money is put into researching and coping with the immediate causes of death, such as finding cures for cancer, than solving contextual problems that give rise to the leading causes of death in the first place, such as reducing pollution and providing people with resources and incentives so they will eat healthier food, exercise more, and stop smoking tobacco.

Few people doubt that we must continue investing heavily in research on the immediate causes of death. Not enough people understand that investing substantially more in solving contextual problems (if necessary, even diverting some funds from medical research) would let the average person live a longer, disease-free life. A dollar spent on prevention saves more lives than a dollar spent on treatment. Ignoring context—failing to think sociologically—kills people (Picard, 2006).[1]

Similarly, by investigating three social contexts in detail—the American inner city, the world of Palestinian suicide bombers, and the hurricane-prone Caribbean basin and the coast of the Gulf of Mexico—we learned much of practical importance for improving the quality of life and increasing life expectancy. We learned, first, that the defiant cry for identity known as hip hop has unfortunate consequences. Hip hop encourages deadly violence. It also diverts attention from mobility strategies that are more likely than gangsterism to meet with success and thus improve the quality of life. We learned, second, that the policy of retaliation that is often involved in suicide bombings and targeted killings deepens the resolve of both sides in the Israeli–Palestinian conflict to kill each other. It thus moves both parties farther away from a negotiated peace. And we learned, third, that the lack of disaster planning in some hurricane-prone regions greatly increases the chance that the most vulnerable members of society will perish. These lessons are sufficiently instructive that I feel wholly justified in claiming that sociology is a life or death issue.

But *caveat emptor*—let the buyer beware. I wouldn't feel comfortable selling you a bill of goods without telling you exactly what the purchase involves. Let me therefore close by offering a thumbnail sketch of how sociologists go about their business. That way, you can make an informed choice about how heavily, if at all, you want to buy into the discipline.

I can best describe what sociologists do by focusing on four terms: values, theory, research, and social policy. As you will now learn, sociologists' ideas about what is good and bad (their **values**) lead them to choose certain subjects for analysis and help them formulate tentative, testable explanations of the social phenomena that interest them (**theories**). Sociologists then systematically collect and analyze data to see if their tentative explanations are valid (**research**). Finally, based on the

---

[1] A century ago, the leading causes of death in North America were pneumonia, influenza, tuberculosis, diarrhea, and other intestinal ailments. From an historical point of view, the invention of antibiotics and increased life expectancy are also important contextual elements in the explanation of how we die.

results of their research, they propose rules and regulations to govern the actions of organizations and governments in the hope of correcting social problems (**social policies**). Individual sociologists may specialize in theory construction, empirical research, or policy analysis, but the sociological enterprise as a whole involves all of these activities.

Doing Sociology

Values

There never has been, nor can there be, any human search for truth without human emotions.

—Vladimir Lenin (1964: 260)

Someone once told Émile Durkheim that the facts contradicted one of his theories. "The facts," Durkheim replied, "are wrong" (quoted in Lukes, 1973: 52). Likewise, when a colleague's experimental evidence appeared to challenge his special theory of relativity, Albert Einstein's reaction was essentially, "so much the worse for the facts" (Clark, 1971: 144). What's wrong with this picture? Aren't scientists' opinions supposed to be governed by respect for evidence? How then could a founding father of sociology and the greatest physicist of the twentieth century react in such a cavalier manner to facts that apparently falsified their views?

Actually, there is nothing wrong with this picture. Great scientists are human beings, and they can be as pig-headed as you and me. Having invested so much time and energy developing pet theories, they may cling to them stubbornly even if evidence suggests that they are wrong. What is intriguing is that, despite such common human failings as obstinacy, vanity, short-sightedness, and narrow-mindedness, scientists routinely arrive at knowledge that is widely considered valid.

They are able to do so because people have designed the *institution* of science to eliminate ideas that can't be supported by evidence. The norms of science require that scientists publicize their findings and their methods of discovery, and that other scientists (with their own pet theories, prejudices, and professional rivalries) carefully scrutinize the work of their colleagues. Science is not quite a blood sport, but it does stimulate a lot of conflict over the validity of ideas and is therefore not recommended for the faint of heart. Out of this conflict there typically emerges a temporary consensus about what constitutes valid knowledge. A higher level of consensus exists in physics than in sociology, but in all disciplines it is the community of scholars playing by the rules of the scientific game that determines the prevailing consensus.[2] You don't get special consideration if you're a Durkheim or an Einstein. Consensus, not authority, rules.

I would not, however, want to leave you with the impression that scientists' values are always a danger to science. To the contrary, values are critically important in the scientific enterprise. They first play a role in determining what we want to study. As Max Weber wrote, we choose to study "only those segments of reality which have become significant to us because of their value-relevance" (Weber, 1949: 76). Values also fire our imagination and our intuition. They shape our ideas about how the parts of society fit together, what the ideal society should look like, which actions and policies are needed to help us reach that ideal, and which theories offer the best explanations for the phenomena that interest us (Edel, 1965). True, when values infuse science they may lead to subjectivity or bias of one sort or another. But that matters little as long as scientists allow their peers to judge the worth of their ideas and form a binding consensus—and as long as outside forces such as governments and corporations don't interfere with their ability to do so. The scientific community's consensus is precisely what is meant by objectivity, and as long as consensus is allowed to crystallize and prevail, bias will be minimized. Thus, values are an invaluable source of scientific creativity. They become problematic only if the scientific community fails to remain vigilant in its scrutiny of theory construction, empirical research, and policy proposals.

Theory and Research

> Practice should always be based upon a sound knowledge of theory....
> [W]ithout it nothing can be done well....
>
> —*Leonardo da Vinci (1956: 910)*

As noted earlier, sociological theories are tentative, testable explanations of some aspect of social life. They state how and why certain social facts are related. For example, in his theory of suicide, Durkheim related facts about suicide rates to facts about social solidarity. Doing so allowed him to explain suicide as a function of social solidarity (see Chapter 1).

---

[2] Because the rewards for innovation are many and scientists are only human, some of them are tempted to break the rules. They may falsify data, for example. But unlike ordinary criminals, who are sometimes able to conceal their illicit activities, scientists work in the open. As a result, the scrutiny of the scientific community almost always ensures that they get caught, usually sooner rather than later.

Nontestable explanations aren't scientifically useful. Some people believe that wealthy, unknown conspirators manipulate the price of gold and benefit from the price swings. Others believe that certain physical ailments are caused by space aliens who routinely abduct earthlings. Such theories are unscientific because they are not testable. Nobody has so far been able to observe, count, analyze, and interpret data that would allow us to decide whether they are valid. Note also that because scientific theories are testable, they are only tentative explanations. Research may disprove them at any time.

A theory may be little more than a hunch drawn from the experience of everyday life (Einstein, 1954: 270). But without some conjecture as to how facts are related it is impossible to conduct meaningful research. That is what Leonardo da Vinci meant when he said that people cannot do anything well if they engage in practice (research, and action based on that research) without theory. Starting research before developing a clear theoretical statement of how the relevant social facts might be related is a recipe for wasting years collecting and analyzing data in the field, the archives, or at a computer terminal. The reverse is also problematic. Theorizing without research is about as useful to science as exercise without movement is useful to the human body. From the comfort of an armchair, one can entertain the wildest of conjectures. The reality check known as research brings theorists down to earth and turns speculation into knowledge.

A stylized version of the sociological research process is presented in Figure 5.1.[3] As you already know, research can begin only when sociologists identify topics that they find significant (step 1) and hypothesize how observable facts central to their topic are related (step 2). Their next task is to review the existing theoretical and research literature (step 3). Reading previous work on the topic of interest stimulates one's sociological imagination and refines one's thinking. Besides, there is no sense rediscovering what researchers have already found. Reviewing the relevant theoretical and research literature is an indispensable means of avoiding duplication of effort and learning from past insights, discoveries, and mistakes.

---

[3] I say "stylized" because research is typically less orderly than Figure 5.1 makes it appear. For example, researchers usually jump back and forth between stage 2 ("formulate a testable theory") and stage 7 ("analyze data") many times before proceeding to stage 8 ("report results").

Figure 5.1 *The Research Process*

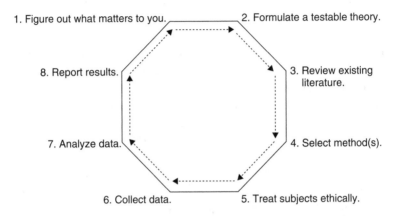

1. Figure out what matters to you.
2. Formulate a testable theory.
3. Review existing literature.
4. Select method(s).
5. Treat subjects ethically.
6. Collect data.
7. Analyze data.
8. Report results.

Different kinds of research questions require different research methods (step 4; Babbie, 2004). In general, sociologists adopt more precise methods when they research topics that are more theoretically refined. Consider surveys, the most widely used research method in sociology. They involve asking a representative sample of people drawn from the population of interest a set of standardized questions about their attitudes, knowledge, and/or behaviour. Surveys may be conducted face-to-face, over the phone, through the mail, or via the Internet. For the most part, the people who respond to surveys ("respondents") are presented with a list of allowable answers from which to choose. But insofar as surveys require that researchers know in advance what questions to ask and the range of possible answers to their questions, surveys are not always an appropriate research tool. Particularly in areas where theory is not highly developed—in "exploratory" research—it usually makes sense to conduct interviews that are less structured and more open-ended. This means that the interviews don't define a range of allowable responses and allow the spontaneous introduction of new questions whose importance emerges only in the course of the interview. In many cases, even conducting formal interviews is jumping the gun. For research where theory is poorly developed and researchers have only a hunch about how observable facts may be related, one or another form of field research is often the method of choice. For example, **participant observation** involves spending considerable time in the social setting of the people who interest the researchers. It allows researchers not just to step back and observe their subjects' milieu from an outsider's point of view but also to step in and develop an understanding of the meaning people attach to the elements that populate their social world. From such observations, researchers may develop precise theoretical formulations that will permit more refined testing of ideas by means of structured interviews and surveys.

Many sociologists regard experiments as too artificial to provide valid knowledge about most forms of social behaviour because they remove people from their social settings (recall our discussion of experiments on the effects of media violence in Chapter 2). As a result, the use of experiments in sociology is probably less widespread now than it was a few decades ago. In contrast, various methods that use historical records and existing documents as data are increasingly popular. For instance, sociologists have interpreted published histories to develop important theories about the uneven spread of industrial capitalism around the world and the turn of some countries to democracy, others to authoritarianism (Moore, 1967; Wallerstein, 1974–89).

Once they leave their offices and begin collecting data, researchers must keep in mind four ethical commandments (step 5):

1. *Respect your subjects' right to safety.* Do your subjects no harm and, in particular, give them the right to decide whether and how they can be studied.
2. *Respect your subjects' right to informed consent.* Tell subjects how the information they supply will be used and allow them to judge the degree of personal risk involved in supplying it.
3. *Respect your subjects' right to privacy.* Allow subjects the right to decide whether and how the information they supply may be revealed to the public.
4. *Respect your subjects' right to confidentiality.* Refrain from using information in a way that allows it to be traced to a particular subject.

Ethical considerations are not restricted to the data collection phase of research (step 6). They come to the fore during the data analysis and reporting phases too. Hence two more commandments:

5. *Do not falsify data.* Report findings as they are, not as you would like them to be.

6. *Do not plagiarize.* Explicitly identify, credit, and reference authors when making use of their written work in any form, including Web postings.

If theories propose conjectures about the way certain social facts are related, data analysis involves determining the degree to which the information at one's disposal conforms to the conjectures (step 7). Information can often be usefully turned into numbers. For example, if the allowable responses to a survey question are "strongly disagree," "disagree," "neither disagree nor agree," "agree," and "strongly agree," the responses can be assigned the numbers 1 through 5, respectively. The advantage of turning information into numbers is that it permits statistical analysis using computers.

You can appreciate why computer-assisted statistical analysis is useful by imagining a spreadsheet with 240 000 cells. Since it is not unusual for surveys to ask 1200 respondents 200 questions each, data matrices of this size are common in sociology (1200 × 200 = 240 000). Each of the spreadsheet's 1200 (horizontal) rows is reserved for an individual respondent. Each of its 200 (vertical) columns is reserved for responses to one survey question. That is a vast amount of information. Human beings don't have the ability to scan, unaided, a spreadsheet with nearly a quarter of a million cells and spot patterns in the numbers that would lead them to conclude that the data conform more or less closely to their theoretical conjectures. Computer-assisted statistical analysis is simply a means of finding patterns in the data matrix—patterns that allow one to see whether one's conjectures hold up. In milliseconds, an ordinary PC equipped with the right software can add up a column of 1200 numbers corresponding to one opinion question in a survey and then divide the sum by the number of respondents who answered the question, telling you the average opinion of the respondents. Or it can compute a statistic that tells you how responses to one opinion question vary with responses to another opinion question, so you can learn how, if at all, the opinions are related. More complex statistical analyses showing, say, the unique and combined effects of class, race, gender, religion, place of residence, and age on political preference might take a few more milliseconds. The point is that having such pattern-finding power at one's disposal increases the researcher's capacity to test, reformulate, and retest theories quickly and creatively.

The final stage in the research process involves publishing the results of one's analysis in a report, a journal, or a book (step 8). Doing so allows other sociologists to pore over the research so that errors can be corrected and better questions can be formulated for future research. It also allows people to apply research findings to social policy.

Some sociological research is conducted with particular policy aims in mind and therefore has a direct impact on the formulation of rules, regulations, laws, and programs by organizations and governments. Most sociological research, however, has only an indirect impact on social policy. For example, no organization or government hired me to write this book, and I entertain no illusion that officials will read it and suddenly decide they need to change the way they do business. Like many sociologists, my aim is to influence the educated public and, in particular, young adults. I hope that my work will contribute, however slightly, to enlightening people about the opportunities and constraints that help shape their thoughts and actions, and assist them in making personal, organizational, and political decisions that will allow them and their fellow citizens to live happier and longer lives than would otherwise be possible. It's an immodest hope but, I think, not entirely unrealistic.

Careers

What about your hopes? Might they include the study of sociology? To make an informed decision on such an important issue, you need information on what you can expect from a sociology degree. It is instructive in this connection to examine the careers pursued by sociology graduates. About 1.35 million Americans and 145 000 Canadians graduate with a bachelor's degree every year. Roughly 29 000 of these people major in sociology. Some 2100 will eventually receive a sociology MA and 650 will earn a sociology PhD (estimated from National Center for Education Statistics, 2004; 2005).[4] What do they do with their degrees?

---

[4] These estimates are based on U.S. data for graduates in the academic year 2002–03. I added 10 percent to the U.S. figures to take account of Canada's population and its slightly lower graduation rate. I also assumed that the ratio of master's to bachelor's graduates and the ratio of doctoral to bachelor's graduates in 2002–03 are equal to the proportion of bachelor's students who eventually graduate with MAs and PhDs.

Most people with a *graduate* degree in sociology teach and conduct research in colleges and universities. Research is a bigger part of the job in more prestigious institutions. In the United States in 2003, average annual earnings stood at about US$38 000 for all occupations, US$49 000 for all white-collar occupations, US$67 000 for all college and university professors, and US$68 000 for sociology professors alone (U.S. Department of Labor, 2004: 73–4).

Many sociologists with a graduate degree conduct research and give policy advice in institutions outside the system of higher education. The number of research- and policy-related jobs for sociologists is growing faster than the number of teaching jobs. In government, sociologists help formulate research-based policy in such areas as health, social welfare, economic and social development, the elderly, youth, criminal justice, science, and housing (for a fascinating case study, see House, 2005). Nongovernmental agencies that employ sociologists include professional and public-interest associations and trade unions. In the private sector, sociologists practise their craft in firms that specialize in public opinion polling, management consulting, market research, standardized testing, and evaluation research, which assesses the impact of policies and programs.

An *undergraduate* major in sociology is excellent preparation for many fields other than sociology (Stephens, 1998). Recent American research shows that about 40 percent of people with a sociology major intend to go to graduate or professional school. Of those who aspire to do so, more than 82 percent expect to choose fields other than sociology (Spalter-Roth, Erskine, Polsiak, and Panzarella, 2005: 24–5). Their top choices in order of popularity:

1. education
2. counselling/psychology
3. applied sociology (MA)
4. social work
5. law
6. criminology
7. sociology (PhD)
8. medicine/nursing
9. marketing/business administration
10. public affairs/public policy
11. communication

Recent Canadian research comparing the earnings of majors in the social sciences and humanities shows that graduates in no field earn significantly more than sociology majors do (Davies and Walters, 2007). However, from the point of view of the job market, the value of a sociology major lies partly in the generic skills it offers rather than any specifically technical skills associated with it (Davies and Walters, 2007). Sociology majors (as well as majors in the other social sciences) tend to be adept in interpersonal relations, communication, decision making, critical thinking, conflict management, the assumption of authority, and the ability to apply abstract ideas to real-life situations. As a result, they can be trained quickly and effectively to do any number of jobs in the quickly growing service sector of the economy. Most employers know that. Consequently, one Canadian study found that the unemployment rate was lower among social science graduates than among science graduates and that there are more new jobs for people with social science degrees than for people with degrees in other fields. As a bonus, the discrepancy between men's and women's income was smallest among social science graduates (Allen, 1999).

Positive and Negative Freedom

Now that I have sketched what sociologists do and how you might fit into the sociological enterprise, there remains the task of summarizing the values, theories, and policies that I have introduced in this book.

Underlying my analyses is a particular conception of human **freedom** that I have come to value highly and that I must first clarify.

Political philosophers distinguish "negative" from "positive" freedom (Berlin, 2002b; MacCallum, 1967). **Negative freedom** is freedom *from* constraints that would otherwise prevent me from doing as I wish. When I have the right to vote, express my opinions publicly, and associate with whomever I wish, I enjoy negative freedom. That is because I can engage in these activities only when nobody prevents me from doing so. Note that noninterference from the state is usually required if I am to enjoy negative freedom.

In contrast, **positive freedom** is the capacity *to* act rationally. It involves taking control of one's life and realizing one's best interests. When I receive a higher education and good medical treatment in the event of ill health, I enjoy positive freedom. That is because I require such benefits if I am to have any hope of realizing my best interests. However, because particular individuals may be incapable of understanding their best interests, it is typically necessary for some higher authority, such as the state, to help define those interests and provide the benefits needed to attain them.

Some political philosophers argue that positive freedom and negative freedom are incompatible. If you have more positive freedom, they say, you must have less negative freedom, and vice-versa. The notion that positive and negative freedoms are rivals was proposed by Sir Isaiah Berlin in the mid-twentieth century (Berlin, 2002b). Berlin argued that if the state tried to define the best interests of the citizenry and provide the benefits it deemed necessary to attain them, it could easily slip into authoritarianism. He pointed to the Soviet Union as a case in point. The rulers of the Soviet Union, guided by communist ideology, claimed to know what was required for the citizenry to realize its best interests. The state provided free education, child-care, medical care, and so on, but people were not free to vote for the party of their choice, express their opinions publicly, or associate with whomever they chose.

In contrast to Berlin's argument, this book is based on the idea that positive and negative freedom *are* generally compatible (Taylor, 1985). Figure 5.2 supports the validity of my claim. It contains data on all 125 countries for which recent data on positive and negative freedom exist. It plots an index of negative freedom (along the horizontal axis) against an index of positive freedom (along the vertical axis). The index of negative freedom combines information on freedom to vote, freedom of the press, freedom of assembly, and other political and civil liberties in each country. It indicates how free people are from state oppression. The index of positive freedom combines information on average level of education, adult literacy, and life expectancy in each country. It indicates how free people are to realize their interests because they have the state support (through education and health care) to do so. If Berlin's argument held, we would expect to discover an inverse relationship between positive and negative freedom; the more of one, the less of the other. But the trend line in Figure 5.2 shows just the opposite. The countries ranking highest on positive freedom also tend to rank highest on negative freedom. The countries ranking lowest on positive freedom also tend to rank lowest on negative freedom. Some countries deviate from this tendency, but the overall association between positive and negative freedom is quite strong.[5] In general, then, and contrary to what Berlin argued, negative and positive freedoms are usually not rivals. In most cases, states that intervene to provide benefits deemed to be beneficial for the citizenry also *remove* political constraints from their citizens. States that constrain their citizens the most tend to provide

Figure 5.2 *Positive by Negative Freedom in 125 Countries*

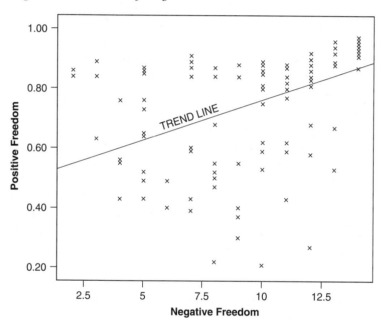

Sources: Compiled from Freedom House (2006); United Nations (2005: 219–22).

Note: Data are for the latest year available. Negative freedom is measured by the index of political and civil liberties, which is calculated annually by Freedom House, a nonpartisan organization that promotes democracy around the world. Positive freedom is measured by life expectancy at birth, the literacy rate for people over the age of 14, and enrollment ratios at all levels of education, as calculated annually by United Nations' social scientists.

[5] The **correlation coefficient** (r) measures the degree of association between variables. It ranges in value from −1 (a perfect inverse correlation, in which a unit increase in one variable is associated with a unit decrease in the other variable) to +1 (a perfect positive correlation, in which a unit increase in one variable is associated with a unit increase in the other variable). An r of 0 indicates no correlation between the two variables. For the two variables arrayed in Figure 5.2, $r = 0.486$, which indicates a moderately strong, positive correlation.

fewest benefits to the citizenry. What gives the trend line in Figure 5.2 its upward slope are the mainly rich and moderately well-off countries in the upper right quadrant that have well-developed state services and are highly democratic; and the mainly moderately well-off and poor countries in the lower left quadrant that have less developed state services and authoritarian regimes.

Putting It All Together

The idea that positive freedom is compatible with negative freedom runs through this book like a multicoloured thread. Consider the main arguments I made in each of the book's substantive chapters.

In Chapter 3, which dealt with suicide bombers, my main theoretical argument boils down to the view that decreasing social solidarity among high-solidarity groups would lower the rate of what Durkheim called altruistic suicide. With good reason, insurgent Palestinian groups believe that they and their people are threatened. Actions that reinforce that belief, such as targeted killings by the Israeli state, encourage some of them to take their own lives for the sake of their people (Brym and Araj, 2007). It follows that decreasing the perceived threat will lower social solidarity and the frequency of suicide attacks. I called for specific state actions to achieve that end: the elimination of targeted killings by Israel and the use of powerful diplomatic and economic levers by the United States to compel both sides to negotiate a settlement that will recognize their territorial and security needs. The positive freedom to live in peace requires such brave and energetic state intervention in my view. I believe, moreover, that, absent their chronic conflict, Palestinians and Israelis would be able to remove restrictions on political and civil liberties that now constrain people in both societies; peace would also allow negative freedom to grow in the Middle East.

The main theoretical argument of Chapter 4 is that when the state provides higher standards of security and well-being to the most vulnerable members of society, it increases their welfare and lowers their chance of death due to natural disasters. At the risk of raising a red flag, so to speak, I made the point by comparing the treatment of vulnerable populations in the United States and Cuba. I fully appreciate that some readers will have reacted negatively to my suggestion that the United States can learn a valuable lesson from a communist country. That is why I emphasized that Japan, too, takes exactly the measures that I think are necessary to protect vulnerable citizens without restricting anyone's negative freedom. The Japanese case demonstrates that freedom from excessive state authority and the freedom of society's most vulnerable members to live in relative safety are not incommensurable.

In Chapter 2's discussion of hip hop, we visited the American inner city, where the sense of community is weak and social institutions, especially families and schools, are crumbling. As Durkheim would lead us to expect in such an anomic social setting, the rate of suicide among inner-city black youth is high and rising quickly. Other forms of violence leading to death, notably homicide, also proliferate, as do cultural products such as hip hop that often glorify violence. Again, I claimed that state intervention could help shore up and provide alternatives to faltering social institutions. More engaging and higher-quality schools, widely accessible child-care programs, and organized after-school athletic activities would, for example, make the inner city less anomic. Gun control would also help. Such policies would increase the positive freedom of residents in the inner city to live more secure lives and enjoy better prospects for upward mobility. They would also increase negative freedom by lowering the constraints on life imposed by coercive violence.

Such are my arguments. I do not ask you to agree with them. I do invite you to engage in a debate with your fellow students and professors on the subjects I have raised, using logic, evidence, and the sociological perspective to add substance to your views. As you do so, you may discover, as I did when I was 19, that sociology is not just a course but a calling.

Glossary

Absolute deprivation refers to longstanding poverty and unemployment.

Altruistic suicide. See **suicide.**

Anomic suicide. See **suicide.**

Citizenship refers to the rights of people to various protections under the law. To varying degrees, citizens of different countries have fought for and won civil rights (free speech, freedom of religious choice, justice under the law), political rights (freedom to vote and run for office), and social rights (freedom to receive a minimum level of economic security and participate fully in social life).

The **correlation coefficient** (r) measures the degree of association between variables. It ranges in value from -1 (a perfect inverse correlation, in which a unit increase in one variable is associated with a unit decrease in the other variable) to $+1$ (a perfect positive correlation, in which a unit increase in one variable is associated with a unit increase in the other variable). An r of 0 indicates no correlation between the two variables.

Culture is the sum total of shared and socially transmitted languages, beliefs, symbols, values, material objects, routine practices, and art forms that people create to help them survive and prosper.

Determinism is the belief that everything happens the way it does because it was destined to happen in just that way.

Egoistic suicide. See **suicide.**

Experiments are carefully controlled artificial situations that allow researchers to isolate presumed causes and measure their effects precisely. Typically, subjects are randomly divided into "experimental" and "control" groups. Only the experimental group is exposed to the presumed cause. The hypothesized effect is measured in the experimental and control groups before and after exposure. By comparing the measures of the effect before and after exposure, in both the experimental and control groups, experimenters can determine how much influence the presumed cause had on the hypothesized effect.

Field research involves systematically observing people in their natural social settings.

Freedom has negative and positive aspects. **Negative freedom** is the absence of constraint. It is freedom *from* obstacles that would otherwise prevent one from doing as one wishes. **Positive freedom** is the capacity to take control of one's life and realize one's best interests. It is freedom *to* act rationally.

The **homicide rate** is the number of murders per 100 000 people in a population in a given period, such as a year.

The **least-squares regression line** (or "trend line") is a straight line in a two-dimensional graph that is drawn so as to minimize the sum of the squared perpendicular distances between each data point and the line itself.

Markets are social relations that regulate the exchange of goods and services. In a market, the prices of goods and services are established by how plentiful they are (supply) and how much they are wanted (demand).

Negative freedom. See **freedom**.

Official statistics are numerical data compiled by state organizations for purposes other than sociological research.

Participant observation research involves spending considerable time in the natural social setting of the people who interest the researchers. This allows researchers to step back and observe their subjects' milieu from an outsider's point of view, and also to step in and develop an understanding of the meaning people attach to the elements that populate their social world.

Positive freedom. See **freedom**.

Power is the ability to realize one's will, even against the resistance of others.

Races are categories of people defined not so much by biological differences as by social forces. Specifically, racial distinctions are typically made and reinforced by advantaged people for the purpose of creating and maintaining a system of inequality.

Rates let you compare groups of different size. To calculate the rate at which an event occurs, divide the number of times an event occurs by the total number of people to whom the event could occur in principle. Then calculate how many times it would occur in a population of standard size (say, 100 000).

Relative deprivation refers to the growth of an intolerable gap between what people expect and what they get out of life.

Research is the process of systematically collecting and analyzing data to test theories.

The **sex ratio** is the number of men per 100 women in a population.

Social action is human behaviour that is meaningful in the sense that it takes into account the behaviour of others.

A **social class** is a position occupied by people in a hierarchy that is shaped by economic criteria including wealth.

Social interaction is a dynamic sequence of social actions in which people (or groups) creatively react to each other.

Social policy refers to the rules and regulations that organizations and governments establish to correct social problems.

Social solidarity refers to the frequency of interaction and the degree of sharing of beliefs, values, and morals in a group.

Social structures are relatively stable patterns of social relations that constrain and create opportunities for the way we think and act.

Suicide, the taking of one's own life, may take several forms according to Durkheim. He called suicides that occur in high-solidarity settings **altruistic**. In contrast, suicide that occurs in low-solidarity settings is egoistic or anomic. **Egoistic suicide** results from a lack of integration of the individual into society because of weak social ties to others. **Anomic suicide** occurs when norms governing behaviour are vaguely defined.

In a **survey,** randomly selected people are asked questions about their knowledge, attitudes, or behaviour. Researchers aim to study part of a group (a "sample") to learn about the whole group of interest (the "population").

Theories are tentative, testable explanations of phenomena.

Upward mobility refers to movement up a system of inequality.

Values are ideas about what is good and bad.

Voluntarism is the belief that people alone control their destiny.

References

Agenda Inc. 2005. "American Brandstand 2005." On the World Wide Web at http://www.agendainc.com/brandstand05.pdf (accessed 27 March 2006).

Allen, Robert C. 1999. *Education and Technological Revolutions: The Role of the Social Sciences and the Humanities in the Knowledge Based Economy.* Ottawa: Social Sciences and Humanities Research Council of Canada.

al-Quds (Jerusalem). 2000–05. [Arabic: *Jerusalem.*]

al-Quds al-'Arabi (London). 2000–05. [Arabic: *Arab Jerusalem.*]

"al-Ra'is: 'Amaliyat Nitanya Juramat did Sha'buna.'" [Arabic: "The President: 'Netanya Operation is a Crime against Our People.'"] 2005. *al-Quds* 12 July: 1A.

American Society of Plastic Surgeons. 2006. "2005 Cosmetic Plastic Surgery Trends." On the World Wide Web at http://www.plasticsurgery.org/public_education/Statistical-Trends.cfm (accessed 14 September 2006).

Anderson, Craig and Brad J. Bushman. 2002. "The Effects of Media Violence on Society." *Science* 295, 5564: 2377–9.

Anderson, Michael. 2003. "Reading Violence in Boys' Writing." *Language Arts* 80, 3: 223–31.

Appleby, John, Maxime Fougère, and Manon Rouleau. 2004. "Is Post-Secondary Education in Canada a Cost-Effective Proposition?" Applied Research Branch, Strategic Policy, Human Resources Development Canada. On the World Wide Web at http://www.11.hrsdc.gc.ca/en/cs/sp/hrsdc/arb/publications/research/2002-000150/page01.shtml (accessed 24 May 2005).

Arian, Asher. 2001. "Israeli Public Opinion in the Wake of the 2000–2001 Intifada." *Strategic Assessment* 4, 2. On the World Wide Web at http://www.tau.ac.il/jcss/sa/v4n2p.Ari.html (15 May 2005).

_____. 2002. "A Further Turn to the Right: Israeli Public Opinion on National Security—2002." *Strategic Assessment* 5, 1. On the World Wide Web at http://www.tau.ac.il/jcss/sa/v5n1p4Ari.html (accessed 15 May 2005).

Associated Press. 2005. "Lil' Kim Sentenced to a Year in Prison." *MSNBC.com* 6 July. On the World Wide Web at http://www.msnbc.msn.com/id/8485039/ (accessed 20 April 2006).

Atran, Scott. 2003. "Genesis of Suicide Terrorism." *Science* 299, 5612: 1534–9.

Auden, W. H. 1940. "September 1, 1939." Pp. 98–101 in *Another Time: Poems*. New York: Random House.

Babbie, Earl. 2004. *The Practice of Social Research*, 10th ed. Belmont CA: Wadsworth.

Bayles, Martha. 1994. *Hole in Our Soul: The Loss of Beauty and Meaning in American Popular Music*. Chicago: University of Chicago Press.

Becker, Ernest. 1971. *The Birth and Death of Meaning: An Interdisciplinary Perspective on the Problem of Man*. New York: Free Press.

_____. 1973. *The Denial of Death*. New York: Free Press.

Berger, Peter L. and Thomas Luckmann. 1966. *The Social Construction of Reality: A Treatise in the Sociology of Knowledge*. Garden City NY: Doubleday.

Berlin, Isaiah. 2002a. "Historical Inevitability." Pp. 94–165 in *Liberty*, Henry Hardy, ed. Oxford: Oxford University Press.

_____. 2002b. "Two Concepts of Liberty." Pp. 166–217 in *Liberty*, Henry Hardy, ed. Oxford: Oxford University Press.

Berube, Alan and Steven Raphael. 2005. "Access to Cars in New Orleans." The Brookings Institution. On the World Wide Web at http://www.brookings.edu/metro/20050915_katrinacarstables.pdf (accessed 30 May 2006).

Block, Fred, Anna C. Korteweg, and Kerry Woodward. 2006. "The Compassion Gap in American Poverty Policy." *Contexts* 5, 2: 14–20.

Blumenthal, Sidney. 2005. "No One Can Say They Didn't See It Coming." *Salon.com* 31 August. On the World Wide Web at http://dir.salon.com/story/opinion/blumenthal/2005/08/31/disaster_preparation/index_np.html (accessed 31 May 2006).

Bourne, Joel. K. 2004. "Gone with the Water." *National Geographic Magazine* October. On the World Wide Web at http://magma.nationalgeographic.com/ngm/0410/feature5/?fs=www3.nationalgeographic.com (accessed 30 May 2006).

Browne, Kevin D. and Catherine Hamilton-Giachritsis. 2005. "The Influence of Violent Media on Children and Adolescents: A Public-Health Approach." *The Lancet* 365, 9460: 702–10.

Brym, Robert J. 1983. "Israel in Lebanon." *Middle East Focus* 6, 1: 14–19.

_____ and Bader Araj. 2006. "Suicide Bombing as Strategy and Interaction: The Case of the Second *Intifada.*" *Social Forces* 84: 1965–82.

_____ and _____. 2007. "Palestinian Suicide Bombing Revisited: A Critique of the Outbidding Thesis." *Political Science Quarterly* 122: Forthcoming.

_____ and John Lie. 2007. *Sociology: Your Compass for a New World*, 3rd ed. Belmont CA: Wadsworth.

Bullard, Robert D. 2006. "Katrina and the Second Disaster: A Twenty-Point Plan to Destroy Black New Orleans." On the World Wide Web at http://www.ejrc.cau.edu/Bullard20pointplan.html (accessed 18 May 2006).

Burdeau, Cain. 2006. "Corps of Engineers Takes Responsibility for New Orleans Flooding." *Associated Press Newswires* 1 June.

"The Celebrity 100." 2005. *Forbes.com* 15 June. On the World Wide Web at http://www.forbes.com/celebrity100/ (accessed 27 March 2006).

Clark, Ronald W. 1971. *Einstein: The Life and Times.* New York: Avon.

Cohn, Marjorie. 2005. "The Two Americas." *Truthout* 3 September. On the World Wide Web at http://www.truthout.org/docs_2005/090305Y.shtml (accessed 26 July 2006).

Combs, Sean "Puffy." 1999. *Forever.* New York: Bad Boy Entertainment (CD).

_____ and the Lox. 1997. "I Got the Power." On the World Wide Web at http://www.ewsonline.com/badboy/lyrpow.html (accessed 22 March 2000).

Comfort, Louise K. 2006. "Cities at Risk: Hurricane Katrina and the Drowning of New Orleans." *Urban Affairs Review* 41: 501–16.

Coser, Lewis. 1956. *The Functions of Social Conflict.* New York: Free Press.

da Vinci, Leonardo. 1956. "Of the Error Made by Those Who Practise without Science." P. 910 in *The Notebooks of Leonardo da Vinci*, Edward MacCurdy, trans. and ed. New York: George Braziller.

Dale, Stephen Frederic. 1988. "Religious Suicide in Islamic Asia: Anticolonial Terrorism in India, Indonesia, and the Philippines." *Journal of Conflict Resolution* 32, 1: 37–59.

Davies, Scott and David Walters. 2007. "The Value of a Sociology Degree." Pp. 10–18 in *Society in Question*, 5th ed., Robert J. Brym, ed. Toronto: Nelson.

Davis, Joyce M. 2003. *Martyrs: Innocence, Vengeance and Despair in the Middle East*. New York: Palgrave Macmillan.

Davis, Mike. 1990. *City of Quartz: Excavating the Future in Los Angeles*. New York: Verso.

Dawsey, Darrell. 2006. "Proof's Death Fits Old Pattern." *The Globe and Mail* 15 April. On the World Wide Web at http://www.theglobeandmail.com/servlet/story/LAC.20060415.RAP15/TPStory/Entertainment (accessed 15 April 2006).

Doberman, John. 1997. *Darwin's Athletes: How Sport Has Damaged Black America and Preserved the Myth of Race*. Boston: Houghton Mifflin.

Durkheim, Émile. 1951 [1897]. *Suicide: A Study in Sociology*, G. Simpson, ed., J. Spaulding and G. Simpson, trans. New York: Free Press.

Dyson, Michael Eric. 2005. "The Culture of Hip-Hop." Pp. 61–8 in *That's the Joint! The Hip-Hop Studies Reader*, Murray Forman and Mark Anthony Neal, eds. New York: Routledge.

_____. 2006. *Come Hell or High Water: Hurricane Katrina and the Color of Disaster*. New York: Basic Civitas Books.

Edel, Abraham. 1965. "Social Science and Value: A Study in Interrelations." Pp. 218–38 in *The New Sociology: Essays in Social Science and Social Theory in Honor of C. Wright Mills*, Irving Louis Horowitz, ed. New York: Oxford University Press.

Einstein, Albert. 1954. *Ideas and Opinions*, Carl Seelig, ed., Sonja Bargmann, trans. New York: Crown.

Elran, Meir. 2006. *Khosen l'Eumi b'Yisrael: Hashpa'ot ha-Intifada ha-Shniya al ha-Khevra ha-Yisraelit*. [Hebrew: *National Resilience in Israel: The Influence of the Second Intifada on Israeli Society*.] Jaffee Center for Strategic Studies, University of Tel Aviv.

Emanuel, Kerry. 2005. "Increasing Destructiveness of Tropical Cyclones over the Past Thirty Years." *Nature* 436, 4: 686–8.

Energy Information Administration, U.S. Department of Energy. 2005. "Hurricane Impacts on the U.S. Oil and Natural Gas Markets." On the World Wide Web at http://tonto.eia.doe.gov/oog/special/eia1_katrina.html (accessed 1 June 2006).

Entine, John. 2000. *Taboo: Why Black Athletes Dominate Sports and Why We Are Afraid to Talk About It*. New York: Public Affairs.

Everett-Green, Robert. 1999. "Puff Daddy: The Martha Stewart of Hip Hop." *The Globe and Mail* 4 September: C7.

"Facts about Lightning." 2006. *LEX18.com*. On the World Wide Web at http://www.lex18.com/Global/story.asp?S=1367554&nav=menu203 _3 (accessed 29 April 2006).

"50 Cent Slams Kanye's 'Bush is Racist' Comment." 2005. *Contactmusic.com* 1 November. On the World Wide Web at http://contactmusic.com/new/xmlfeed.nsf/mndwebpages/50%20cent%20 slams%20kanyes%20bush%20is%20racist%20comment (accessed 23 May 2006).

Forman, Murray. 2001. "It Ain't All about the Benjamins: Summit on Social Responsibility in the Hip-Hop Industry." *Journal of Popular Music Studies* 13: 117–23.

Frank, Thomas and Matt Weiland, eds. 1997. *Commodify Your Dissent: Salvos from the Baffler*. New York: W.W. Norton.

Frankl, Viktor E. 1959. *Man's Search for Meaning: An Introduction to Logotherapy*, I. Lasch, trans. Boston: Beacon Press.

Freedman, Jonathan L. 2002. *Media Violence and Its Effect on Aggression: Assessing the Scientific Evidence*. Toronto: University of Toronto Press.

Freedom House. 2006. "Freedom in the World 2006." On the World Wide Web at http://www.freedomhouse.org/uploads/pdf/ Charts2006.pdf (accessed 1 July 2006).

George, Nelson. 1998. *Hip Hop America*. New York: Penguin.

Goddard Institute for Space Studies. 2006. "Global Surface Air Temperature Anomaly (C) (Base: 1951–1980)." http:// www.giss.nasa.gov/data/update/gistemp/graphs/Fig.A.txt (accessed 24 April 2006).

Government of Canada. 2002. "Study Released on Firearms in Canada." On the World Wide Web at http://www.cfc-ccaf.gc.ca/media/news_releases/2002/survey-08202002_e.asp (accessed 29 December 2005).

Gracyk, Theodore. 2001. *I Wanna Be Me: Rock Music and the Politics of Identity*. Philadelphia: Temple University Press.

Gross, Michael L. 2003. "Fighting by Other Means in the Mideast: A Critical Analysis of Israel's Assassination Policy." *Political Studies* 51: 350–68.

Gurr, Ted Robert. 1970. *Why Men Rebel*. Princeton NJ: Princeton University Press.

Hajdu, David. 2005. "Guns and Poses." *New York Times* 11 March. On the World Wide Web at www.nytimes.com (accessed 11 March 2005).

Hamilton, Maxwell J., Elaine de Valle, and Frances Robles. 2005. "Damage Extensive Across Island." *Miami Herald* 10 July. On the World Wide Web at http://www.latinamericanstudies.org/cuba/extensive.htm (accessed 26 May 2006).

Hamlin, Cynthia and Robert J. Brym. 2006. "The Return of the Native: A Cultural and Social-Psychological Critique of Durkheim's *Suicide* Based on the Guarani-Kaiowá of Southwestern Brazil." *Sociological Theory* 24: 42–57.

Harding, David J., Cybelle Fox, and Jal D. Mehta. 2002. "Studying Rare Events through Qualitative Case Studies: Lessons from a Study of Rampage School Shootings." *Sociological Methods and Research* 31: 174–217.

Hirsh, Arnold R. and Joseph Logsdon. 1992. "Introduction to Part III." Pp. 189–200 in *Creole New Orleans: Race and Americanization*, Arnold R. Hirsch and Joseph Logsdon, eds. Baton Rouge LA: Louisiana State University Press.

Holmes, Tamara E. 2005. "Blacks Underrepresented in Legal Field: ABA Report Shows Stark Contrasts in the Career Tracks of Lawyers." *Black Enterprise* August 2005. On the World Wide Web at http://www.findarticles.com/p/articles/mi_m1365/is_1_36/ai_n15674277/pg_2 (accessed 30 April 2005).

House, J. D. 2005. "Change from Within the Corridors of Power: A Reflective Essay of a Sociologist in Government." *Canadian Journal of Sociology* 30: 281–314.

Huesmann, L. Rowell, Jessica Moise-Titus, Cheryl-Lynn Podolski, and Leonard D. Eron. 2003. "Longitudinal Relations between Children's Exposure to TV Violence and their Aggressive and Violent Behavior in Young Adulthood: 1977–1992." *Developmental Psychology* 39, 2: 201–21.

Hunter, Shireen T. 1998. *The Future of Islam and the West: Clash of Civilizations or Peaceful Coexistence?* New York: Praeger.

Huntington, Samuel P. 1996. *The Clash of Civilizations and the Remaking of the World Order*. New York: Simon and Schuster.

Ignatieff, Michael. 2005. "The Broken Contract." *New York Times Magazine* 25 September: 15–17.

Intergovernmental Panel on Climate Change. 2001. *Climate Change 2001: Synthesis Report*. Cambridge UK: Cambridge University Press. On the World Wide Web at http://www.grida.no/climate/ipcc_tar/vol4/english/index.htm (accessed 23 May 2006).

International Policy Institute for Counter-Terrorism. 2004. On the World Wide Web at http://www.ict.org.il (accessed 1 November 2004).

Israeli Ministry of Foreign Affairs. 2004. "Palestinian Violence and Terrorism Since September 2000." On the World Wide Web at http://www.mfa.gov.il/MFA/Terrorism-+Obstacle+to+Peace/ Palestinian+terror+since+2000/Palestinian%20violence%20and% 20terrorism%20since%20September (accessed 1 November 2004).

James, William. 1976. *The Varieties of Religious Experience: A Study in Human Nature*. New York: Collier Books.

"Jim Crow Laws: Louisiana." 2006. On the World Wide Web at http:// www.jimcrowhistory.org/scripts/jimcrow/insidesouth.cgi?state= Louisiana (accessed 29 May 2006).

Johnson, Jeffrey G., Patricia Cohen, Elizabeth M. Smailes, Stephanie Kasen, and Judith S. Brook. 2002. "Television Viewing and Aggressive Behavior during Adolescence and Adulthood." *Science* 295, 5564: 2468–71.

Johnston, W. Robert. 2003. "Chronology of Terrorist Attacks in Israel, Part IV: 1993–2000." On the World Wide Web at http://www.johnstonsarchive.net/terrorism/terrisrael-4.html (accessed 25 October 2004).

Karl, Thomas R. and Kevin E. Trenberth. 1999. "The Human Impact on Climate." *Scientific American* 281, 6: 100–5.

Katz, Bruce, Matt Fellowes, and Mia Mabanta. 2006. *Katrina Index: Tracking Variables of Post-Katrina Reconstruction*. Washington DC: The Brookings Institution. On the World Wide Web at http://www.brookings.edu/metro/pubs/200604_KatrinaIndex.pdf (accessed 24 April 2006).

King, G. and R. Bendel. 1995. "A Statistical Model Estimating the Number of African-American Physicians in the United States." *Journal of the National Medical Association* 87, 4: 264–72.

Knutson, Thomas R. and Robert E. Tuleya. 2004. "Impact of CO_2-Induced Warming on Simulated Hurricane Intensity and Precipitation: Sensitivity to the Choice of Climate Model and Convective Parameterization." *Journal of Climate* 17: 3477–95.

Kolbert, Elizabeth. 2006. *Field Notes from a Catastrophe*. London: Bloomsbury.

Krupa, Michelle. 2006. "Presumed Missing." *The Times-Picayune* 6 March. On the World Wide Web at http://www.nola.com/news/ t-p/frontpage/index.ssf?/base/news-5/1141545589263750.xml (accessed 30 May 2006).

Kubrin, Charis E., Tim Wadsworth, and Stephanie DiPietro. 2006. "Deindustrialization, Disadvantage and Suicide among Young Black Males." *Social Forces* 84: 1559–79.

Kurzweil, Ray. 1999. *The Age of Spiritual Machines: When Computers Exceed Human Intelligence.* New York: Viking Penguin.

Lapchick, Richard. 2004. *2004 Racial and Gender Report Card.* Orlando FL: University of Central Florida. On the World Wide Web at http://www.bus.ucf.edu/sport/public/downloads/2004_Racial_Gender_Report_Card.pdf (accessed 29 April 2006).

Laqueur, Walter. 2004. *No End to War: Terrorism in the Twenty-First Century.* New York: Continuum.

Lenin, Vladimir I. 1964. "Book Review: N. A. Rubakin, *Among Books...*" Pp. 259–61, Vol. 20, *Collected Works*, 45 vols. Moscow: Foreign Languages Publishing House.

Lenton, Rhonda L. 1989. "Homicide in Canada and the U.S.A." *Canadian Journal of Sociology* 14: 163–78.

Logan, John R. 2006. "The Impact of Katrina: Race and Class in Storm-Damaged Neighborhoods." Department of Sociology, Brown University. On the World Wide Web at http://www.s4.brown.edu/Katrina/report.pdf (accessed 24 April 2006).

Logdon, Joseph and Caryn Cossé Bell. 1992. "The Americanization of Black New Orleans." Pp. 201–61 in Arnold R. Hirsch and Joseph Logsdon, eds. *Creole New Orleans: Race and Americanization.* Baton Rouge LA: Louisiana State University Press.

Lukes, Steven. 1973. *Émile Durkheim, His Life and Work: A Historical and Critical Study.* London: Penguin.

MacCallum, Gerald C., Jr. 1967. "Negative and Positive Freedom." *The Philosophical Review* 76: 312–34.

Mahoney, Jill and Alan Freeman. 2005. "Rebuilt City Likely to be a Lot Smaller—and Whiter." *The Globe and Mail* 17 September: A22.

Margalit, Avishai. 2003. "The Suicide Bombers." *New York Review of Books* 50, 1. On the World Wide Web at http://www.nybooks.com/articles/15979 (accessed 1 September 2004).

Marshall, T. H. 1965. "Citizenship and Social Class." Pp. 71–134 in *Class, Citizenship, and Social Development: Essays by T. H. Marshall,* T. H. Marshall, ed. Garden City NY: Anchor.

Martin, Susan Taylor. 2005. "Can We Learn from Cuba's Lesson?" *St. Petersburg Times* 9 September. On the World Wide Web at http://www.sptimes.com/2005/09/09/Worldandnation/Can_we_learn_from_Cub.shtml (accessed 26 May 2006.)

Mattern, Mark. 1998. *Acting in Concert: Music, Community, and Political Action*. New Brunswick NJ: Rutgers University Press.

McWhorter, John. 2005. *Winning the Race: Beyond the Crisis in Black America*. New York: Gotham Books.

Mead, George Herbert. 1934. *Mind, Self and Society*. Chicago: University of Chicago Press.

Mills, C. Wright. 1959. *The Sociological Imagination*. New York: Oxford University Press.

Mokdad, Ali H., James S. Marks, Donna F. Stroup, and Julie L. Gerberding. 2004. "Actual Causes of Death in the United States, 2000." *Journal of the American Medical Association* 291, 10: 1238–45.

Moore, Barrington, Jr. 1967. *Social Origins of Dictatorship and Democracy: Lord and Peasant in the Making of the Modern World*. Boston: Beacon Press.

National Center for Education Statistics. 2004. "Table 303. Degrees awarded by degree-granting institutions, by control, level of degree, and state or jurisdiction: 2002–03." On the World Wide Web at http://nces.ed.gov/programs/digest/d04/tables/dt04_303.asp (accessed 2 July 2006).

_____. 2005. "Table 294. Earned degrees in economics, history, political science and government, and sociology conferred by degree-granting institutions, by level of degree: Selected years, 1949–50 to 2002–03." On the World Wide Web at http://nces.ed.gov/programs/digest/d04/tables/dt04_294.asp (accessed 2 July 2006).

National Center for Injury Prevention and Control. 2006. "WISQARS Leading Causes of Death Reports, 1999–2003." On the World Wide Web at http://webappa.cdc.gov/sasweb/ncipc/leadcaus10.html (accessed 15 April 2006).

National Rifle Association. 2005. "Guns, Gun Ownership, & RTC at All-Time Highs, Less 'Gun Control,' and Violent Crime at 30-Year Low." On the World Wide Web at http://www.nraila.org/Issues/FactSheets/Read.aspx?ID=126 (accessed 29 December 2005).

National Weather Service. 2005. "The Saffir-Simpson Hurricane Scale." On the World Wide Web at http://www.nhc.noaa.gov/aboutsshs.shtml (accessed 2 June 2006).

Neal, Mark Anthony. 1999. *What the Music Said: Black Popular Music and Black Public Culture*. New York: Routledge.

New York Times. 2000–06. East Coast Final Edition.

Nordheimer, Jon. 2002. "Nothing's Easy for New Orleans Flood Control." *New York Times* 30 April: F1.

Oliver, Anne Marie and Paul Steinberg. 2005. *The Road to Martyrs' Square: A Journey into the World of the Suicide Bomber.* Oxford UK: Oxford University Press.

Oreskes, Naomi. 2004. "The Scientific Consensus on Climate Change." *Science* 306: 1686.

Pape, Robert A. 2005. *Dying to Win: The Strategic Logic of Suicide Terrorism.* New York: Random House.

Perina, Kaja. 2002. "Suicide Terrorism: Seeking Motives beyond Mental Illness." *Psychology Today* 35, 5: 15

Picard, André. 2006. "The West Is Where the Heart Does Best." *The Globe and Mail* 5 July: A15.

Piven, Frances Fox, and Richard A. Cloward. 1977. *Poor People's Movements: Why They Succeed, How They Fail.* New York: Vintage.

_____ and _____. 1993. *Regulating the Poor: The Functions of Public Welfare,* updated ed. New York: Vintage.

Polanyi, Karl. 1957. *The Great Transformation: The Political and Economic Origins of Our Time.* Boston: Beacon Press.

Quaschning, Volker. 2003. "Development of Global Carbon Dioxide Emissions and Concentration in Atmosphere." On the World Wide Web at http://www.volker-quaschning.de/datserv/CO2/index_e.html (accessed 2 March 2005).

Reuter, Christoph. 2004. *My Life Is a Weapon: A Modern History of Suicide Bombing,* Helena Ragg-Kirkby, trans. Princeton NJ: Princeton University Press.

Reuters News Agency. 2005. "Hurricane Dennis Killed 16 in Cuba—Castro." On the World Wide Web at http://www.planetark.org/dailynewsstory.cfm/newsid/31634/newsDate/13-Jul-2005/story.htm (accessed 26 May 2006).

Ricolfi, Luca. 2005. "Palestinians, 1981–2003." Pp. 77–129 in *Making Sense of Suicide Missions,* Diego Gambetta, ed. Oxford: Oxford University Press.

Samuels, David. 2004. "The Rap on Rap: The 'Black Music' that Isn't Either." Pp. 147–53 in *That's the Joint! The Hip-Hop Studies Reader,* Murray Forman and Mark Anthony Neal, eds. New York: Routledge.

Schiermeier, Quirin. 2005a. "Hurricane Link to Climate Change Is Hazy." *Nature* 437, 22: 461.

_____. 2005b. "Trouble Brews Over Contested Trend in Hurricanes." *Nature* 435, 23: 1008–9.

Sen, Amartya. 1990. "More than 100 Million Women Are Missing." *New York Review of Books* 20 December: 61–6.

_____. 2001. "Many Faces of Gender Inequality." *Frontline* 18: 27 October–9 November. On the World Wide Web at http://www.hinduonnet.com/fline/fl1822/18220040.htm (accessed 20 April 2005).

Sexton, Richard and Randolph Delehanty. 1993. *New Orleans: Elegance and Decadence.* San Francisco: Chronicle Books.

Silverman, Adam L. 2002. "Just War, Jihad, and Terrorism: A Comparison of Western and Islamic Norms for the Use of Political Violence." *Journal of Church and State* 44, 1: 73–92.

Simmel, Georg. 1950. *The Sociology of Georg Simmel,* Kurt H. Wolff, trans. and ed. New York: Free Press.

Spalter-Roth, Roberta, William Erskine, Sylvia Polsiak, and Jamie Panzarella. 2005. *A National Survey of Seniors Majoring in Sociology.* Washington DC: American Sociological Association. On the World Wide Web at http://www.asanet.org/galleries/default-file/B&B_first_report_final.pdf (accessed 12 December 2005).

Springhall, John. 1998. *Youth, Popular Culture and Moral Panics: Penny Gaffs to Gangsta-Rap, 1830–1996.* New York: Routledge.

Sprinzak, Ehud. 2000. "Rational Fanatics." *Foreign Policy* 120: 66–73.

Stephens, W. Richard, Jr. 1998. *Careers in Sociology.* New York: Allyn & Bacon. On the World Wide Web at http://www.abacon.com/socsite/careers.html (accessed 3 July 2006).

Stern, Jessica. 2003. *Terror in the Name of God: Why Religious Militants Kill.* New York: Ecco/HarperCollins.

Strong, Nolan. 2006. "Lil Kim's Reality Show Scores Highest Debut in BET History." *Allhiphop.com* 14 March. On the World Wide Web at http://www.allhiphop.com/hiphopnews/?ID=5460 (accessed 23 April 2006).

Sullivan, Mercer L. 2002. "Exploring Layers: Extended Case Method as a Tool for Multilevel Analysis of School Violence." *Sociological Methods and Research* 31, 2: 255–85.

"Survey of Hurricane Katrina Evacuees." 2005. *The Washington Post* and the Henry J. Kaiser Family Foundation and the Harvard School of Public Health. On the World Wide Web at http://www.washingtonpost.com/wp-srv/politics/polls/katrina_poll091605.pdf (accessed 24 April 2006).

Taarnby, Michael. 2003. *Profiling Islamic Suicide Terrorists: A Research Report for the Danish Ministry of Justice.* Aarhus, Denmark: Centre for Cultural Research, University of Aarhus. On the World Wide Web at http://www.jm.dk/image.asp?page=image&objno=71157 (accessed 1 September 2004).

Taylor, Charles L. 1985. "What's Wrong with Negative Liberty?" Pp. 211–29 in *Philosophy and Human Sciences: Philosophical Papers 2.* Cambridge: Cambridge University Press.

Tidwell, Mark. 2004. *Bayou Farewell: The Rich Life and Tragic Death of Louisiana's Cajun Coast.* New York: Vintage.

_____. 2005. "It's Time to Abandon New Orleans." *Winnipeg Free Press* 9 December: A15.

United Nations. 2004a. "Cuba: A Model in Hurricane Risk Management." On the World Wide Web at http://www.un.org/News/Press/docs/2004/iha943.doc.htm (accessed 26 May 2006).

_____. 2004b. *Reducing Disaster Risk: A Challenge for Development.* New York. On the World Wide Web at http://www.undp.org/bcpr/disred/documents/publications/rdr/english/rdr_english.pdf (accessed 18 May 2006).

_____. 2005. *Human Development Report 2005.* On the World Wide Web at http://hdr.undp.org/reports/global/2005/ (accessed 1 July 2006).

_____. 2006. "Cartographic Section." On the World Wide Web at http://www.un.org/Depts/Cartographic/english/index.htm (accessed 2 May 2006).

U.S. Census Bureau. 2002a. "Table 1. United States—Race and Hispanic Origin: 1790 to 1990." On the World Wide Web at http://www.census.gov/population/documentation/twps0056/tab01.xls (accessed 29 April 2006).

_____. 2002b. "Table 3. Black or African American Population, by Age and Sex for the United States: 2000." On the World Wide Web at http://www.census.gov/population/cen2000/phc-t08/tab03.xls (accessed 29 April 2006).

_____. 2005. "Hurricane Katrina Disaster Areas." On the World Wide Web at http://ftp2.census.gov/geo/maps/special/HurKat/Katrina_Reference_v2.pdf (accessed 30 May 2006).

_____. 2006. "Entire Data Set." On the World Wide Web at http://www.census.gov/popest/datasets.html (accessed 15 April 2006).

U.S. Department of Labor. 2004. *National Compensation Survey: Occupational Wages in the United States, July 2003*

Supplementary Tables. Washington DC: Bureau of Labor Statistics. On the World Wide Web at http://www.bls.gov/ncs/ocs/sp/ncbl0636.pdf (accessed 3 July 2006).

U.S. Geological Survey. 2006. "Earth Resources Observation and Science (EROS)." On the World Wide Web at http://edc.usgs.gov/products/elevation/gtopo30/gtopo30.html (accessed 23 April 2006).

U.S. House of Representatives, Select Bipartisan Committee to Investigate the Preparation for and Response to Hurricane Katrina. 2005. *A Failure of Initiative: The Final Report of the Select Bipartisan Committee to Investigate the Preparation for and Response to Hurricane Katrina.* On the World Wide Web at http://katrina.house.gov/ (accessed 24 April 2006).

Victor, Barbara. 2003. *Army of Roses: Inside the World of Palestinian Women Suicide Bombers.* New York: Rodale Press.

Wallerstein, Immanuel. 1974–1989. *The Modern World-System,* 3 vols. New York: Academic Press.

"Washing Away: Special Report from the *Times-Picayune.*" 2002. 23–27 June. On the World Wide Web at http://www.nola.com/hurricane/?/washingaway/ (accessed 1 June 2006).

Weber, Max. 1946. "Class, Status, Party." Pp. 180–95 in *From Max Weber: Essays in Sociology,* Hans Gerth and C. Wright Mills, trans. and eds. New York: Oxford University Press.

_____. 1947. *The Theory of Social and Economic Organization,* T. Parsons, ed., A. M. Henderson and T. Parsons, trans. New York: Free Press.

_____. 1949. "'Objectivity' in Social Science and Social Policy." Pp. 49–112 in *The Methodology of the Social Sciences,* Edward A. Shils and Henry A. Finch, trans. and eds. New York: Free Press of Glencoe.

Webster, P. J., G. J. Holland, J. A. Curry, and H.-R. Chang. 2005. "Changes in Tropical Cyclone Number, Duration, and Intensity in a Warming Environment." *Science* 309: 1844–6.

Wilson, William Julius. 1987. *The Truly Disadvantaged: The Inner City, the Underclass, and Public Policy.* Chicago: University of Chicago Press.

Zogby, James J. 2002. *What Arabs Think: Values, Beliefs and Concerns.* Utica NY: Zogby International/The Arab Thought Foundation.

Index

Changing Inequality

THE AARON WILDAVSKY FORUM FOR PUBLIC POLICY

Edited by Lee Friedman

This series is to sustain the intellectual excitement that
Aaron Wildavsky created for scholars of public policy everywhere.
The ideas in each volume are initially presented and discussed
at a public lecture and forum held at the University of California.

AARON WILDAVSKY, 1930–1993

"Your prolific pen has brought real politics to the study of budgeting, to the
analysis of myriad public policies, and to the discovery of the values underlying the political cultures by which peoples live. You have improved every
institution with which you have been associated, notably Berkeley's Graduate
School of Public Policy, which as Founding Dean you quickened with your
restless innovative energy. Advocate of freedom, mentor to policy analysts
everywhere." (Yale University, May 1993, from text granting the honorary
degree of Doctor of Social Science)

Changing Inequality

Rebecca M. Blank

UNIVERSITY OF CALIFORNIA PRESS

Berkeley   Los Angeles   London

University of California Press, one of the most distinguished university presses in the United States, enriches lives around the world by advancing scholarship in the humanities, social sciences, and natural sciences. Its activities are supported by the UC Press Foundation and by philanthropic contributions from individuals and institutions. For more information, visit www.ucpress.edu.

University of California Press
Berkeley and Los Angeles, California

University of California Press, Ltd.
London, England

Library of Congress Cataloging-in-Publication Data

Blank, Rebecca M.
    Changing inequality / Rebecca M. Blank.
        p.   cm. — (The Aaron Wildavsky forum for public policy ; 8)
    Includes bibliographical references and index.
    ISBN 978-0-520-26692-6 (cloth : alk. paper)
    ISBN 978-0-520-26693-3 (pbk. : alk. paper)
    1. Income distribution—United States.   2. Equality—Economic aspects—United States.   3. United States—Economic conditions.   I. Title.
    HC110.I5B497   2011
    339.20973—dc22   2011005495

Manufactured in the United States of America

20 19 18 17 16 15 14 13 12 11
10 9 8 7 6 5 4 3 2 1

This book is printed on Cascades Enviro 100, a 100 percent postconsumer waste, recycled, de-inked fiber. FSC recycled certified and processed chlorine free. It is acid free, Ecologo certified, and manufactured by BioGas energy.

To Hanns and Emily

CONTENTS

ILLUSTRATIONS

TABLES

FIGURES

ACKNOWLEDGMENTS

This manuscript began as a lecture delivered as part of the Aaron Wildavsky Forum for Public Policy, University of California–Berkeley, in March 2009. I thank those who attended the initial lecture and the follow-up discussion for their excellent questions and comments, particularly Lee Friedman, Michael Hout, Steve Raphael, and Robert Reich.

Thanks are due to Howard Lempel for excellent research assistance and data analysis; his assistance is visible throughout these pages.

Introduction

The United States is in an extended period of rapidly rising inequality. Starting in the mid-1970s, all measures of U.S. economic inequality have risen, including inequality in wages, income, and wealth. This development has made income distribution and income inequality a topic of substantial interest among researchers and policy analysts who focus on economic and social issues in the United States. This book adds to the discussion about inequality in two ways. Part 1 provides a comprehensive look at changes in the level and distribution of income since 1979. Part 2 discusses the forces that drive changes in inequality.

Whereas most research on inequality has focused on wages, the first part of this book shows how changes in the distribution of wages combine with changes in hours and weeks of work to affect annual earnings among workers. In turn, changes in the distribution of annual earnings combine with changes in government income and other income to affect the distribution of total income among families and individuals.

I focus on the changing distribution of per person income available to nonelderly persons between 1979 and 2007. Changes in income distribution are affected not just by changes in income sources but also by changes in the family choices made by men and women deciding to marry (or not) and to have children (or not). The analysis in this book investigates the impact on the overall income distribution of changes in the demographic choices of families and individuals, as well as changes in income components.

It is well known that inequality has risen sharply over the last three decades. The results of this detailed analysis indicate that changes in family composition and family size account for about 15 percent of the rise in U.S. income inequality, while changes in income account for the remaining rise in inequality. Most of this rise is due to increases in wage inequality.

Many readers may be surprised at the extent to which per person income has risen for nonelderly adults in the United States. This is true across the income distribution, so that the whole distribution has shifted upward even as it has spread out and become more unequal. The only exception occurs at the very bottom of the income distribution, where there has been an increase in the number of persons at the lowest levels of income. Some of this increase in per person income is due to declining family size, but the primary reason for this change is more hours of work in the labor market among women. This shift in women's work behavior has increased income in married-couple and in single-female-headed families. After adjusting for inflation, median per person income among nonelderly adults has risen 24 percent since 1979, to $36,900 in 2007. Of course, adults in married-couple families have higher incomes than those who live singly or who are in single-headed families.

Hence, rising inequality is occurring in a framework of rising overall incomes for most nonelderly adults, which may be one reason why the policy concern with inequality has remained muted. These changes, however, are not due to increases in wages for many persons, but are due to increases in the work effort within families, and particularly by women. Although such increases in work effort may give women more financial independence and reflect a decline in labor-market barriers, this also means that a higher share of women's time is dictated by the demands of market work.

The second part of this book examines the forces that drive changes in inequality. Economic inequality is affected by economic shocks, which can be immediate (a natural disaster, a pandemic, or a war) or can unfold slowly over time (global warming, the introduction of computer technology, or the rise of public universities). These forces can shift the availability of human skills and physical capital in ways that change access to income and shift the income distribution. These economic changes are mitigated by political institutions and policy choices. As historical examples indicate, the effects of economic shocks on inequality depend upon the institutional environment in which they occur, so that similar economic shocks can result in quite different long-term distributional effects.

After a review of how some past economic shocks may have affected inequality, I look at the potential impact of future economic changes. Reversing the rapid increase in inequality over the past three decades will be difficult; even large equalizing future changes in work effort or family composition (changes that are unlikely to occur) would not bring inequality back to its 1979 levels. This suggests that higher inequality is likely to remain a feature of the economic landscape in the United States for many decades to come.

WHY SHOULD WE CARE ABOUT INEQUALITY?

Although rapid changes in any aspect of the U.S. economy are always of interest to economists, changes in inequality may generate broader concern, because rising inequality can have effects on a host of other economic and social outcomes. At least four effects of rising inequality are most commonly mentioned.

First, if increases in inequality reflect declines in the well-being of those at the bottom of the income distribution, this raises questions about the well-being of the poor in a rich, developed nation. Adjusted for inflation, wages fell among less-skilled male workers in the 1980s and have only partly recovered in the years since then (Autor, Katz, and Kearney, 2008). The effects of falling wages have been much discussed, with particular attention on the extent to which declining wages have led to declines in male labor-force participation and in marriage rates among the less skilled—both of which are associated with higher poverty.

Second, widening inequality may lead to reduced economic mobility if greater inequality makes economic gains harder for those at the bottom of the income distribution or if it reinforces the economic position of those at the top. Economic mobility is often viewed as a measure of openness and opportunity in a society. High degrees of inequality may be more acceptable if economic hierarchies are not stagnant and people at the bottom of the distribution move to the top of the distribution with some degree of frequency.

There is evidence that intergenerational economic mobility in the United States has been lower than in other highly industrialized countries over the past several decades (Jäntti et al., 2006). Whereas mobility reductions may have limited short-run effects, over time they can intensify economic and social stratification. Since a disproportionate share of low-income families are headed by people of color or by single mothers (of all colors), children from these families may face particularly reduced economic opportunities in a time of rising inequality, intensifying racial differences as well. Of course, these economic changes may also affect social roles and increase the sense of social distance or class difference between groups.

Third, inequality may have an effect on aggregate economic growth over time, although both the sign and size of this effect are disputed. Milton and Rose Friedman (1979) argue that greater inequality can spur ambitious work effort by those who want the larger rewards available to top earners, and that this can lead to higher economic productivity. Others argue that a growing group of poorer and non–upwardly mobile persons create economic costs and can impede aggregate growth. For instance, in a recent book Richard Freeman (2007) argues that rising wage inequality may reduce productivity. He reports on experiments showing that as rewards become more unequal, the efforts of those at the bottom are reduced because they believe they have no chance of achieving these rewards.

There is an ongoing debate in the empirical literature about the relationship between economic inequality and growth in both poor and rich countries. Much of the quantitative research on the relationship between inequality and growth suggests that the relationship is relatively weak and that other factors have greater effects on growth (Barro, 2000). These are difficult relationships to measure, however, because they unfold only over long periods of time, and it is hard to isolate the causal effects of shifting inequality when other things are changing at the same time.

Finally, rising economic inequality may affect civic and social behavior outside the realm of economics. For instance, there is evidence that inequality in the rate of voting in the United States has widened at the same time that economic inequality has increased (Freeman, 2004). If widening differences in economic experience lead to different perceptions about who has won or lost from past policy changes, it may become harder to hold a common civic conversation about public policy concerns. Widening inequality may increase social discontent among lower-income groups or reduce the empathy that higher-income groups have for lower-income groups. Regardless of its effect on social discontent, areas with higher inequality appear to have lower rates of self-reported happiness (Glaeser, Resseger, and Tobio, 2008).

While some are concerned about the effects of widening inequality, others may believe that wide differences in economic outcomes are, per se, undesirable. For instance, the "Scandinavian model" of social welfare is often associated with a belief that a more equitable economic distribution of income is a desirable social goal. In general, however, Americans are less concerned with levels of inequality than are Europeans, and tend not to place a high value on greater economic equality in itself.[1] Hence, the discussion about inequality in the United States has focused more on whether rising inequality has undesirable economic or social side effects rather than on the fairness of these changes.

WHAT'S IN THIS BOOK?

For all of these reasons, rising economic inequality within the United States has drawn ongoing attention. The primary goal of the book is to describe shifts in the distribution of income among working-age adults over the last three decades and to consider how and why inequality might change in the future. The book looks at how these shifts have differed by gender and by the type of family in which adults live. The analysis explores reasons for these changes, investigating the different components of income and looking at the forces that are driving widening inequality in overall income levels.

Although much research has focused on changes in hourly or weekly wage inequality, there has been less attention to other components of income. Changes in annual earnings inequality among workers are the result of changing inequality in hourly wages and in hours of work, and of the interaction between these two components of earnings. Changes in total-income inequality depend upon changes in family size, changes in the number of workers in a family and their wages, and the correlations between these factors. They also depend upon changes in inequality in other (i.e., unearned) income.

In the first part of this book, I look at the trends in inequality over the past three decades in all of these components of individual earnings and of family income, to identify which of the components that determine income have contributed the most to rising economic inequality. Chapter 1 provides a brief description of the data that I use in this study. I describe the groups that I am looking at and the years over which I study changes in inequality. I focus solely on nonelderly adults, because I am interested in the relationship between labor-market changes (where wage inequality has widened markedly) and overall changes in the level and distribution of income available to individuals within their family units.

Chapter 2 focuses on the labor market, looking at shifts in wages among workers. The results in this chapter underscore the different ways in which the distribution and level of earnings have changed among employed men and women. Although I replicate the evidence showing widening inequality between more- and less-skilled workers, the overall growth in skill levels in the U.S. workforce has shifted wages upward. Furthermore, women are working much more than before, so their annual earnings have grown markedly, largely due to increases in weeks worked per year. While hourly wages have become much more unequal, this rising inequality in wages has been somewhat off-set by falling inequality in work effort among workers, with more workers working full-time and full-year. The result is that the overall distribution of annual earnings among workers has shifted upward, even while wage inequality rose. Some may be surprised to learn that annual earnings have grown among work-ers in the bottom half of the earnings distribution. This is almost entirely due to greater work effort on the part of women.

Chapter 3 turns from wages and earnings to the distribution of total income among all nonelderly adults. I look at shifts in the distribution of total income among single individuals and among persons living in married-couple families and single-headed families. I also look at comparative changes in the three primary components of annual income—namely, annual earn-ings, government income, and all other unearned income. Strik-ingly, both for earnings and for total income, I find that increases in inequality are accompanied by a substantial upward shift in most of the income distribution, so that overall incomes are growing at the same time that their distribution is becoming more spread out. Incomes among those in the middle of the dis-tribution have risen substantially, although there has been an increase in the share of persons with very low incomes. Rising inequality around an increasing median leads to an income dis-tribution in 2007 in which almost everyone has higher incomes than persons at equivalent points in the income distribution in 1979, except for the very lowest income group. Rising inequality is typically viewed as less of a problem when it occurs in a context where most people are doing better.

Chapter 4 explores the reasons behind these changes in the distribution of total income and discusses what they might mean for overall well-being among American adults. I look at the effects of changing family composition and family size, as well as the effects of shifts in the distribution of earnings and other income components. About three-quarters of the increase in inequality in the overall distribution of income occurred because of increases in the inequality of income components—primarily, increases in annual earnings inequality. This, in turn, occurred because of increases in wage inequality.

Much of the increase in median income occurred because of increases in earnings due to increased female work effort. Hence, understanding the effect of increasing work effort on overall income is very important in analyzing the effects of rising inequality on the well-being of Americans. Increases in work effort are not unambiguously positive in their effects on overall well-being, even if they do result in higher incomes. This result might be evaluated very differently from increases in median earnings that are the result of rising wages.

About 14 percent of the rise in inequality is due to shifts in family demographics, including shifts in family size as well as in the type of families where individuals reside. A decline in married-couple families has been matched by increases in single-person households and in families with single heads. (A high share of the growth in single-headed families is among single-mother families.)

This first part of the book emphasizes the importance of

understanding changes in the labor market in order to understand changes in overall income distribution. It also underscores the importance of family composition choices for economic well-being. The results in this section provide a comprehensive view of the long-term changes in the level and distribution of economic resources available to nonelderly Americans.

The second part of the book steps back from data analysis to consider the forces that create, sustain, or alter long-term trends in inequality. Long-term trends toward rising or falling inequality over time within countries often come to an end at some point. It is not clear what triggers changes in the trends toward or away from long-term inequality. Indeed, economists continue to argue over the causes of recent rises in U.S. wage inequality.

Chapter 5 looks at evidence from past history, largely but not entirely within the United States, to indicate how major economic shocks appear to affect income distribution over time. Economic shocks include catastrophic events that occur at a particular point in time, such as a deep recession, a war, or a major health crisis that causes substantial deaths. But economic shocks may also refer to major economic changes that unfold more slowly over time, such as new technologies that expand productivity and create new opportunities for wealth creation, or the opening up of new frontiers and the availability of additional land and mineral resources. Whereas there is substantial ongoing attention to the effects of such economic changes on overall economic growth, there has been much less attention to the effects of such changes on economic inequality.

Chapter 5 goes on to suggest ways in which economic shocks can influence long-run trends toward increasing or decreasing inequality. Most important, the historical evidence indicates that the effects of a given economic shock are rarely predetermined but may be heavily influenced by the political institutions and the political economy of the nation when the shock occurs. Hence, the opening up of frontiers can consolidate additional wealth within an elite group of families, or it can provide new wealth to previously lower-income groups. Large economic shocks often influence public attitudes and political structures, creating new patterns in the distribution of economic resources as well as political access.

Chapter 6 focuses on the current economic environment and looks at some simple simulations that indicate how particular behavioral, economic, demographic, or policy changes might alter the current distribution of economic resources. Most of these changes are focused on raising incomes among those at the bottom of the distribution. (Most of the rise in inequality is occurring because those at the top are experiencing very fast increases in earnings, but I assume that reducing their earnings is much less politically palatable than raising income at the bottom.) The changes that I simulate include economic changes that would reduce the proportion of low-skilled workers in the population, raise wages and labor-force participation among lower-wage workers, or reduce investment income among upper-income workers. I also look at demographic changes that would increase marriage and reduce the number of single persons and single-headed families in the population. And I look at policy changes that would redistribute resources and raise the incomes of poor workers and poor families.

These simulations provide a comparative sense of the effect these different types of changes would have on the overall distribution and level of income among nonelderly American adults. In general, the results suggest that none of these changes, by themselves, would have major effects on income distribution, but a number of them together could indeed produce both higher income levels and a more equal distribution of economic resources. Even quite large changes, however, leave income inequality closer to its 2007 level than its 1979 level, suggesting that a major reversal in inequality is unlikely in the absence of substantial and currently unforeseen changes.

The final chapter, chapter 7, focuses explicitly on the current economic environment. Given that we have recently experienced a severe global economic recession, I discuss the possible ways in which this major economic shock might influence long-term trends in inequality. The most likely outcome is that the current trends will persist and that the forces that have been driving increased inequality over the past three decades will continue to operate. But there are possible economic and political changes that may emerge from a deep and sustained recession that could alter the recent trend toward increased inequality and equalize incomes in the years ahead.

If there is any one central message in this second part of the book, it is that rising inequality is not the inevitable result of unchangeable forces. Economic change interacts with the political economy and the set of rules, regulations, and policies enforced within the economy. Particularly in developed countries, with effectively functioning governments, the political system shapes economic outcomes. There are things that we can do in the United States to reduce economic inequality and offset some of the economic forces that have produced greater inequality. In fact, we have chosen to adopt a number of policies that have done this, such as the expansion of the Earned Income Tax Credit to low-wage earners in low-income families with children. Whether we do more is our choice.

As a final note, I should make it clear that my primary interest in this book is in the more developed economies. There is a deep and ever-growing literature on the relationship between growth and inequality in poor countries,[2] which I will occasionally reference in this book. However, I am interested in wealthier countries that have effectively functioning governments, high levels of human capital, and technologically advanced physical capital. The famous "Kuznets curve" suggests that inequality will rise in poorer countries (as the growth process benefits some more than others) and decline in richer countries (as the benefits of growth spread more widely). Although sharp declines in inequality in the mid-twentieth century in many of the highly industrialized countries seemed to support this theory, inequality rose in the United States and in a number of other high-income countries at the end of the twentieth century (Atkinson, 2003). This suggests that high rates of industrial development and per capita income do not guarantee declining inequality.[3] The second part of this book pushes beyond Kuznets's hypothesis to discern the factors that may lead to rising or falling economic inequality in the developed world.

PART I

Changes in Income and Earnings

ONE

A Broader Look at Changing Inequality

The next several chapters of this book provide a detailed comparison of the composition and distribution of income in the United States in 1979 and in 2007. I am interested in looking at the pretax income available to all nonelderly adults, which I refer to as the *total-income distribution*. Surprisingly, there is almost no research that takes an approach as comprehensive as that taken in this book, looking as it does at changes in the distribution of total income and its sources. There are a large number of papers that investigate changes in wage inequality over the past several decades, often focusing on either hourly or weekly wages.[1] Very few researchers have looked at how changes in hours or weeks of work interact with wage inequality, however, or at how total-income inequality has changed in comparison to earnings inequality.

THE LITERATURE ON RECENT TRENDS IN U.S. INCOME INEQUALITY

The literature on changes in aggregate-income inequality is not extensive. All of these papers indicate that income inequality in the United States has been widening in recent decades. Most of this literature focuses either on married-couple families or on families with children, and ignores individuals who live alone or in other types of families. For instance, Juhn and Murphy (1997) look at changes in patterns of earnings within married-couple families, focusing particularly on the growing positive correlation between wives' and husbands' earnings. Pencavel (2006) updates and extends this work.[2] Reed and Cancian (2001) simulate the effects of changes in husbands' and wives' earnings and capital income on the family income distribution.[3] Gottschalk and Danziger (2005) look at male and female wage rates, earnings, and family income. Ahituv and Lerman (2007) are concerned with the effect of changes in family structure and work behavior on inequality. Other papers look at the role of family structure changes in explaining growing family income inequality.[4]

One past paper that is more comprehensive is by Karoly (1996), who looks at changes in income among the entire U.S. population between 1973 and 1993. A more recent paper, by Heathcote, Perri and Violante (2010), looks at the historical relationship between labor-force behavior, wages, and total household income using a variety of different data sets. Their focus is on the macroeconomic implications of these relationships.

This book investigates how the distribution of income among all persons has been affected by changes in labor-force behavior, family structure, wages, and unearned income. In contrast to earlier papers, this book looks at all nonelderly adults, including those who live alone as well as those in families headed by married couples or single individuals. I investigate changes in the distribution of earnings and relate changes in earnings by gender to changes in the distribution of wages, taking account of simultaneous changes in the distribution of work hours. I also look at total income available to individuals and analyze the effects of changes in the distribution of earnings, governmental income, and other unearned income. In short, this quantitative analysis attempts to be more comprehensive, providing a better overall look at shifts in inequality among all of the components of earnings and income, and including a broader slice of the total population in the analysis.

THE DATA ON WHICH THIS ANALYSIS IS BASED

The remainder of this chapter describes the data on which all of the analysis in this book is based. Those who are most interested in the results and conclusions can skip to chapter 2, although I encourage even those readers to skim through the remainder of this chapter so that they may better understand the nature and the limitations of this analysis.

The primary years of comparison in this paper are 1979 and 2007. These years are comparable points in the business cycle and are both end years of economic expansion (the peak of the cycle); both were followed by a deep and extended recession. Rising wage inequality in the United States started in the mid- to late-1970s, so 1979 represents a time before people became concerned with increasing inequality. These two endpoints provide almost three decades of comparison.

The data analysis throughout this book is based on the Current Population Survey (CPS)—a large, random national sample of the population. For each primary year, I use the March data from the following year. These data include the Annual Social and Economic Supplement,[5] which asks a variety of questions about individual and family income and work effort among all civilian adults during the previous year. Hence, my data is taken from the March 1980 and March 2008 CPS, providing information on 1979 and 2007, respectively.[6]

I use data for all eighteen- to sixty-four-year-old adults in each year.[7] I focus on nonelderly individuals because this group is typically considered the working-age population, and I am particularly interested in how changes in the distribution of wages over the past thirty years have affected changes in aggregate income. In part because nonelderly adults are attached to the work force, the policy options that one might consider to address inequality among this population are also very different from those that one would discuss if looking at income inequality among the elderly. Throughout the analysis, I use individuals as the key unit of observation—not families. Like the CPS, however, I assume that individuals share income with all other coresident persons who are related by marriage, adoption, or birth. Persons or families that live together but are not related to each other I assume to be separate income units.

I will use the term "family unit" to refer to the group with whom an individual shares income. I use this, rather than the more common term "family," because a family in CPS terminology includes at least two related individuals. Since I include single individuals who rely solely on their own income in my analysis, a "family unit" can refer either to a group of related individuals or to a single individual.[8]

One of the most difficult problems in the CPS for distributional analysis is the use of "top-coding" for various income variables.[9] Not only do I not have information on actual income among those at the top of the distribution, but the top-codes change from year to year, so the extent of missing information varies across years. Furthermore, because top-coding occurs by income source, even individuals whose total income is not at the top of the income distribution may be top-coded on one particular income variable. Burkhauser et al. (2008) show that failure to account for these top-coding issues greatly affects estimates of trends in income inequality.

Fortunately, Larrimore et al. (2008) have recently completed an extensive analysis of the impact of top-coding in the CPS. They were able to access internal Census data, and they provide information on the mean values for top-coded data by income source for the Current Population Surveys fielded in each year from 1976 through 2007. For wages and self-employment income, they provide these mean values by gender, race, and full-time/part-time status. This allows me to adjust for top-coding in wages and self-employment income, and in the income families receive from Social Security, other government assistance programs, Unemployment and Workers' Compensation, interest, dividends, pensions, and a host of other income sources.[10]

One of the problems in the data is the presence of negative income, typically because of negative earnings or negative net rental income. Self-employed individuals may report negative earned income when their business is doing poorly, for instance. I set all of these negative earnings or rental-income reports to zero.[11]

A further problem is that some individuals are in family units that report zero income for the entire year. I have looked closely at these individuals and am persuaded that many of them are actually in this situation. They may be supported by someone outside their family unit or may be living on savings for the year. In 1979, this group represented 0.45 percent of the sample, but that figure increased to 1.74 percent of the sample for 2007. About two-thirds of these zero-income persons are in single-person family units in both years. In both years, about 80 percent say they are taking care of either home or family (perhaps taking care of a relative they do not live with), claim they are ill or disabled (although they report no disability income), claim they are going to school, or report themselves unable to find work. They have disproportionately low levels of education. I have repeated the analysis in chapters 2 and 3, both including and excluding the zero-income family units. Excluding them makes no difference to any of the data trends that I discuss. They are included in all of the results reported in this book.

It is worth emphasizing that all of the analysis in this book is based on cash income as reported to the government. Some types of income tend to be underreported in government surveys. For instance, there appears to be underreporting of cash-assistance programs among lower-income persons. But the most significant underreporting probably occurs among higher-income individuals, particularly those who are self-employed or engaged in illegal activities. My guess is that the inclusion of unreported or illicit income would result in an even wider distribution of income than these data indicate. But we know little about the trends in unreported income, and it is hard to say whether taking them into account would accentuate or offset the widening income inequality of the past thirty years.

Since this analysis is based on cash income, these data take no account of taxes. As I note in chapter 4, taxes are generally progressive, and the after-tax distribution of income is less unequal than the before-tax distribution of income. These data also do not include noncash benefits from employers (such as pension payments, sick days, and health-insurance subsidies) or from the government (such as assistance for housing, food, and child-care costs). In chapter 4, I return to these concerns and indicate how the inclusion of tax and noncash benefits might affect my conclusions.

ADJUSTING FOR DIFFERENCES IN FAMILY SIZE

I look at the distribution of income and income components at the individual level. This assumes that the key question is how economic well-being is distributed among persons. When discussing earnings and its components, I can look at individual earnings among workers. But when I turn to a discussion of total income and its components (earnings, government income, and other income), I must allocate the income within a family unit to each individual. One option is make a simple per person income calculation, dividing total income by family size. This is not a satisfying approach, however. Individuals live in different-size family units, and there are economies of scale within these units.

For this reason, most economists make an adjustment for economies of scale when calculating per person income. Such an adjustment assumes that the additional income needed to keep family well-being at the same level will decline as more and more persons are added to the family. Said in another way, to keep a family unit equally well off as family size increases, income has to increase more when a second person joins the family than it does when a third person enters; it has to increase more when a third person enters than it does when a fourth person enters; and so on.

I adjust for these differences in economies of scale by dividing family income by the square root of family size. This is the equation:

$$Y_i = Y_f / \sqrt{N_f} \tag{1-1}$$

where Y_i is the per person income allocated to person i; Y_f is the total income available in the family unit where person i resides; and N_f is the number of persons in this family unit. If this is a single individual who lives alone, his or her income constitutes the total income in the family unit. If this is an individual who lives with others, he or she will be allocated a share of income from the family unit—a share that decreases as family-unit size rises, but that does so at a slower rate than it would if I did not account for economies of scale.[12]

Table 1 shows how this adjustment affects per person income, showing how per person income changes as family size grows. Column 1 shows total family income, column 2 shows family size, column 3 indicates the result of a simple per person income calculation, and column 4 shows per person income adjusted for economies of scale. As column 1 indicates, I assume that family income equals $100,000. With only one person in the family unit, per person income equals $100,000 regardless of how it is calculated. When a second person enters the family unit, a simple per person income calculation would give each person $50,000. But the family size adjustment assumes there are economies of scale when two people live together and share rent, food, and other purchases. This means that adjusted per person income for this two-person household is $70,711 each. This is the equivalent amount of income each person would have to have to be as well off if they lived alone as they are living together in a family unit with $100,000 in income.

The remaining columns show how this calculation changes as family size rises. With four people in the household, each person has the equivalent of $50,000 in per person income in my calculation, which is the amount they would need to live alone at the same level of well-being as they achieve living together as a four-person family.

This adjusted per person income calculation allows me to di-rectly compare the economic well-being of individuals no mat-

TABLE I

Example of Family Size Adjustment on Per Person Income

Family Income ($)	Family Size	Per Person Income, Not Adjusted for Economies of Scale ($)	Per Person Income, Adjusted for Economies of Scale ($)
(1)	(2)	(3)	(4)
100,000	1	100,000	100,000
100,000	2	50,000	70,711
100,000	3	33,333	57,735
100,000	4	25,000	50,000
100,000	5	20,000	44,721
100,000	6	16,667	40,825

ter what their living arrangements might be. Hence, rather than comparing total family income levels, I will compare adjusted per person income levels and will look at how the distribution of adjusted per person income is changing over time. A single individual whose total income equals $50,000 is assumed to be as well off as an individual living in a family of four whose total income is $100,000. Both of these individuals have $50,000 in adjusted per person income.

MEASURING INEQUALITY

Throughout this book I look at three different measures of inequality in the distribution of income and its components. First, I report the *Gini coefficient,* a measure of statistical dispersion that rises as income inequality rises. In a situation of perfect equality, where all incomes are equal, the Gini coefficient equals zero. At extreme inequality (where one person has all the income and everyone else has zero), the Gini coefficient equals one.

Hence, as the Gini coefficient rises, income inequality increases. Gini coefficients for the distribution of family income in most advanced industrialized nations have historically been between 0.22 and 0.40.[13]

Second, I show the *coefficient of variation* (CV), which is the standard deviation of the data divided by its mean. The CV provides a measure of how dispersed the data are around their mean. Like the Gini coefficient, it equals zero when all incomes are equal and rises with growing inequality. Highly unequal incomes can result in CVs that are well above one, however. For any significant changes in inequality, one would expect the Gini and the CV to move together; by looking at both of them I can confirm that the trends in the data do not vary with measurement choice.

Third, I report comparisons of the data at several different points in the distribution, typically looking at the 90/10 ratio, which compares the data at the ninetieth percentile in its distribution with the data at the tenth percentile. Growing inequality means a rising 90/10 ratio. I will also look at the 90/50 ratio and the 50/10 ratio (the fiftieth point in the distribution is the median), in order to see if rising inequality is concentrated at the top or the bottom of the distribution. As noted earlier, changes in inequality driven by rises in top incomes may be viewed differently from changes in inequality driven by declines in bottom incomes. If inequality is changing only slightly or only at certain points in the distribution, these measures might provide conflicting information. If inequality is shifting across the entire distribution, all of these measures should indicate rising inequality.

TWO

Changing Inequality in Annual Earnings and Its Components

Most of the research on inequality in the past three decades has focused on rising inequality in hourly or weekly wages, particularly the rapid increases in wages among more-skilled workers in contrast to stagnant or falling wages among less-skilled workers. In this chapter, focusing on workers only, I look at changes in hourly wages as well as changes in weeks and hours of work. These components combine to produce changes in total annual earnings. The results show that annual earnings have changed in ways that are quite different from the better-known changes in hourly wages. It is particularly interesting to observe the large differences between how men's earnings and women's earnings have changed over time. As this chapter demonstrates, increases in labor-market effort, particularly among women, have offset inequality in hourly wages and shifted the whole earnings distribution upward.

ANNUAL EARNINGS AND ITS COMPONENTS

Annual labor-market earnings for any person depend upon three components: how much is earned per hour; how many hours are worked per week; and how many weeks are worked per year. Expressed mathematically, for an individual i,

$$E_i = w_i \cdot h_i \cdot k_i \qquad (2\text{--}1)$$

where E_i represents total annual earnings for person i, w_i represents hourly wages, h_i represents hours worked per week, and k_i represents weeks worked per year. All of these components have been changing. I start by looking at changes in the distribution of total annual earnings and then discuss distributional changes in each of its three components.

Throughout this section, I focus only on the distribution of annual earnings and its components among eighteen- to sixty-four-year-old civilian workers. Hence, there are no adjustments for family size in any of the data in this section. I merely report earnings per worker and its components among those who work. The results of this chapter, which focuses on what has been happening to individual workers within the labor market, are highly important in understanding the shifts in family income discussed in the next chapter, where I expand the analysis to look at all nonelderly adults.

One problem with looking only at workers, however, is that the share of workers has shifted in the population. Women's labor-force participation[1] has risen from 67 percent to 73 percent over this time period, for instance, so "workers" in 2007 include a wider swath of the female population. At the same time, men's labor-force participation has declined from 91 percent to 85 percent, so male workers are less representative of the overall male population in 2007. This means that the characteristics of workers may be shifting over this twenty-eight year period, and changes in the earnings distribution will reflect changes in who is working as well as changes in the labor-market opportunities available to workers. I will discuss the impact of changing labor-force participation at the end of this chapter.

CHANGES IN INEQUALITY IN ANNUAL EARNINGS

Hourly wage inequality has been rising steadily over the past thirty years—a fact documented extensively in the research literature on the U.S. labor force. The rise in inequality in annual earnings is much less marked than the rise in inequality in hourly wages, however, as we shall see in a minute.

Table 2 provides information on key measures of inequality for annual earnings in 1979 (column 1) and in 2007 (column 2). Part A of table 2 focuses on all workers, while part B looks only at male workers and part C looks only at female workers. Between 1979 and 2007, median real annual earnings rose by $6,000—from $25,000 to $31,000. (All income and earnings data are in 2007 dollars, calculated using the GDP deflator for personal consumption expenditures.) The data for male and female workers suggest that much of this increase in median earnings occurred because of a substantial increase in median annual earnings among female workers—from $16,000 to $26,000. In contrast, median annual earnings among men rose much less—from $35,000 to $37,000.

At the same time that the midpoint in the distribution of earnings among all workers was rising, inequality (the dispersion of earnings around the median) rose somewhat. The Gini coefficient crept up, and the CV rose. Whereas the 90/50 ratio

TABLE 2
Measures of Inequality for Annual Earnings and Its Components

	Total Annual Earnings		Hourly Wages		Hours per Week		Weeks per Year	
	1979	2007	1979	2007	1979	2007	1979	2007
	(1)	(2)	(3)	(4)	(5)	(6)	(7)	(8)
PART A. ALL WORKERS								
Median	$25,002	$31,000	$13.22	$16.15	40	40	52	52
Gini coefficient	0.45	0.46	0.36	0.45	0.14	0.14	0.14	0.09
Coefficient of variation	0.90	1.15	1.01	3.84	0.30	0.28	0.31	0.23
90/10 ratio	16.13	11.43	4.89	5.77	2.27	2.00	2.74	1.73
90/50 ratio	2.42	2.58	2.18	2.38	1.25	1.25	1.00	1.00
50/10 ratio	6.67	4.43	2.24	2.42	1.82	1.60	2.74	1.73
PART B. MALE WORKERS								
Median	$35,003	$37,000	$16.87	$17.79	40	40	52	52
Gini coefficient	0.39	0.46	0.34	0.45	0.11	0.12	0.10	0.07
Coefficient of variation	0.78	1.12	0.85	3.47	0.25	0.26	0.25	0.22
90/10 ratio	9.67	10.00	4.77	6.00	1.57	1.72	2.00	1.53
90/50 ratio	2.07	2.70	1.99	2.43	1.38	1.38	1.00	1.00
50/10 ratio	4.67	3.70	2.40	2.47	1.14	1.25	2.00	1.53

PART C. FEMALE WORKERS

Median	$15,922	$26,000	$10.33	$14.42	40	40	52	52
Gini coefficient	0.43	0.44	0.33	0.45	0.16	0.15	0.19	0.10
Coefficient of variation	0.83	1.09	1.25	4.36	0.33	0.30	0.38	0.25
90/10 ratio	18.62	13.00	4.08	5.44	2.22	2.40	4.00	2.00
90/50 ratio	2.34	2.50	1.96	2.33	1.00	1.20	1.00	1.00
50/10 ratio	7.96	5.20	2.08	2.33	2.22	2.00	4.00	2.00

NOTE: Earnings and wages in 2007 dollars. The sample includes all civilian workers aged eighteen to sixty-four.

rose, the 90/10 ratio fell, as did the 50/10 ratio. This suggests that the top of the distribution rose faster than the median but that earnings at the bottom also rose faster than the median, with only a small overall rise in inequality. I show the distribution of total earnings in 1979 and 2007 visually in figure 1-A. Whereas the share of workers with quite high earnings increases between these two years, the share of workers with very low earnings decreases substantially. Dispersion in the bottom half of the distribution is a bit lower, while the overall median is rising, so there are fewer people in the lower "bins" in figure 1-A.[2]

These results may seem puzzling to those who know that wages fell among lower-skilled male workers in the United States over this time period. When I look at annual earnings among men only (part B in table 2), I see much steeper increases in inequality, with noticeably larger increases in the Gini coefficient and the CV for male earnings. Yet even for men, the 50/10 ratio for annual earnings falls somewhat. Figure 2-A shows these patterns among men.

Women show the same pattern, but with a much greater decline in inequality between the middle and the bottom of the distribution of annual earnings. (See part C in table 2; also see figure 3-A.) Women show increases in the overall dispersion of annual earnings, but these increases in inequality are concentrated in the top half of the distribution. Earnings dispersion at the bottom of the women's earning distribution falls markedly, as shown by the declining 50/10 ratio. Figure 3-A indicates that over these three decades there was a noticeable shift among women out of lower-earnings categories, and a substantial increase in annual female earnings of more than $30,000.

Clearly, annual earnings inequality is following a somewhat different pattern than wage inequality, which previous research suggests has become more unequal at both the top and the bottom of the wage distribution. Earnings inequality has widened at the top but has grown more equal at the bottom. This is largely because of increases in annual earnings, particularly among women, that have reduced the number of workers with very low earnings levels. In the absence of any changes in earnings dispersion, an increase in median earnings will reduce the share of workers in low-earnings categories and increase the share in high-earnings categories. Combined with an increase in dispersion at the top end of the earnings distribution, the net effect has been a small increase in overall earnings inequality but unambiguous improvement in earnings levels as fewer and fewer workers are found in low earnings categories.

Changes in annual earnings reflect offsetting changes in hours and weeks of work, as well as changes in hourly wages. As we shall see, increasing dispersion in wages is being offset by decreases in dispersion in other components of earnings, leading to less overall dispersion in annual earnings than in hourly wages. I turn next to these components of earnings.

CHANGES IN HOURLY WAGE INEQUALITY

Columns 3 and 4 of table 2 confirm that these data show the same patterns of rising wage inequality throughout the distribution that other researchers have found. All measures of hourly wage inequality in table 2 rise between 1979 and 2007. This includes increases in the 90/10 ratio, the 90/50 ratio, and the 50/10 ratio, suggesting that the wage distribution has spread out at both the top and the bottom. Figures 1-B, 2-B, and 3-B show this pattern graphically for hourly wages among all workers and for male and female workers.

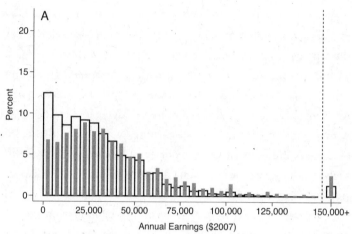

Each bin is a $5,000 interval except the last, which includes all workers making at least $150,000.

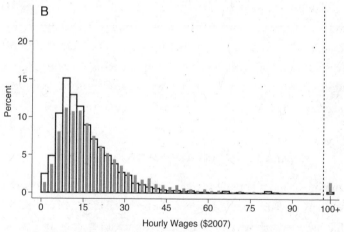

Each bin is a $2.50 interval except the last, which includes all workers making at least $100/hr.

1979   2007

Figure 1. Distribution of annual earnings and its components, all workers: A. Distribution of annual earnings in 1979 and in 2007; B. Distribution of hourly wages in 1979 and in 2007; C. Distribution of hours worked per week in 1979 and in 2007; D. Distribution of weeks worked in 1979 and in 2007. Each graph includes all civilian workers aged eighteen to sixty-four.

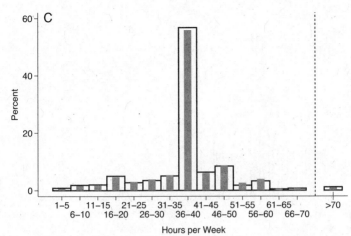

Hours per Week

Each bin is a 5 hour interval except the last, which includes all workers working more than 70 hrs/wk.

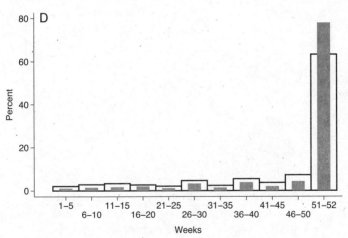

Weeks

Each bin is a 5 week interval.

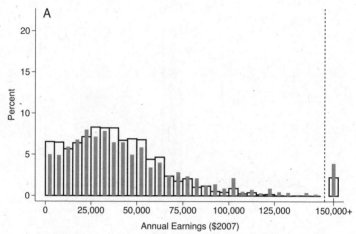

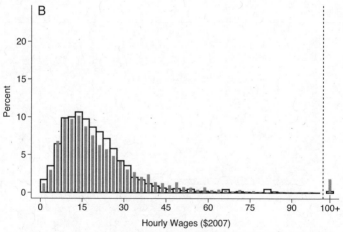

Figure 2. Distribution of annual earnings and its components, male workers: A. Distribution of annual earnings in 1979 and in 2007; B. Distribution of hourly wages in 1979 and in 2007; C. Distribution of hours worked per week in 1979 and in 2007; D. Distribution of weeks worked in 1979 and in 2007. Each graph includes all civilian workers aged eighteen to sixty-four.

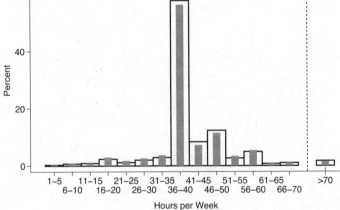

Hours per Week

Each bin is a 5 hour interval except the last, which includes all workers working more than 70 hrs/wk.

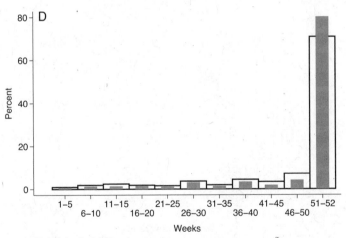

Weeks

Each bin is a 5 week interval.

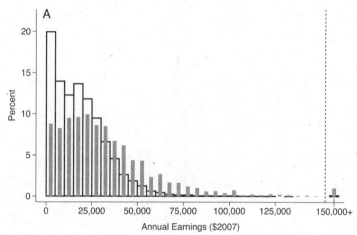

Each bin is a $5,000 interval except the last, which includes all workers making at least $150,000.

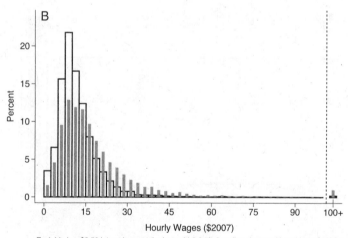

Each bin is a $2.50 interval except the last, which includes all workers making at least $100/hr.

Figure 3. Distribution of annual earnings and its components, female workers: A. Distribution of annual earnings in 1979 and in 2007; B. Distribution of hourly wages in 1979 and in 2007; C. Distribution of hours worked per week in 1979 and in 2007; D. Distribution of weeks worked in 1979 and in 2007. Each graph includes all civilian workers aged eighteen to sixty-four.

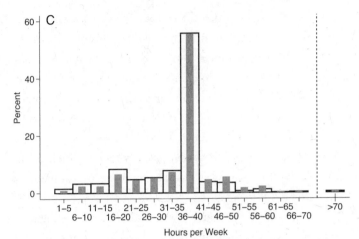

Hours per Week

Each bin is a 5 hour interval except the last, which includes all workers working more than 70 hrs/wk.

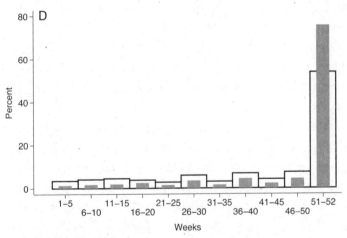

Weeks

Each bin is a 5 week interval.

1979   2007

Our data also suggest that the increase in dispersion in wages at the top of the distribution is bigger than the increase at the bottom, as other researchers have noted. Particularly among men, the 90/50 ratio rises much more than the 50/10 ratio over this period. This is consistent with recent work by Lemieux (2008, 2010), which indicates that male wages grew most rapidly below the twentieth percentile and above the sixtieth percentile of the wage distribution between 1989 and 2004. Much of the ground lost by the lowest-wage workers in the 1980s was made up in the following fifteen years.

It is worth noting that much of the research on wage inequality separates workers by skill level, whereas the results in table 2 show wage changes among all persons, without distinguishing education levels. The number of people with no education beyond a high school degree has declined between 1979 and 2007. Among men, the share of the civilian workforce with just a high school degree or less fell from 61 percent to 43 percent between 1979 and 2007; among women this share fell from 64 percent to 34 percent.[3]

In Figure 4, I confirm that my data show the same patterns of wage changes by skill as others have reported. Figure 4-A shows the percent change in median real hourly wages by education level among all workers between 1979 and 2007. Figure 4-B shows the patterns by education level for male workers only, and Figure 4-C shows the patterns among female workers. For men, wages fall among high school dropouts as well as among those with only a high school degree. They are flat among those with some college. Only men with a four-year college degree or graduate education have shown real wage growth. For female workers, wages grew at all skill levels, but they grew much faster among more-educated women.

This increase in the return to education has been attributed to skill-biased changes in demand, driven by new technologies that have sharply increased the demand for the most-skilled workers. Although rising, the supply of highly skilled workers has not kept up with this increased demand in recent decades, resulting in steady upward pressure on wages among these workers. An ever-growing literature explores some of the issues behind the technological and demand-related shifts that have been driving wage changes over the past three decades.[4]

There is a substantial rise in the share of workers in high-wage categories in figure 1-B. This occurs because of small declines in the share of workers in low-wage categories among men and quite large declines among women (figures 2-B and 3-B). In short, even though wage changes among less-skilled men have been negative (and they have been small for less-skilled women), this group constitutes a declining share of all workers. When looking at the full distribution of workers, there are fewer low-wage workers because there are fewer less-skilled persons in the workforce. This decline in the share of low-skilled workers would have been faster but has been slowed by relatively high rates of immigration among lower-skilled persons since the 1980s.[5]

Furthermore, wages have been growing among even less-educated women. Median hourly wages rose from $10.33 to $14.42 among all women workers over this time period, shifting the entire distribution of women's wages upward. Other research suggests that this is because of increases in women's experience in the labor market over this period, since women work for more of their adult years, and this gain in experience results in higher wages (Blau and Kahn, 1997; Blau and Kahn, 2006). The negative effects of children and marriage on women's wages have decreased as well. Whereas married women and women

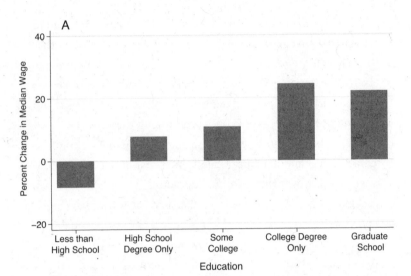

Figure 4. *(above and opposite)* Percent change in median hourly wages from 1979 to 2007 by education level—all workers and by gender: A. All workers; B. Male workers; C. Female workers. Each graph includes all civilian workers aged eighteen to sixty-four.

with children earned less than their single peers in 1979 (holding education and experience constant), the negative effects of marriage and children on women's earnings behavior became much smaller by the mid-2000s (Blank and Shierholz, 2006). This has also contributed to rising wages among women.

CHANGES IN INEQUALITY
IN HOURS WORKED PER WEEK

Weekly hours of work have been relatively stable over this period, with median weekly hours equal to forty for all workers in both years. This stability hides different distributional trends by gender, however. The distribution of women's weekly

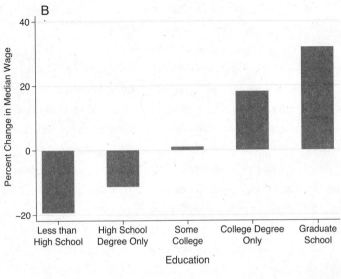

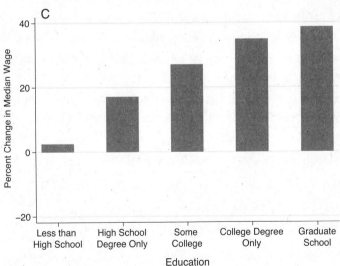

hours of work has shifted upward, while the distribution of men's weekly hours has shifted downward slightly.

Columns 5 and 6 of table 2 and figures 1-C, 2-C, and 3-C show trends in the distribution of weekly hours among all workers and male and female workers. Weekly hours are heavily grouped between thirty-six and forty hours per week. In fact, more than 50 percent of both men and women report working exactly forty hours per week. This makes for a relatively tight distribution.

Although weekly hours among men show a slight increase in overall inequality among all measures in table 2, weekly hours among women show a slight decline in overall inequality. This is because fewer women report very low weekly hours of work in 2007, as the declining 50/10 ratio for women indicates. At the same time, there is an increase in the number of women reporting higher hours in the top part of the hours distribution in 2007. Conversely, men at the bottom of the distribution are now working fewer hours per week, although there has been little change at the top of the distribution.

Overall, hours of work are changing relatively little over this time period. There is a slight decline in inequality, due to the declines in dispersion among female workers. Hours of work are not driving the changes in earnings inequality, however.

CHANGES IN INEQUALITY
IN WEEKS WORKED PER YEAR

The final component of total earnings is the numbers of week worked each year. This is a somewhat different variable than weekly hours, wages, or earnings, because weeks are necessarily capped at fifty-two each year, and a high share of workers work full-year. In fact, the median number of weeks of work for all workers is fifty-two. Hence, any change in the distribution of weeks must be due to changes in the extent of part-year work.

As columns 7 and 8 of table 2 indicate, inequality in weeks of work has declined among all workers and among both male and female workers. This is entirely due to a decline in the number of low-week workers, especially among women.[6] These shifts are visible in figures 1-D, 2-D, and 3-D. Figure 3-D shows the distribution of weeks among women in 1979 and 2007, with a substantial reduction in the number of women reporting that they work less than fifty weeks each year.

Hence, equalizing shifts in the distribution of weeks of work have offset rises in wage inequality. One reason why annual earnings inequality has increased less than wage inequality is that lower-wage workers are working more weeks each year.

COMPARISONS BY RACE

Although the tables shown here include all workers, I have looked separately at black and white workers by gender. In 1979 there are too few Hispanic workers to break this group out separately by gender.

The trends for black and white women are strikingly similar. In both years, the distribution of annual earnings among black and white female workers looks quite similar, with similar Gini coefficients and coefficients of variation. This means that black women show the same substantial upward shift in their earnings distribution as white women, and the same decline in the number of persons in low-wage categories. This is despite the fact that black women have lower overall hourly wages. In 2007, black women's median hourly wages are $13.35, whereas white women's are $14.53. These lower wages are somewhat offset by a greater number of hours of work among black women. Both black and white women show substantial increases in the share working full-time at fifty-two weeks per year.

The racial differences among men are much greater, with substantial differences in the distribution of both annual earnings and hourly wages between black and white men in both years. Changes in the distribution of earnings and wages over time are similar in both groups, however. Like white men, black men show a substantial decline in the number of workers in low-earnings categories, but in both years black men's wages are clustered in much lower wage categories. Median hourly wages among black men are $14.42 in 2007, while they are $18.27 among white men. Median annual earnings among black men are $30,000 in 2007, while they are $39,000 among white men. The dispersion in earnings is also less for black men, since there are many fewer of them are in high-earnings categories.

Black men's wages and earnings increase faster than white men's, even if they remain much lower at the end of the period. Inequality would have grown even more among men if these greater increases among black men had not occurred.

For both white and black women, inequality in annual earnings increases only slightly between 1979 and 2007, with increases in inequality in hourly wages offset by rising work effort. Inequality among white men is increasing faster than among black men, however, largely because the top white male wage earners move into much higher hourly wage categories over these years. Yet despite these differences, the general conclusions about changes over time in earnings and their distribution are quite similar for both black and white workers. There are substantial differences by gender in both groups, with women's greater work effort leading to very different changes in their earnings distribution.

ACCOUNTING FOR THE DIFFERENT PATHS
OF EARNINGS AND WAGES

The previous discussion reinforces the fact that annual earnings and wages have not followed identical patterns over the past three decades. In fact, when looking at the distribution of annual earnings among all workers, it appears that workers throughout the earnings distribution in 2007 were largely better off than workers at an equivalent point in the earnings distribution in 1979. The share of workers in low earnings categories has fallen noticeably, while the share in high earnings categories has risen. Overall measures of inequality in annual earnings have edged up only slightly, and the gap between the middle and the bottom of the distribution appears to have closed somewhat. There are three primary reasons for these differences in the earnings distribution relative to the wage distribution.

First, while hourly wage inequality has increased markedly, inequality in hours per week has changed relatively little (and decreased among women), while inequality in weeks per year has declined. These hours-related changes have offset changes in wages.

Second, while wages have fallen among less-educated men and risen little among less-educated women, less-educated workers are a declining share of the workforce. The result is that hourly wages have risen across the wage distribution, and particularly among female workers, among whom they are up by more than four dollars per hour over this time period.

Third, increasing wages, hours per week, and weeks per year among women have also helped reduce inequality in the distribution of total earnings. These changes have led to greatly increased annual earnings for women over the past three decades, especially at the bottom of the distribution, where many female workers were part-time or part-year workers in 1979.

In summary, changes in the gender, education, and hours of the workforce may have offset increases in wage inequality, so earnings inequality increased less than wage inequality. However, we would still like to know how rising wage inequality has affected the earnings distribution. In particular, we would like to know what earnings inequality would look like in a world where increases in wage inequality were not offset by other changes in the labor force.

To estimate this effect, I run simulations that hold work behavior and the gender and educational makeup of the workforce constant at their 1979 levels but allow the distribution of wages within levels of education to change over these years as they actually did for both men and women. This simulation indicates how much of the change in the level and the distribution in annual earnings is due to changes in the distribution of hourly wages alone, with no shift in hours or labor-force shares among men or women by education level.

It is not entirely realistic to look at a world where the distribution of wages changes but work behavior does not, since these changes in the distribution of wages may have *caused* many of the changes in work behavior.[7] If one of the ways in which changes in the wage distribution affected earnings inequality was by generating important changes in work behavior, this channel should be included in any estimate of wage changes' impact on earnings inequality. Nonetheless, this simulation tells us something about the relative importance of distributional shifts in wages relative to shifts in work behavior. The exact details of how this simulation is calculated are given in appendix 1.

Table 3 shows the results of this simulation. Columns 1, 4, and

7 show actual 1979 values at the median and for various measures of inequality among all workers and among male and female workers. Columns 2, 5, and 8 show the actual percent change in these measures between 1979 and 2007. Columns 3, 6, and 9 show the simulated change if the work behavior of both men and women workers is held constant at its 1979 level within skill categories.

When both the gender and skill mix of workers and their hours of work are held at their 1979 levels, there are substantially different changes in the level and distribution of earnings in 2007. Absent workforce changes, the median level of earnings grows relatively little—by only 4 percent rather than 24 percent between 1979 and 2007. Inequality grows much faster based on the Gini coefficient, with faster growth in the 90/50 ratio and less of a decline in the 50/10 ratio.

With little growth in the median, there is less of an upward shift in the entire distribution. More workers stay in the low-earnings categories. At the same time, rising wages at the top of the wage distribution pull up the top of the earnings distribution, and this effect is not offset by greater work effort among women, so the 90/50 ratio grows faster among women (and among all workers). In short, widening wage inequality leads to widening earnings inequality; without offsetting changes in work effort, there is less growth in overall earnings levels.

This is particularly visible in the simulation for male earnings. Without any changes in work behavior or education level, overall median male earnings fall about 6 percent between 1979 and 2007, while the distribution widens. In actuality, median male earnings rose about 6 percent. In contrast, among women, there is real earnings growth even without any increase in hours of work or education, with median earnings rising by 20 percent

TABLE 3

Simulation Showing the Effect on Annual Earnings When Labor Force Behavior Is Held Constant at Its 1979 Level

	All Workers			Male Workers			Female Workers		
	1979 Value	Percent Change 1979–2007		1979 Value	Percent Change 1979–2007		1979 Value	Percent Change 1979–2007	
		Actual	Simulated		Actual	Simulated		Actual	Simulated
	(1)	(2)	(3)	(4)	(5)	(6)	(7)	(8)	(9)
Median	$25,002	24.0	4.0	$35,003	5.7	-5.7	$15,922	63.3	19.9
Gini coefficient	0.45	3.7	8.3	0.39	17.7	17.2	0.43	2.9	10.5
90/10 ratio	16.13	-29.2	-0.9	9.67	3.4	11.2	18.62	-30.2	4.2
90/50 ratio	2.42	6.6	12.4	2.07	30.5	24.3	2.34	6.8	11.6
50/10 ratio	6.67	-33.6	-11.8	4.67	-20.7	-10.6	7.96	-34.7	-6.6

NOTE: The sample includes all civilian workers aged eighteen to sixty-four. These simulations hold constant the shares in the workforce of male and female workers by education level. Two education levels are distinguished, where less-educated workers are those with a high school degree or less and more-educated workers are those with at least some college. The simulations also hold constant the distribution of hours among workers within each of the four gender/education cells. See appendix 1 for details.

in the simulation. In reality, median earnings rose much faster—by 63 percent. When hours of work and skill level are held constant, widening wage inequality among women causes greater increases in the 90/50 ratio and less of a decline in the 50/10 ratio.

SUMMARIZING CHANGES IN
THE DISTRIBUTION OF ANNUAL EARNINGS

To sum up the results of this entire section on earnings changes: if one judges worker well-being on the basis of annual earnings, the results here suggest that equivalent workers are doing better in 2007 than in 1979. The midpoint of the distribution of earnings has risen. Earnings in the bottom of the distribution have risen faster than the median, with declines in the 50/10 ratio of earnings. Earnings in the top of the distribution have moved up more quickly than the median, increasing inequality. Rising inequality that occurs in the context of overall earnings increases may be viewed less negatively than if the bottom of the distribution were declining.

However, these gains in overall earnings levels have occurred largely because of increases in full-time work, especially among women, that in turn increased women's earnings throughout their distribution. Population shifts to a more skilled workforce also added to these gains. Without these changes in labor-force behavior, median earnings would have declined among men and grown much less among women.[8] (Of course, given rising wages among the most-skilled workers, earnings would have grown at the top of the distribution regardless of shifts in work behavior.) In short, earnings growth among female workers has helped mitigate the economic effects of growing inequality. But this earnings growth is not happening because wages are growing substantially for most workers, but because the population—especially the female population—is working more hours. As I discuss at more length in chapter 4, the welfare implications of this are uncertain. There are gains from greater earnings and perhaps greater economic independence among women, but these gains may be offset by the costs of spending more time in market work.

THREE

Changing Inequality in Total Income and Its Components

In this chapter, I look at changes in the distribution and level of total income available to individuals—from their own earnings, from the earnings of others with whom they live and share income, and from the receipt of unearned income from government programs, private assets, alimony payments, and other sources. Earnings are the primary source of income for most individuals and families, but most people receive some unearned income. As a result, earnings and total income need not always move together.

MEASURING TOTAL INCOME AND ITS COMPONENTS

Total family income is the sum of earnings, government income, and unearned income from other sources. Throughout this chapter, I am interested in the well-being of individuals and how it is changing over time; hence I translate family income into individual economic well-being by looking at per person income, adjusted for family size. This calculation assumes that all related people who live together pool their income and share it equally. As discussed in chapter 1, the family size adjustment acknowledges that larger families can live more economically, so that income need not increase linearly as family size grows for per person income to remain constant.

More formally, I define total per person income for individual i as:

$$Y_i = Y_f/\sqrt{N_f} = (E_f + G_f + O_f)/\sqrt{N_f} \qquad (3\text{–}1)$$

where Y_f is total income received by the family unit f in which individual i lives. E_f represents total earnings among all workers in the family unit, G_f represents total income from government sources, and O_f represents other unearned income sources. As before, N_f is the total number of persons in the family unit. As explained in chapter 1, I adjust for differences in family size by dividing total family income by the square root of N.

Government income includes income from means-tested programs (such as cash support through the Supplemental Security Income program or the Temporary Assistance to Needy Families program) as well as other government programs (such as Social Security disability).[1] Other income includes investment income (such as dividends or interest) and income from private income sources (such as work disability).[2]

Earnings, government income, and other unearned income received by any individual are assumed to be shared among all persons in the family unit. This means that all adults in the same family unit are considered equally well off. Hence, if a wife works more hours and earns more income, all individuals in that family unit will be assigned higher income.

Note that family-unit income is based upon the income from all sources in the family, so if elderly parents live with the family, their Social Security income is included. This is true even though I do not include these elderly parents in my sample of nonelderly adults. I assume that their income makes their coresident (nonelderly) children better off and should be counted. Children and elderly adults are also included in my calculation of a family's size.

All of the income data reported in this section will refer to per person income based on total family-unit income adjusted for family-unit size. Therefore, the income levels shown here are not the same as family income (which reports total income inside a family unit), nor are they the same as per capita income within a family, which does not account for economies of scale as family size grows. This should be kept in mind in interpreting the dollar amounts shown in the tables.

THE TYPES OF FAMILY UNITS
IN WHICH INDIVIDUALS RESIDE

Although I am primarily concerned with changes in the distribution of income among all individuals, I also separate individuals into three groups, depending upon the type of family unit in which they live. *Single persons* are those individuals who live in one-person family units, residing with no other related persons (although they could share living quarters with unrelated individuals).³ *Persons in single-headed family units* live with relatives, but in a family unit headed by a single individual and not a married couple. The majority of adults in single-headed family units are family heads, but these families may also include other adults who are related to the head. The final family category is *persons in married-couple family units.* These are individuals who live in family units headed by married couples. The majority of these persons are either the husband or the wife in the married couple, but there may be other nonelderly adults in these families (this can include adult children as well as other relatives). All nonelderly adults in these family units are considered persons in married-couple families in my calculations.

Part A of table 4 describes the distribution of persons across these family types. In 1979, 13 percent of all nonelderly adults were in single-person family units, 12 percent were in single-headed family units, and 75 percent were in married-couple family units. As expected, by 2007 the share of persons in single-headed family units had increased, while the share of those in married-couple family units had declined. There has also been an increase in the share of those in single-person family units.

Parts B through D of table 4 describe the breakdown of persons within each family type. In both years, men were more likely than women to be in single-person family units, while men and women were equally represented in married-couple family units. Women were much more likely to reside in single-headed family units—not surprising, since many of these families are headed by females. Within married-couple family units, between 15 and 16 percent of the adults were not part of the married couple that heads the family. These additional adults could be adult children of the married couple, parents, or other relatives. A much higher share of the adults in single-headed family units were not themselves the family-unit head—between 45 and 47 percent. This reflects the lower income levels of single-headed families, and the greater likelihood that they share living space with other related adults, including unmarried partners.

It is also worth noting that family-unit size has fallen noticeably over the 1979–2007 period. The last row of Part A in table 4 indicates that the mean family had 3.3 people in 1979 but only

TABLE 4

Share of Persons by Family Type

	1979	2007
PART A. PERCENT OF ALL PERSONS IN:		
Single-person family units	13.4	21.0
Single-headed family units	11.9	16.9
Married-couple family units	74.7	62.2
Mean family-unit size (all family units)	3.29	2.92
PART B. AMONG PERSONS IN SINGLE-PERSON FAMILY UNITS		
Percent male	54.7	55.7
Percent female	45.3	44.3
Mean family-unit size	1.00	1.00
PART C. AMONG PERSONS IN SINGLE-HEADED FAMILY UNITS		
Percent male	33.3	40.3
Percent female	66.7	59.7
Percent in family unit but not head	44.6	47.0
Mean family-unit size	3.26	3.12
PART D. AMONG PERSONS IN MARRIED-COUPLE FAMILY UNITS		
Percent male	49.9	50.0
Percent female	50.1	50.0
Percent in family unit but not part of married couple	15.1	16.0
Mean family-unit size	3.71	3.51

NOTE: The sample includes all persons aged eighteen to sixty-four; however, children and the elderly are included when the family size of each member of the sample is calculated.

2.9 people in 2007. This is due to two changes. First, there has been a shift to smaller types of family units, with more individuals in single-person family units (where the family unit size is one by definition) or single-headed family units. Second, family size within both married-couple and single-headed family units has fallen. This is largely because of a decline in the number of children in these family units. Holding income constant, declines in family size within married-couple or single-headed family units will increase the economic well-being of persons in these family types, since this means that family income will be shared among fewer people. Shifts across family types that move people into smaller (and typically poorer) families with fewer adult earners have uncertain effects on overall economic well-being. The effect of changes in family size on the income distribution among nonelderly persons is explored further in the next chapter.

Figures 5-A through 5-D provide a quick look at the availability of the three income sources (earnings, government income, and other unearned income) for persons in each decile in the distribution of total income. Figure 5-A shows these income components among all persons, and figures 5-B through 5-D show these income components among persons in each of the three family types. Each figure shows the mean percentage of income that comes from earnings, government income, and other unearned income at each decile in the *overall* income distribution. That is, I line all persons up by their total income level and divide them into ten equal-sized groups. I then take the income shares for each income component for each family, and calculate the mean within each decile.[4] The black lines show the shares for 1979, and the gray lines show the shares for 2007. The thick solid lines represent earnings, the dashed lines represent government income, and the thin solid lines represent other unearned income.

Figure 5-A shows income components by income decile for all persons. Earnings constitute about half of all income at the bottom decile of the income distribution but rise to over 80 percent of all income by the third decile. Government income is quite high at the bottom of the distribution and very low at the top, as expected. The share of income from government has shrunk noticeably among those at the bottom of the distribution between 1979 and 2007. Other unearned income is relatively constant throughout the distribution—at about 10 percent of all income—although the composition of other unearned income varies over the distribution, with higher-income persons more likely to have income from investments.

As noted in chapter 1, the changes in government income shown here are based on cash income from the government and therefore do not represent all government assistance. Excluded are in-kind benefits from such programs as the Supplemental Nutrition Assistance Program (previously known as Food Stamps) and public housing assistance. Also excluded is the value of any publicly provided health care through the Medicaid program. In addition, because this information is based on total reported cash income, it ignores taxes. For instance, the Earned Income Tax Credit (EITC) increases the cash available to lower-income working families through refundable tax credits. Hence, the government income sources shown in figure 5 (and discussed throughout this paper) reflect the direct cash payments to individuals from government means-tested programs, primarily through the Temporary Assistance to Needy Families program, the Supplemental Security Income program, and Social Security (disability, survivors, or retirement). Changes in

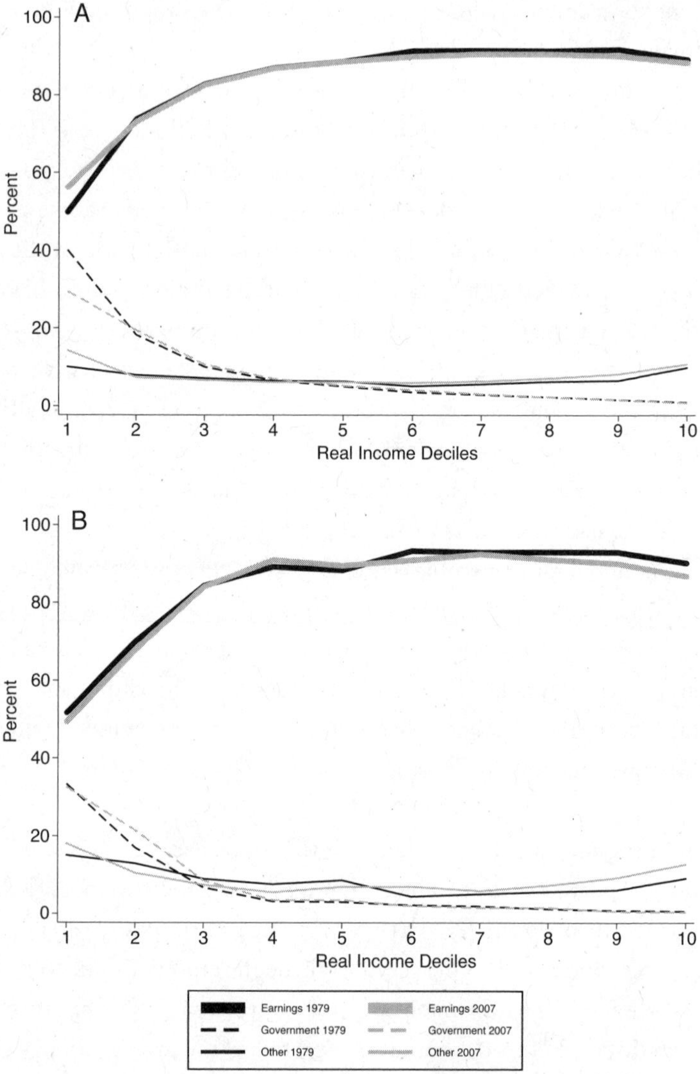

Figure 5. Percent of family income from each source by income decile—all persons and by family type: A. All people; B. Single individuals; C. Persons in single-headed family units; D. Persons in married-couple family units. Each graph includes all persons aged eighteen to sixty-four.

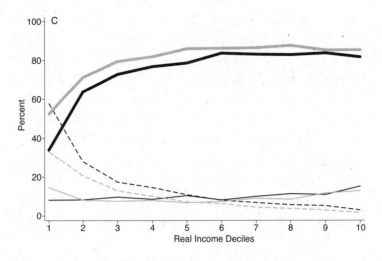

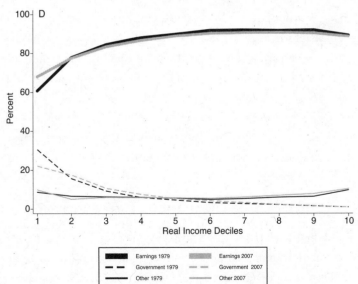

▬ Earnings 1979	▬ Earnings 2007
- - Government 1979	- - Government 2007
— Other 1979	— Other 2007

government income reflect changes in direct cash payments, not changes in other forms of government assistance.

Figures 5-B through 5-D also show income shares by source of income for persons in each of the three family types. Individuals in single-person and married-couple family units have patterns of income from these income sources very similar to each other and to the pattern among all persons in figure 5-A. Persons in single-headed family units have a lower share of their income from earnings. Among persons in the lower deciles of income in single-headed family units, government cash assistance constitutes a significant share of their income. In 1979, government income was a higher share of total income than earnings in the bottom decile; in 2007, earnings were more important. This reflects the changes in support for low-income families that occurred with welfare reform as cash assistance was restricted and single mothers were encouraged to enter the labor market. Single-mother families increased their work and earnings significantly, while their access to monthly cash payments dropped sharply.

In the four following sections, I discuss the distribution of total income and its components among all persons and then among persons in each of the three family types.

CHANGES IN TOTAL INCOME INEQUALITY

I look first at changes in the distribution of total income and its components among all persons. In comparison to the previous analysis of wages and earnings, which was based only upon those working, this analysis is based upon all nonelderly adults, working or not. Each adult's per person income, adjusted for family size, provides one point on the distribution of income among all persons.[5]

The top part (part A) of table 5 provides information on various measures of income inequality among all persons. The first two columns show inequality measures in 1979 and 2007 for total annual income; columns 3 and 4 show inequality measures in these two years for annual earnings; columns 5 and 6 show inequality measures for cash government income; and the final two columns show these measures for other unearned income. Figures 6-A through 6-D show the distribution of total income and its three components in both years.[6]

The median person in my sample has almost $36,900 in per person income (adjusted for family unit size) in 2007. This has increased by more than $7,000 since 1979. Total annual income inequality among all persons clearly rises over this time period. There is an increase in the Gini coefficient, in the CV, and in the 90/50 and 50/10 ratios. With such a strong upward shift in the median income level, this widening dispersion is occurring around an upward-shifting distribution. It is clear from figure 6-A that the whole distribution has become much flatter by 2007. There are more people in the lowest income bin in 2007, fewer people in the middle bins, and substantially more at higher income levels. There is a particularly large increase in the share of people whose per person (family size adjusted) total income exceeds $150,000.[7]

Earnings inequality is increasing even more rapidly. Note that the data on earnings in table 5 are different from those in table 2. Table 2 looked only at workers, whereas table 5 includes all persons, a number of whom are not working. Table 5 allocates earnings to individuals based on total earnings in the family unit. Even a nonworking adult will be allocated some earnings if there are other working adults in the family. This is because of the assumption that all related adults share income, making it

TABLE 5

Measures of Inequality for Total Annual Income[1] and Its Components

	Total Annual Income		Annual Earnings		Government Income		Other Income	
	1979	2007	1979	2007	1979	2007	1979	2007
	(1)	(2)	(3)	(4)	(5)	(6)	(7)	(8)
PART A. ALL PERSONS								
Median	$29,753	$36,897	$26,835	$32,909	$0	$0	$177	$57
Gini coefficient	0.35	0.43	0.39	0.47	0.84	0.88	0.84	0.86
Coefficient of variation	0.70	0.95	0.74	1.02	2.29	2.61	3.38	2.86
90/10 ratio	5.98	8.91	14.90	33.75	n/a^2	n/a^2	n/a^2	n/a^2
90/50 ratio	2.02	2.41	2.08	2.46	n/a^2	n/a^2	37.27	177.13
50/10 ratio	2.97	3.69	7.16	13.71	n/a^2	n/a^2	n/a^2	n/a^2
PART B. SINGLE INDIVIDUALS								
Median	$24,210	$28,000	$21,502	$25,000	$0	$0	$50	$0
Gini coefficient	0.41	0.47	0.47	0.52	0.88	0.91	0.88	0.90
Coefficient of variation	0.84	1.11	0.92	1.21	2.70	3.13	3.52	3.42
90/10 ratio	8.99	14.60	n/a^2	n/a^2	n/a^2	n/a^2	n/a^2	n/a^2
90/50 ratio	2.23	2.61	2.33	2.70	n/a^2	n/a^2	118	n/a^2
50/10 ratio	4.03	5.60	n/a^2	n/a^2	n/a^2	n/a^2	n/a^2	n/a^2

Median	$18,679	$23,336	$13,789	$18,984	$1,533	$0	$88	$1
Gini coefficient	0.41	0.44	0.51	0.51	0.64	0.79	0.82	0.84
Coefficient of variation	0.83	1.02	1.01	1.17	1.27	1.86	3.10	2.65
90/10 ratio	8.52	10.54	n/a[2]	n/a[2]	n/a[2]	n/a[2]	n/a[2]	n/a[2]
90/50 ratio	2.33	2.57	2.77	2.79	5.38	n/a[2]	71.84	6530.50
50/10 ratio	3.65	4.10	n/a[2]	n/a[2]	n/a[2]	n/a[2]	n/a[2]	n/a[2]

Median	$32,276	$44,159	$29,631	$40,000	$0	$0	$225	$150
Gini coefficient	0.32	0.39	0.35	0.42	0.86	0.89	0.84	0.84
Coefficient of variation	0.65	0.85	0.66	0.91	2.56	2.75	3.38	2.70
90/10 ratio	4.70	6.52	6.64	8.99	n/a[2]	n/a[2]	n/a[2]	n/a[2]
90/50 ratio	1.95	2.26	1.97	2.25	n/a[2]	n/a[2]	30.06	77.36
50/10 ratio	2.42	2.89	3.37	4.00	n/a[2]	n/a[2]	n/a[2]	n/a[2]

NOTE: The sample includes all persons aged eighteen to sixty-four.

1. Annual income for each person is per person income based on family-unit income adjusted for family size.

2. The symbol n/a (not applicable) indicates that the denominator of the ratio is zero at this point in the distribution.

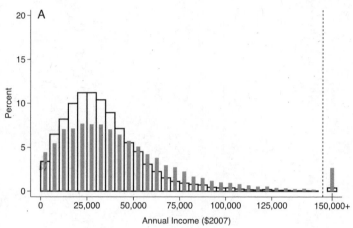

Each bin is a $5,000 interval except the last, which includes all people with at least $150,000 in income.

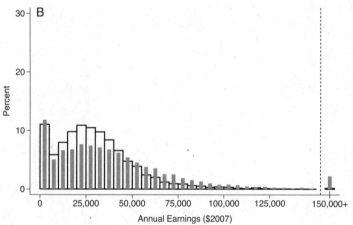

Each bin is a $5,000 interval except the last, which includes all people making at least $150,000.

☐ 1979   ▨ 2007

Figure 6. Distribution of annual income and its components, all people: A. Distribution of total income in 1979 and in 2007; B. Distribution of earnings in 1979 and in 2007; C. Distribution of government income in 1979 and in 2007; D. Distribution of other income in 1979 and in 2007. Each graph includes all people aged eighteen to sixty-four; annual income for each person is per person family-unit income adjusted for family size.

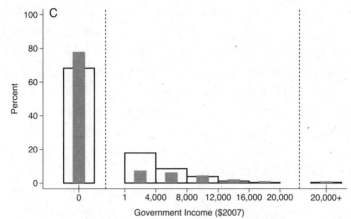

Government Income ($2007)

Each bin is a $4,000 interval except the first, which includes all people receiving no money, and the last, which includes all people receiving more than $20,000.

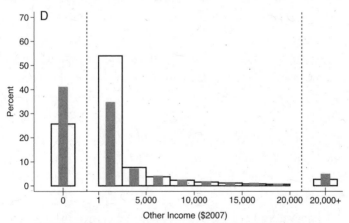

Other Income ($2007)

Each bin is a $2,500 interval except the first, which includes all people receiving no money, and the last, which includes all people receiving more than $20,000.

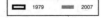

appropriate to allocate total earnings among the adults. Hence, the economic status of a nonworking wife is affected by the earnings level of her husband. As I discussed earlier, there have been significant increases in labor-force involvement among women, which will increase total earnings in family units and thereby increase the earnings that are allocated to each person.

Per person income from earnings increased by over $6,000 between 1979 and 2007, to almost $33,000. Figure 6-B shows the change in the distribution of earnings among persons between these two years. The widening inequality in earnings is clearly visible, with a slight increase in the share of persons with very low access to earnings but an upward shift in the share of persons at higher earnings levels. There is a substantial upward shift in per person earnings levels, even as the distribution becomes more spread out.

For persons in the middle of the income distribution, median income from government sources is zero in both years. Government income shows widening inequality as measured by the Gini coefficient and the CV. Because more than 50 percent of all persons live in families that report no government income, I cannot calculate any income ratios. The share receiving no cash government income has increased over time. This is clear from figure 6-C.

Changes in the distribution of other unearned income show mixed patterns over the past three decades. The Gini coefficient goes up slightly, but the CV goes down. More than 10 percent of all family units receive no other unearned income, so I cannot calculate 90/10 or 50/10 ratios. But I can calculate 90/50 ratios. These show a very large increase in the disparity between income at the ninetieth percentile and the median. How can this occur without rapid increases in overall inequality? The

90/50 ratio is very sensitive to changes in the median when the median is a small number. In this case, the median level of other unearned income falls from $177 to $57—a change that results in a large increase in the 90/50 ratio. One way of saying this is that the increase in the number of people with zero other unearned income swamps the increase in high levels of other unearned income among those who receive this income. Figure 6-D shows these patterns.

It is notable that the share of persons receiving other unearned income has declined markedly between 1979 and 2007. This decline in the receipt of other unearned income is almost entirely concentrated among those reporting interest income. In 1979, 67 percent of all persons reported some interest income (typically, very small amounts); by 2007, only 48 percent report interest income. Because interest income was the only source of other unearned income for many families in 1979, this decline in reported interest income results in fewer people reporting other unearned income. No other category of other unearned income has declined (and most categories have increased slightly). The result is far more persons with zero levels of other unearned income, but much higher levels of other unearned income among the 59 percent of persons who report receiving this type of income in 2007.

Overall, most individuals in 2007 who compared the level of their economic well-being to the well-being of persons at an equivalent point in the 1979 income distribution would be likely to conclude that they were better off based on total income levels. The overall distribution of income shifted up over these years, with more people in the upper-income categories. There is, however, an increase in the number of people at the very bottom of the distribution of total income and earnings, suggesting that the group of very low income persons has risen even as the share of higher-income persons has risen as well.

If individuals in the bottom half of the distribution in 2007 made *relative* comparisons between themselves and those who were better off, however, they might have felt worse off in 2007 than they were in 1979. The median pulled ahead of the bottom of the distribution, and the higher percentiles pulled away from the median. Those in the middle of the distribution became relatively worse off, even if they were absolutely better off.

CHANGES IN INEQUALITY
AMONG SINGLE INDIVIDUALS

Changes in aggregate income inequality and its components for persons living as single individuals are shown in part B of table 5, as well as in figures 7-A through 7-D. Changes in the distribution of income for individuals in single-person family units look broadly similar to changes in the distribution of income for all persons.

Overall, income inequality is rising among individuals in single-person family units, around a rising median. Median per person income rose from $24,200 to $28,000 between 1979 and 2007. Figure 7-A shows the spreading out of the distribution of total income for these single individuals between 1979 and 2007. Although there are fewer single individuals in most low-income categories, there was a substantially higher share of single individuals in the lowest category (those with incomes below $5,000.)

Earnings are by far the most important income component for single individuals, and their median level of earnings rose from $21,500 to $25,000. Earnings have become more unequal, driving overall income inequality. More than 17 percent of single individuals have no earnings, so I cannot calculate income ratios using the tenth percentile of the distribution. The graph in figure 7-B shows rising inequality in earnings, with an increase in the share of nonworkers as well as an increase in those with higher earnings.

Relatively few single individuals have government income (less than 25 percent in either year). Few safety-net programs are available to nonelderly, nondisabled individuals without children, who compose the majority of this category. And the share of all single individuals who report no other unearned income but live entirely on earnings or government income rises to over 50 percent by 2007. The large number of persons without government income or other income makes it harder to interpret changes in the Gini coefficient and the CV for these two income components. In general, in 2007 there are more single individuals receiving no government income (figure 7-C) or other unearned income (figure 7-D), but those who *do* receive income from these sources receive higher amounts.

CHANGES IN INEQUALITY AMONG PERSONS IN SINGLE-HEADED FAMILY UNITS

There has been growing interest in the economic well-being of single female-headed families, since more and more children and adults are residing in these families. Furthermore, these families are disproportionately likely to receive some sort of public assistance. The changes in the 1990s in programs for lower-income families greatly increased work and decreased cash public-assistance receipt among these single-mother families. Although single-headed family units are composed of many types of families—some with and some without children, and some with male rather than female heads—female-headed families with children

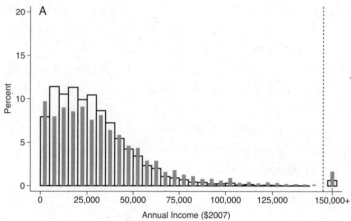

Each bin is a $5,000 interval except the last, which includes all people with at least $150,000 in income.

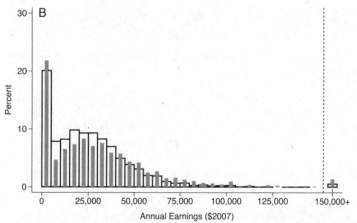

Each bin is a $5,000 interval except the last, which includes all people making at least $150,000.

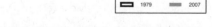

Figure 7. Distribution of annual income and its components, single individuals: A. Distribution of total income in 1979 and in 2007; B. Distribution of earnings in 1979 and in 2007; C. Distribution of government income in 1979 and in 2007; D. Distribution of other income in 1979 and in 2007. Each graph includes all single individuals aged eighteen to sixty-four; annual income for each person is per person family-unit income adjusted for family size.

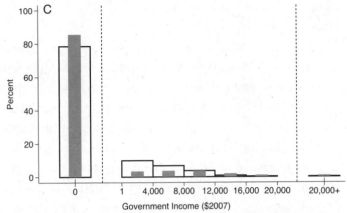

Government Income ($2007)

Each bin is a $4,000 interval except the first, which includes all people receiving no money, and the last, which includes all people receiving more than $20,000.

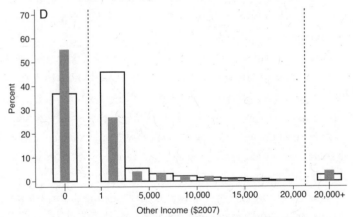

Other Income ($2007)

Each bin is a $2,500 interval except the first, which includes all people receiving no money, and the last, which includes all people receiving more than $20,000.

under age eighteen constitute well over half of the family units in this category.[8]

Part C of table 5 shows changes in income equality among persons in single-headed family units, and figures 8-A through 8-D provide a graphical depiction of the distribution of total income and its components in the two key years. As with other groups, income inequality increased among persons in single-headed family units, with the whole distribution becoming flatter. The increase in inequality was smaller among this group than any other, however. As figure 8-A indicates, there was a decline in the share of persons in very low income single-headed family units, and an increase in those in the higher-income bins. This is the only group with a significant decline in the share of persons in the bottom income category, with less than $5,000 in per person income.

Persons in these families had low incomes compared with those in other family types. Although their median income grew by almost $5,000 over this time period, it was only $23,300 in 2007. This is consistent with other evidence that shows growing income among single-mother families following welfare reform, as their increased earnings more than replaced their decreased cash public-assistance benefits (Blank, 2006).[9]

This is the one group for whom earnings inequality shifted very little. The share of single-headed family units with working adults rose (the share without earnings fell from 15 percent to 12 percent), consistent with other evidence showing that work behavior increased following welfare reform among lower-skilled women who head families with children.

Inequality in government cash income rose for persons in single-headed family units, primarily driven by an increase in the share of adults in single-headed family units that received no government income. This share rose from 42 percent in 1979 to 65 percent in 2007, again consistent with the effects of welfare reform that resulted in many women leaving the welfare rolls. As government income fell, both earnings and other unearned income became a higher share of total income among these family units.

CHANGES IN INEQUALITY AMONG PERSONS IN MARRIED-COUPLE FAMILY UNITS

Married-couple families are often considered separately from other family units because of the unique aspect that selection into marriage plays in their economic prospects. Not only do we believe that married-couple families share income, but we also believe that they make joint labor-supply decisions. As a result, many papers that investigate shifts in income distribution focus on changes in the behavior of wives and husbands in married-couple families.[10] This issue is particularly important as the female labor supply increases and the male labor supply declines. The extent to which couples have changed their joint labor-supply patterns is quite important in understanding inequality in income among married couples.

In particular, as others have noted, married women are working more and earning more over this period, and these changes are more concentrated among the wives of higher-earning men. Figures 9-A through 9-C demonstrate the nature of these changes.[11] Figure 9-A plots the probability that a wife works, based on the earnings decile of her husband, in each of the two years. Wives of high-earning husbands were less likely to work than wives of middle- or low-earning husbands in 1979. Their labor-force participation increases much faster over the next

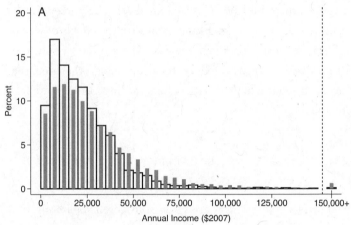

Each bin is a $5,000 interval except the last, which includes all people with at least $150,000 in income.

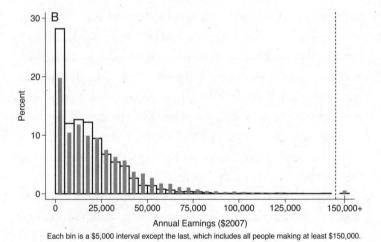

Each bin is a $5,000 interval except the last, which includes all people making at least $150,000.

1979   2007

Figure 8. Distribution of annual income and its components, persons in single-headed family units: A. Distribution of total income in 1979 and in 2007; B. Distribution of earnings in 1979 and in 2007; C. Distribution of government income in 1979 and in 2007; D. Distribution of other income in 1979 and in 2007. Each graph includes all members of single-headed families aged eighteen to sixty-four; annual income for each person is per person family-unit income adjusted for family size.

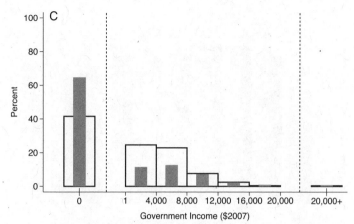

Each bin is a $4,000 interval except the first, which includes all people receiving no money, and the last, which includes all people receiving more than $20,000.

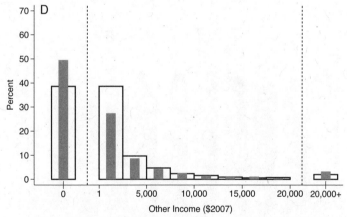

Each bin is a $2,500 interval except the first, which includes all people receiving no money, and the last, which includes all people receiving more than $20,000.

1979   2007

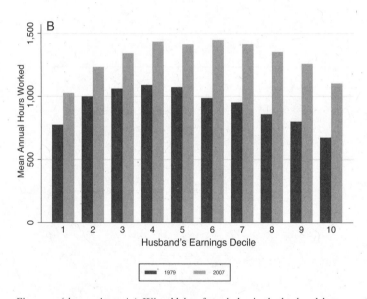

Figure 9. *(above and opposite)* Wives' labor force behavior by husbands' earnings decile: A. Wives' labor-force participation; B. Wives' mean hours worked; C. Wives' mean earnings. Each graph includes all husbands and wives who head married-couple family units and where the husband is aged eighteen to sixty-four.

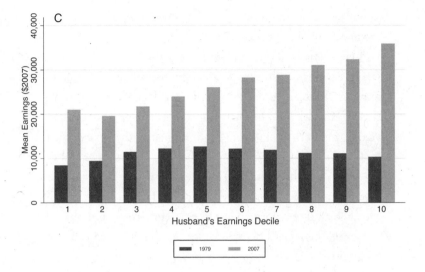

several decades, however, so that labor-force participation in 2007 is relatively similar among the wives of middle- and high-earning husbands. By 2007, the wives of high-earning husbands are far more likely to work than the wives of low-earning husbands—something that was not true in 1979.

Figure 9-B plots wives' average hours of work against the earnings decile of their husbands and shows that the wives of higher-earning men also increased their working hours more over these decades; this suggests that the increase in labor-force participation among wives of high-earning husbands is not driven by an increase in part-time work. Finally, figure 9-C plots wives' annual earnings by the earnings decile of their husbands. This shows large changes in earnings among all wives, but relatively larger increases among the wives of higher-earning men.

The result is that changing work behavior among wives is raising the income of persons in families with higher-earning husbands more than it is raising income among those persons in households with lower-earning husbands. This has increased income inequality over time.[12]

The changes shown in figure 9, with larger increases in wives' earnings within higher-income households, are due to a number of forces. In part, this reflects changes in the distribution of education within marriage. Over the past twenty-eight years, women have become more educated than men, with a higher share of women than men holding high school and college degrees. More-educated men tend to marry more-educated women (and vice versa, depending on who you think is doing the choosing). As more educated women become available, the number of marriages in which both mates hold college degrees (or graduate degrees) is growing. In 1979, only 22 percent of married men held a college or graduate degree. Among these, 47 percent were married to women who held a college or graduate degree. By 2007, 35 percent of married men had at least a college education, and 68 percent of them had college-educated wives.[13]

The fact that more college-educated men are married to college-educated women will pull up the relative earnings among these households in two ways. First, labor-force participation among college-educated women has expanded more rapidly than among other groups over the past three decades, reflecting the large increase in access to high-paying jobs among well-educated women as social norms have changed and discrimination against women in the labor force has declined. Second, as the economic returns to education grow, earnings among highly educated women are growing more rapidly than among other women (see figure 4-C). The combination of more work and higher wages among college-educated women means that the families in which these women reside have seen substantial income increases.

Wives' earnings are also maintaining family income among

those married to low-earning husbands. As earnings among less-skilled men have actually fallen (see figure 4-B), women's earnings have replaced rather than reinforced men's earnings in these married-couple families. Furthermore, marriage rates among less-skilled men and women have declined much more than among more-skilled men and women, in part due to less-skilled men's declining wages. Hence, this group is simply less represented among married couples. Whereas the share of persons who lived in married-couple family units was very similar among the more and less educated in 1979, by 2007 only 58 percent of working-age people with a high school degree or less were in married-couple family units, compared with 65 percent of more-educated persons. As a result, by 2007 less-skilled men and women were more likely to live as single individuals or in single-headed family units, which reduced the overall income available to them.

Part D of table 5, and figures 10-A to 10-D, show how the distribution of income has changed among persons in married-couple family units. These persons are generally better off than those in other family types, and their economic advantage rose over this time period. Persons in these families experienced a very large increase in their median per person income, of almost $12,000 over these twenty-eight years—from $32,300 to $44,200. This reflects the rise in earnings available to persons in these families through increased female labor supply and the "dropping out" of marriage among lower-earning persons. This change shifts the entire distribution of income well to the right over time. Figure 10-B shows large declines in the share of persons in married-couple families in lower earnings categories.

At the same time, table 5 indicates that all measures of inequality in total income are increasing among persons in married-couple family units. Both the 90/50 and the 50/10 ratios are rising

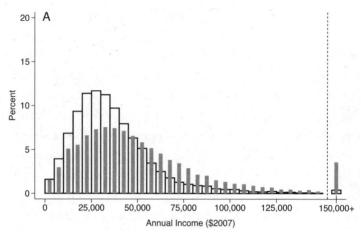

Each bin is a $5,000 interval except the last, which includes all people with at least $150,000 in income.

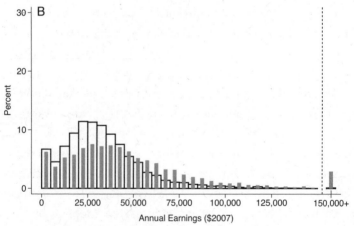

Each bin is a $5,000 interval except the last, which includes all people making at least $150,000.

Figure 10. Distribution of annual income and its components, persons in married-couple family units: A. Distribution of total income in 1979 and in 2007; B. Distribution of earnings in 1979 and in 2007; C. Distribution of government income in 1979 and in 2007; D. Distribution of other income in 1979 and in 2007. Each graph includes all members of married-couple-headed families aged eighteen to sixty-four. Annual income for each person is per person family-unit income adjusted for family size.

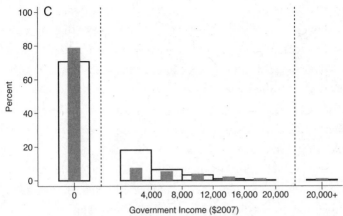

Each bin is a $4,000 interval except the first, which includes all people receiving no money, and the last, which includes all people receiving more than $20,000.

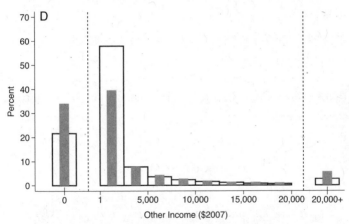

Each bin is a $2,500 interval except the first, which includes all people receiving no money, and the last, which includes all people receiving more than $20,000.

for persons in these families. This is a rise in inequality around a rapidly growing median, however, which suggests that most persons in these types of families have become better off over time.

Overall, earnings among adults in married-couple families show very similar patterns as overall income. Not surprisingly, earnings are rising rapidly among persons in married-couple families, and earnings inequality is also rising. Despite this, income inequality and earnings inequality are lower among persons in married-couple families than they are among single individuals or persons in single-headed families. Although there is a long upper tail on earnings within married-couple families, there are fewer married-couple families with extremely low earnings levels.

A high share of persons in married-couple families report themselves as not receiving government income. The rates are over 70 percent in both years. A growing share (about 35 percent) also report receiving no other unearned income in 2007, although other unearned income increased significantly among those who report it. Changes in inequality in these two income sources are relatively small.

COMPARISONS BY RACE

The patterns of change in the distribution and level of per person total income among black and white persons are generally similar. Both groups show increasing income inequality with rising overall income levels. The actual amounts of income in the black population are much lower, but their income grows faster over this time period. (I cannot look at equivalent numbers for the Hispanic population because their sample is too small in 1979 for reliable comparisons.)

Median per person income among all black individuals rose from $18,900 in 1979 to $26,400 in 2007. Among white individuals, median per person income rose from $31,000 in 1979 to $38,700 in 2007. The income gap between blacks and whites fell over this time period, and this reduced inequality on average. The per person income distribution among blacks is lower in both years, however, and more clustered in the lower income categories. The increase in persons in the lowest income categories (seen in figure 6) occurred entirely within the white population, however. The share of persons in the lower income categories among blacks between 1979 and 2007 has fallen in every category. Despite these differences, both groups have shown relatively similar increases in overall income inequality.

Changes in the distribution of earnings and of government income are quite similar in the white and black populations, although black persons have lower earnings and somewhat more government income. The share of blacks with zero other unearned income is much higher than in the white population, reflecting lower black wealth levels and more limited sources of other unearned income.

These aggregate patterns are mirrored among different family types. Among persons in married-couple families, single individuals, and persons in single-parent families, the distribution of income among blacks is significantly lower than among whites, although they show similar changes in income inequality.

In short, the overall story of how the income distribution is changing is very similar, even when looking separately at the income distribution among black and white persons. This is true even though black income levels are noticeably lower across all groups.

CONCLUSIONS

In this chapter, which focuses on trends in total income, it is clear that overall income levels have risen even while overall income inequality has increased. This trend is apparent among persons in married-couple families and those who live as single individuals. The only exception occurs among persons in single-parent families, who have shown income increases but only small increases in inequality.

This chapter, which looks at total annual income, indicates that earnings changes were the primary cause of rising income levels and widening income equality. The previous chapter showed that rising earnings were predominantly driven by increases in work effort among women. These increases in women's earnings were key to higher incomes among both single-headed family units and married-couple family units.

Except for the increase in the share of persons in the very lowest income category, there was a decline in the share of the population in the lower income categories and an overall upward shift of the entire income distribution. This means that most persons are better off in 2007 than were persons who were at a similar point in the income distribution in 1979. But, because of the rapid growth in top incomes, which led to increasing dispersion in the income distribution, most people in 2007 were further below the top income earners than were equivalent people in 1979.

Understanding the implications of these shifts requires knowing more about exactly why they occurred. The next chapter turns to this question, investigating the combination of demographic and economic factors that resulted in these changes.

FOUR

Understanding These Changes

In this chapter, I look at the reasons why total-income inequality is changing and why the overall distribution of total income is shifting upward. Some of these changes are due to shifts in family composition and size; some are due to changes in the level and distribution of income components within family types. I finish this chapter by talking about what these changes in total income and its distribution might signal about overall well-being among individuals.

There are three factors underlying the shifts in total income that I observed in the last chapter. First, within each family type, family size is shifting. Since family size is declining (except among single individuals, who are always one person per family), if nothing else changes this will raise per person income within single-headed family units and married-couple family units. Second, the share of the population living in each family type is changing. As we saw in the previous chapter, there are fewer people in married-couple families and more people in single-person and single-headed family units. This will further reduce average family size, since these types of families have fewer people in them. But this shift will work to reduce per person income, since these growing family types typically have lower incomes.

Finally, holding family size and type constant, the distributions of income and its components are shifting within each type of family. For instance, because of the market changes discussed in chapter 2, earnings inequality is rising. Within married-couple family units, overall earnings levels are rising as both spouses are more likely to work. Within single-headed family units, earnings have increased while government income has decreased.

In the next three sections I will sequentially look at the importance of each of these factors—family size, family type, and earnings—in explaining changes in the distribution of total income. I start by looking at the effects of changes in family size and family type.

HOW IMPORTANT ARE CHANGES IN FAMILY SIZE AND TYPE FOR THE LEVEL AND DISTRIBUTION OF TOTAL INCOME?

Family size has steadily declined among single-headed and married-couple family units, in part because of falling fertility and in part because fewer adult children or elderly parents live in the family household. Within each family type, the effect of changes in family size between 1979 and 2007 can be simulated to see what family incomes would look like if family size had not changed. Details of this simulation are described in appendix 3.

Table 6 shows how the Gini coefficient and median incomes for the total-income distribution would have changed within each family type if family size had been constant after 1979. The first column shows the 1979 value for the specific measure, the second column shows the actual change between 1979 and 2007, and the third column shows the simulated change, holding family size constant. Part A shows the results for persons in single-headed family units. The first row indicates that mean family size among people in these family units was 3.26 people in 1979, and this figure fell by 4.4 percent (to 3.12 people) by 2007. In contrast, the simulation is designed so that there is no change in family size.[1]

The second row indicates that median income grew by 25 percent after 1979 among persons in single-headed family units. It would have grown by 23 percent if family size had not fallen, suggesting that the decline in family size among single-headed families accounts for a modest 7 percent of the overall growth in median income among persons in these families.

The third row indicates that the Gini coefficient grew by a little over 8 percent over this time period among single-headed family units, and is little changed by holding family size constant. The fact that the Gini is largely unaffected when family size is held constant suggests that the declines in family size have had little effect on inequality.

Part B makes equivalent calculations for persons in married-couple families. These persons were in families with an average of 3.7 people in 1979, which declined to 3.5 people (down 5.2 percent) by 2007. Median income among persons in married-couple families rose by 37 percent from 1979 to 2007, but would have risen by only 33 percent if family size hadn't changed. Hence, changes in family size explain about 10 percent of the rise in median income within these families. As with persons in single-headed families, the changes in family size did not have

TABLE 6

Simulation Showing the Effect of Holding the Distribution of
Family Size Constant within Each Family Type at Its 1979 Value

| | 1979 Value | Percent Change, 1979–2007 | |
| | | *Actual* | *Simulated* |
	(1)	(2)	(3)
PART A. SINGLE-HEADED FAMILY UNITS			
Mean family size	3.26	−4.4	0.0
Median annual income	$18,679	24.9	23.2
Gini coefficient	0.41	8.3	8.5
PART B. MARRIED-COUPLE FAMILY UNITS			
Mean family size	3.71	−5.2	0.0
Median annual income	$32,276	36.8	33.2
Gini coefficient	0.32	20.7	21.0
PART C. SINGLE INDIVIDUALS			
Mean family size	1.00	0.0	—
Median annual income	$24,210	15.7	—
Gini coefficient	0.41	15.9	—

NOTE: The sample includes only those family units headed by a person aged
eighteen to sixty-four. Annual income for each person is per person income
based on family-unit income adjusted for family size. See appendix 3 for details.

any important effect on the Gini coefficient, which is largely
unchanged in the simulation.

Part C of table 6 shows the data for single individuals, as a
comparison. These individuals are all in one-person family
units in both years, so by definition they face no changes in family size, and there is no simulation to be done.

The results in table 6 indicate that reductions in family size
among persons in single-headed and married-couple family

types had an effect on median income levels. They explain one-tenth to one-fifteenth of the increase in median income within these groups. These family-size changes have little effect on income inequality, however, indicating that family-size declines were as large in higher-income families as in lower-income families.

So far I have looked at family-size changes only within family types. But family size is also affected by the decreased share of people living in (larger) married-couple families and the increased share of people living in (smaller) single-headed families or as single individuals. In my next simulation, I look at the impact on the total-income distribution of changes in the share of persons across these family types and discuss how this shift interacts with the change in family size within family type.

Appendix 3 gives details about how I simulate income in 2007 if there were no shift in the distribution of persons across family types after 1979. This simulation raises the share of married couples in 2007 to its 1979 level, and lowers the share of people living as single individuals or in single-headed family units to their 1979 levels.

As we saw in the last chapter, income inequality is lower among persons in married-couple family units than among persons in other family types, and median incomes are higher. Shifting family shares away from married-couple households since 1979 should have decreased overall income levels. The net effect on inequality is uncertain, however, since this would have decreased the share of the population in higher-income family units, which tends to reduce inequality. But it shifted the population into family types with a more unequal income distribution, which would tend to increase inequality. Furthermore, this shift by itself should have lowered family size, because it involves a shift from larger to small types of family units. In the simulation, I show first the effects of holding the share of persons within each family type constant at its 1979 levels, and then show the additional effects of also holding family size within family type constant at its 1979 levels (as I did in table 6).

Table 7 reports the results of these simulations, showing how total income and earnings would have changed if there had been no demographic shifts across family types or across family size. I show changes in mean family size, in median income and earnings, and in the Gini coefficients on total income and earnings. Column 1 shows the 1979 value of the specified measure, while column 2 shows its actual percent change between 1979 and 2007. Column 3 shows the simulated change if I hold constant the share of eighteen- to sixty-four-year-olds living in each family type. Column 4 shows the simulated change if I hold family-type shares constant and also hold family size within each family type constant at its 1979 level. This last column shows the total effect of these demographic changes, including both changes in population shares across family types and changes in family size within family types.

The first row in table 7 shows how family size shifts in these simulations. The mean person in 1979 lived in a family of 3.29 people. This figure declined by 11 percent by 2007. The majority of this decline in family size is due to the decline in the share of people living in married-couple family units. If I hold family-type shares constant, family size would have declined by only 5 percent. This 5 percent decline is due to changes in family size within family type. If I hold this constant, family size is unchanged (column 4). Hence, 56 percent of the decline in family size is due to shifts across family types, while the remaining 44 percent is due to shifts in family size within family types.

TABLE 7

Simulations Showing the Effect of Holding the Share
of Each Family Type in the Population and the Distribution
of Family Size within Each Family Type Constant at Their 1979 Values

	1979 Value	Percent Change, 1979–2007		
		Actual	*Holding Constant the Share of Each Family Type in the Population*	*Holding Constant Family-Type Shares and Family Size within Family Type*
	(1)	(2)	(3)	(4)
Mean family size	3.29	−11.3	−4.9	0.0
Median annual income	$29,753	24.0	32.3	29.3
Median annual earnings	$26,835	22.6	31.4	29.1
Gini coefficient— total income	0.35	22.2	18.8	18.9
Gini coefficient— total earnings	0.39	19.2	15.4	15.5

NOTE: The sample includes all persons aged eighteen to sixty-four. Annual income for each person is per person income based on family-unit income adjusted for family size. See appendix 3 for details.

Row 2 shows the changes in median income under these simulations, and row 3 shows the changes in median earnings. Median income rose by 24 percent between 1979 and 2007. If there had been no population shift to lower-income family types, it would have risen even faster—by 32 percent. Hence, the shift away from married-couple families slowed the overall growth in income. This is offset, however, by declining family size within family type, which has increased per person median income growth as married-couple and single-headed families became smaller. If family-size changes were held constant as well as family-type shares, median income would have grown by 29.3 percent.

The combined effect of the demographic shifts that occurred in both family size and family types lowered median income gains from 29 percent to 24 percent between 1979 and 2007, with the income-decreasing effects of a shift to lower-income family types having a larger effect than the income-increasing effects of reductions in family size within family types.

Changes in total earnings are quite similar to the changes in total income. The shift away from married-couple family units substantially reduced the growth in median total earnings (from a simulated 31 percent without this shift to an actual change of 23 percent). This was somewhat offset by the reductions in family size, however. If both family size and the distribution of family types are held constant, median earnings would have grown by 29 percent.

Rows 4 and 5 show the change in the Gini coefficient for total income and total earnings from these simulated demographic changes. The shift away from married-couple families had an inequality-increasing effect on the total-income distribution. If it had not occurred, the Gini coefficient would have risen by only 19 percent rather than 22 percent. The shift to smaller family sizes had little further effects on inequality, as we saw in table 6. The shifts in the Gini coefficient for total earnings are quite similar.

These demographic changes explain 15 percent of the rise in the Gini coefficient for total income between 1979 and 2007, and 19 percent of the rise in the Gini coefficient for total earnings. Hence, widening inequality in earnings and other income sources is only part of the reason why income inequality rose among all persons over these decades. Some of the increase was due to demographic shifts in family composition toward smaller families and away from married-couple families.

Although much of the discussion of widening inequality has focused on economic changes that have affected earnings opportunities, this section of the chapter indicates that demographic factors also played a role in increasing inequality. The social changes that led to increased divorce, later marriage, greater child-bearing outside marriage, and smaller families would have produced some widening in income inequality even if no economic changes had occurred.

By themselves, these changes would have resulted in overall declines in income and earnings, due to the move to lower-income family units and away from married couples. The fact that income and earnings rose suggests that these demographic effects on income levels were more than offset by other economic changes.

It is worth emphasizing the limitations of these simulations. They focus on demographic changes, assuming that changes in earnings, government income, and other unearned income within each family type all occur independently of demographic shifts. In other words, they assume that the level and distribution of income among (for example) married couples was not affected by marriage's decline. In reality, marriage became more selective over these twenty-eight years, with higher marriage rates among more-educated persons. Ideally, I would simulate a world with higher marriage rates among the (mostly less educated) people who would have married in 1979 but did not get married in 2007. By increasing the share of married couples in 2007, I increase the population share of the group that is married in 2007 instead of returning to the same marital patterns as in 1979. This results in an increase in the skill level of the population.

HOW IMPORTANT ARE CHANGES IN THE DISTRIBUTION OF EARNINGS AND OTHER INCOME SOURCES FOR THE LEVEL AND DISTRIBUTION OF TOTAL INCOME?

The previous section simulated the effect of demographic shifts on the distribution of total income and earnings. This section focuses on the effect of shifts in earnings and other income sources but disregards changes in family composition and size. In the next section, I put both of these changes together and compare their relative sizes.

In this simulation I allow the composition and size of family types to evolve between 1979 and 2007, but I hold constant the distribution of various income components at their 1979 levels within each family type. Essentially, I ask what the effect on total income would have been if the distribution of earnings, government income, and other unearned income within each family type had not shifted between 1979 and 2007 but the demographic shifts in family types and family size did take place. This necessarily assumes that the behavioral shifts in work behavior among women and men did not occur. The details of how this simulation is done are given in appendix 3.

Table 8 presents the results of this simulation. Columns 1 through 3 look at the results for all individuals. Columns 4 through 6 show the effects of the simulation for single individuals, columns 7 through 9 show the effects on persons in single-headed family units, and columns 10 through 12 show the effects on persons in married-couple family units. The three columns under each sample show (in order) the 1979 value of each measure, its actual change from 1979 to 2007, and its simulated change when the distribution of income components is held constant.

Part A shows the results when only the distribution of earnings is held constant at its 1979 levels (but government income and other unearned income are allowed to change). Row 1 shows the effects on median income levels, and row 2 shows the effects on the Gini coefficient.

Shifts in the earnings distribution explain virtually all of the increase in median income that occurs between 1979 and 2007. Median income would have declined by 0.5 percent (rather than increasing by 24 percent) among all persons if the earnings distribution had not shifted upward, for all of the reasons discussed in the previous chapters. For single individuals, median income would have increased by only 2 percent (versus its actual increase of 16 percent) when the earnings distribution is unchanged from its 1979 levels. For persons in single-headed family units, median income would have declined by 3 percent rather than growing by 25 percent if the earnings distribution were unchanged. For persons in married-couple families, median income would have increased by only 6 percent rather than 37 percent. These results underscore the importance of shifts in the earnings distribution not just on income inequality, but on income levels. Increases in annual earnings (driven largely by increases in hours, as we saw earlier) are the primary reason why incomes have risen.

Rising inequality in the earnings distribution also explains most of the rise in the Gini coefficient between 1979 and 2007. The Gini for income among all persons would have increased by only 9 percent if the earnings distribution had not shifted, compared with its actual increase of 22 percent. Hence, changes in the earnings distribution explain 60 percent of the rising Gini coefficient over this time period.

This effect varies substantially across family types, however. Changes in the earnings distribution alone explain most of the rise

TABLE 8

Simulations Showing the Effect of Holding the Distribution
of Various Income Components Constant at Their 1979 Levels

	All Persons			Single Individuals		
	1979 Value	Percent Change 1979–2007		1979 Value	Percent Change 1979–2007	
		Actual	*Simulated*		*Actual*	*Simulated*
	(1)	(2)	(3)	(4)	(5)	(6)
PART A. SIMULATION 1: HOLDING THE DISTRIBUTION OF ANNUAL EARNINGS AT ITS 1979 PATTERN[1]						
Median income	$29,753	24.0	-0.5	$24,210	15.7	2.3
Gini coefficient	0.35	22.2	9.0	0.41	15.9	2.6
PART B. SIMULATION 2: HOLDING THE DISTRIBUTION OF TOTAL INCOME AT ITS 1979 PATTERN[1]						
Median income	$29,753	24.0	-2.9	$24,210	15.7	-0.2
Gini coefficient	0.35	22.2	5.7	0.41	15.9	0.0

NOTE: The sample includes all persons aged eighteen to sixty-four.

1. Held constant is the distribution of earnings or total income, unadjusted for family size. The simulated data are then adjusted for actual family size. See Appendix 3 for details.

in the Gini coefficient among single individuals and among persons in married-couple family units. It explains far less of the increase in the Gini coefficient among single-headed families, however. This is consistent with the results in chapter 3 that indicated less of an increase in earnings inequality among persons in single-headed family units than among persons in other family types.

	Persons in Single-headed Family Units			Persons in Married-Couple Family Units		
1979 Value	Percent Change 1979–2007		1979 Value	Percent Change 1979–2007	
	Actual	*Simulated*		*Actual*	*Simulated*
(7)	(8)	(9)	(10)	(11)	(12)
$18,679	24.9	-3.0	$32,276	36.8	5.7
0.41	8.3	6.5	0.32	20.7	5.1
$18,679	24.9	0.6	$32,276	36.8	2.0
0.41	8.3	-1.2	0.32	20.7	3.4

Holding just the earnings distribution constant is a somewhat unsatisfactory simulation. We know that changes in earnings are correlated with changes in other income sources. For instance, when government income (welfare payments) became less available to single mothers, their earnings rose sharply. As a result, it is probably more informative to look at the effect of changes in all sources of income together, thereby controlling for correlations in the receipt of different income components.

Part B of table 8 does this by simulating the effect of holding the distribution of all income sources constant between 1979 and 2007. While still allowing demographic changes to occur, this simulation looks at the effect on total income if income components and their distribution (within each family type and before adjusting for family size) had not shifted between these years.

The effect on median income of holding the distribution and level of all income sources unchanged from 1979 are quite striking. Median income would have fallen by 3 percent among all persons (rather than rising by 24 percent) if the level and distribution of earnings and other income sources had not risen. This is consistent with the results in table 7, which show that demographic changes alone would have reduced income levels. Changes in the distribution of income sources explain virtually all of the rise in median income among single individuals and persons in single-headed family units, and most of the rise among persons in married-couple family units.

Changes in the level and distribution of income sources explain much of the rise in the Gini coefficient as well. Among all persons, the Gini coefficient would have risen by only 6 percent rather than 22 percent if the underlying distribution of income sources hadn't changed, suggesting that 74 percent of the rise in overall inequality is due to shifts in the distribution of income components. These shifts also explain most of the rise in inequality among individuals within family types as well.

In general, the results in table 8 suggest that the majority—but not all—of the changes in inequality are due to shifts in the underlying distribution of income components, particularly earnings. All of the increases in median income levels are due to shifts in income components.

Just as demographic changes can affect income, so income changes can affect demographic choices. So this simulation separates income changes and demographic changes more neatly than we can do in reality. For instance, declines in government welfare income to single mothers (and the resulting increase in labor-force participation and earnings) could have affected both fertility and marriage decisions, although, as it turns out, these policy shifts appear to have had few such effects.[2] There is evidence to suggest that some economic changes, such as the decline in earnings among less-skilled men, have reduced marriage rates, although this does not appear to be a major factor in their long-term decline.[3] Not accounting for these interactions means that the simulation results in table 8 are only a partial approximation of the effect of changes in income inequality on the total-income distribution.

UNDERSTANDING THE COMPARATIVE EFFECTS OF CHANGES IN INCOME SOURCES AND CHANGES IN FAMILY COMPOSITION

The previous discussion looked separately at the effects of demographic shifts versus shifts in income components. In this section, I combine these effects in two final simulations. The first one starts with the results in table 8, estimating first the effect of changes in income components and then estimating the effects of demographic changes. The second simulation starts with the results in table 7, estimating first the effects of demographic changes and then estimating the effects of changes in income components. The factor that is introduced first, whether income or demographics, will capture some of the interaction between income and family size. This means that the results are slightly different depending upon which effect is controlled for first. The two simulations provide a range that allows us to bound the effects of each of these factors on median income and Gini coefficients. These simulations estimate each of these shifts as separable and independent changes. The residual in each of these simulations is due to the correlation between demographic shifts and income shifts, and shows how much of the change in income levels and inequality occurred because of simultaneous interactions between demographic and income changes that are not controlled for in these simulations.

Table 9 shows the results of these two simulations. The first column focuses on changes in the Gini coefficient between 1979 and 2007, and the second column focuses on changes in median income. Part A simulates the effect of holding the distribution and level of income components constant at their 1979 levels (but allowing family size and composition to change) and then simulates the additional effects of also holding family size and composition constant. Part B reflects the same simulations but switches the order, first simulating the effects of holding family size and composition constant at their 1979 levels and then simulating the effect of holding the level and distribution of income constant.

These simulations provide a range to bound the effects of each of these changes. The results in column 1 suggest that about three-quarters (73 to 74 percent) of the change in the Gini coefficient is due to changes in the distribution of earnings and other income components, whereas just under 15 percent is due to changes in family size and composition. In short, both family demographic shifts and income shifts were driving income

TABLE 9

Simulations Showing the Relative Importance of Changes in
Income Distribution versus Changes in Family Size and Composition

	Gini Coefficient	Median Income
	(1)	(2)
Percent change 1979–2007	22.2	24.0

PART A. SIMULATING INCOME CHANGES FIRST AND DEMOGRAPHIC CHANGES SECOND

Share of percent change 1979–2007 resulting from:		
Income distribution changes	74.4	112.2
Family size and composition changes	13.8	−10.1
Residual	11.8	−2.1

PART B. SIMULATING DEMOGRAPHIC CHANGES FIRST AND INCOME CHANGES SECOND

Share of percent change 1979–2007 resulting from:		
Income distribution changes	73.5	124.0
Family size and composition changes	14.8	−21.9
Residual	11.8	−2.1

NOTE: The sample includes all persons aged eighteen to sixty-four. See appendix 3 for details.

inequality upward. The 12 percent residual suggests that behavioral changes due to the correlation of demographic choices and income receipt also worked to increase inequality.

The results in column 2 suggest that increases in income and its components would have led to even greater increases in median income than are observed, but these were offset by income-reducing demographic changes (primarily shifts away from married-couple family units, as discussed earlier). The correlation between demographic and income changes somewhat offsets these increases in median income as well.

These simulations emphasize that there were two important changes occurring in the distribution of total income among all persons over the past three decades. One was a shift in the income available to persons because of changes in the level and distribution of income from the labor market, from unearned-income sources, and from government income. The second is a shift in family composition that resulted in changes in the mix of family types and in the size of families within single-headed and married-couple families. Although the first change had the bigger effect on the overall distribution of income, both of them were important.

The changes in income and its distribution, exclusive of changes in family composition, were the most important reason why income inequality was rising. Income from all sources, but particularly from earnings, became more unequally distributed between 1979 and 2007, with a wider distribution due to faster rises at the top and stagnation at the very bottom. But it is important to emphasize that rising inequality is only part the story of why the income distribution changed. At the same time that the distribution of income was becoming more dispersed, the distribution was shifting upward, with substantial increases in median income among all family types. The median person gained more than $7,000 in total per person income, which can be entirely explained by a rise in earnings within family units over these three decades.

This increase in the median puts the rising inequality in a somewhat different perspective. While the distribution of income did widen, with particular increases in the share of persons in high-income categories, the rising median means that the share of persons in lower-income categories shrank significantly over the past three decades. These gains in median income occurred to persons in all types of family units, although they were largest among persons in married-couple family units. Figure 6-A shows a strong upward shift in the distribution of total income, so that many fewer people were in the lower-income categories in 2007 than in 1979. Even in the face of widening inequality, the equivalently ranked person in 2007 had substantially more income than in 1979. Except for the very lowest category, this is true at the bottom of the distribution as well as at the top.

The primary reason for these increases in the median of the income distribution was rising earnings. This is closely related to increases in hours worked within households by adult women, as discussed in chapter 2.

The analysis throughout this section of the book provides some insight into why rising inequality has not been a major political issue in the United States. If people are comparing their well-being with the well-being of others like them twenty-eight years earlier (perhaps looking at their parents compared with themselves), they will find that an equivalent person in 2007 is better off. Rising inequality has occurred around increases in overall per person income. Of course, if people are comparing themselves with others at the same point in time, those above them in the income distribution have become relatively richer (as the upper tail has grown), and this might make them feel worse off. It is likely that people observe both their relative location in the income distribution and their absolute level of well-being over time. The fact that absolute and relative comparisons would lead to different conclusions about changing well-being suggests one reason why concern about inequality has been more muted in this country.

HOW ARE THESE NUMBERS AFFECTED BY CONSIDERING TAXES AND NONCASH COMPENSATION?

The calculations in this book are based on cash income before taxes. Both taxes and noncash benefits, including those received from one's employer (such as health insurance and pension benefits) and those received from the government through transfer programs (such as food subsidies and Medicaid), can have a significant effect on the income available to a family. There have been significant changes in taxes and in noncash benefits and transfers between 1979 and 2007. Ideally, one might want to look at a measure of disposable (after-tax) income that includes noncash compensation. Though it is beyond the scope of this book to estimate the effect of taxes, government benefits, and noncash compensation, this section briefly summarizes what we know about changes over time in taxes and other benefits.

The government system of taxes is explicitly designed to generate public funds that may be used to redistribute income and other benefits from one group to another. Federal income taxes are progressive; that is, they tax top income earners at a higher rate than bottom income earners. In contrast, Social Security and Medicaid taxes are set at a fixed rate for all taxpayers; Social Security taxes end above a certain dollar limit, so those taxes impose higher tax burdens on low-income families than on higher-income families. Most researchers who have looked at the aggregate effect of the federal tax system find that its net effect is progressive, with somewhat higher rates on higher-income families. This suggests that the net effect of federal taxes is to lower inequality.

Federal tax rates have fallen for all groups over the past several decades, particularly in the early 2000s, when the Bush administration enacted across-the-board tax cuts. Over the period from 1979 to the mid-2000s, tax rates fell most substantially for lower-income families and for very high income families. At the bottom end, expansions in tax benefits, such as the Earned Income Tax Credit (EITC), have left many low-income families with negative federal tax rates because they receive income subsidies through the EITC. At the top end, rates were cut substantially in the tax reform of the mid-1980s and cut further in the early 2000s. The available research indicates that the net effect of these changes is a slightly less progressive system than in the late 1970s, so after-tax income has widened along with pretax income.[4]

These results suggest that the inclusion of taxes in the analysis would serve only to reinforce the findings discussed here. A less progressive tax system would reinforce the widening inequality observed in the pretax cash-income data. At the same time, the overall decline in tax rates would increase after-tax incomes over this time period and shift the distribution of after-tax income upward.

Of course, people not only pay taxes, but also receive benefits from the government. If these benefits come in the form of cash payments (such as farm-subsidy payments or cash welfare payments), they are included in the earlier analysis. Some government benefits also arrive in the form of lower tax rates (among those paying mortgage interest or among recipients of the EITC, for instance). These benefits are counted in the tax analysis just discussed. Lower-income groups, however, typically receive other benefits in the form of noncash assistance through so-called in-kind programs, such as the Supplemental Nutrition Assistance Program (previously known as Food Stamps), rent subsidies, and child-care subsidies.[5] In these programs, the purchase of food and housing is subsidized, but the payments are made directly to those who provide these goods rather than to the low-income families. Hence, they do not show up as part of cash income to families.

There is no research that compares the redistributional effects of in-kind government transfers in 1979 to the mid-2000s on all nonelderly individuals. Ziliak (2008) indicates that means-tested benefits had a smaller poverty-reducing effect in 1999 than they did in 1979 for poor families, with particularly large declines among single-parent households with children. Scholz, Moffitt, and Cowan (2009) show that benefits from means-tested programs for single parents declined from 1984 to 2004 among the lowest-income families, although they rose somewhat for families at the poverty level and above.[6] In short, there is no reason to believe that noncash government benefits for food and housing have changed in ways that would reduce income inequality since 1979.

Of course, the government is not the only source of noncash compensation. Many workers receive compensation from their employers that does not show up in their monthly paychecks, primarily through pension and health-care benefit payments. These payments are hard to track since there is no data source that collects such information at an individual level. The best source of information is the Employment Cost Index, calculated from firm-level data that track the cost of all employee compensation by employers, including wage costs. A comparison between total costs and wage costs provides information on non-wage benefits. In 2007, 27 percent of the total employment costs paid by employers to employees went for nonwage benefits. The largest expenses went to retirement payments, both to Social Security and for private pension plans. The next largest payments were to health-insurance plans.

Brooks Pierce (2010) looks at the trend in these data between

1987 and 2007 and concludes that nonwage benefits grew over this time period. Furthermore, the cost of employee benefits grew more in high-wage jobs than in low-wage jobs. His conclusion is that inequality in full compensation grew more than inequality in wage compensation. Growing pension contributions particularly benefited higher-wage workers. Health-insurance costs grew the most for middle-wage workers. This suggests that the inclusion of nonwage benefits would also emphasize the trends we saw in cash income—namely, a growing level of overall income, combined with growing inequality.

Although the inclusion of taxes, noncash government benefits, and noncash employer compensation would change the levels of per person income reported earlier, this short review suggests that their inclusion would not alter the trends in pretax cash income. Tax rates have generally fallen and nonwage employee compensation has risen, further reinforcing the trend toward higher overall income levels during this time period. At the same time, the federal tax system and nonwage employee compensation have both changed in ways that resulted in a more unequal distribution of compensation once these factors are taken into account. This, too, would reinforce the trend toward widening inequality over the past three decades.

CAN THIS TELL US SOMETHING ABOUT INDIVIDUAL WELL-BEING?

These data show that per person income among nonelderly adults rose significantly even as income became more unequally distributed. This suggests that most people were better off, if well-being is measured by cash income.

Of course, income is only a partial measure of well-being. In this section, I discuss the limitations of these income numbers as a measure of overall economic well-being. As I discussed in previous chapters, incomes are increasing largely because more adults are working in the labor market, particularly adult women. The effect on well-being depends upon how families and individuals feel about trading away time at home (spent on child care, home work, and leisure) for time spent in paid employment that leads to increased income. These income increases could have left some women who preferred to stay home feeling worse off if they felt forced into market work because of inadequate earnings by their husbands; but others could have found market work more attractive. In addition to looking at time use, I also quickly review the literature on reports of overall life satisfaction to see how these correlate with the rising income levels and rising inequality we see in the income data.

For many women, the alternative to market work is work at home rather than leisure. It is not clear that a movement from home work to market work leaves someone worse off. Women who provide a rising share of family income may have gained increased independence, strengthening their decision-making power within families. In the end, the gains from higher family income and greater economic independence among women workers must be weighed against the losses from more time at work and less time at home.

Because the number of hours in the day is fixed, changes in market work are directly related to changes in home work and leisure time. Aguiar and Hurst (2007, 2009) indicate that leisure has increased since the mid-1960s, using a variety of different definitions of what "leisure" might mean. This is true for both men and women. These increases in leisure were more marked between 1965 and 1985. Since the mid-1980s, leisure has increased only slightly among men, and declined slightly among women. For men, this increase was almost entirely driven by an increase in leisure among less-educated men. Reduced employment among these men explains 82 percent of the increase in their leisure time. In contrast, more-educated men have reduced their leisure time over the past several decades. Hence inequality in leisure is increasing, but to the benefit of lower-income groups. Among women, the increases in time spent in paid market work are matched by declines in other types of unpaid home work, although there is no decline in time spent caring for children.

Economists typically assume that leisure time has a positive effect on overall satisfaction (or "utility," as economists usually call it). In this case, leisure-time trends have improved well-being, and have increased well-being the most among those men who have lost wages. Hence, this increase in leisure may, to some extent, offset the negative effects of wage declines on men's satisfaction with their lives.

For highly educated women married to highly educated men, whose increased labor-force participation has occurred along with significant increases in earnings and family income, these changes are likely to have left their families better off. The movement of educated women into a wide range of jobs and professions has increased their life opportunities and almost surely left them better off. Indeed, many of these women could have chosen to remain at home (given rising income levels among more-educated men), but they clearly did not.

For less-educated women, who are less likely to be married and whose income (even with greater earnings) remains relatively low, these increased hours of market work may signal more-ambiguous changes in well-being. The low levels of income on which many of these women must rely suggest that they have few alternatives to low-wage market work, particularly as welfare-to-work programs reduced public assistance options in the mid-1990s. Some have argued that rises in single parenting indicate that women prefer work to marriage and so must be better off. The alternative view is that deteriorating marriage options (as lower-income men's wages decline and as incarceration rates have risen, particularly among black men) mean that increased work among low-wage women is a forced response to a worsening set of options.

OTHER MEASURES OF WELL-BEING

This analysis finds that incomes are increasing, but so is income inequality, particularly wage inequality. Women's additional market work is a primary reason why incomes have increased, and this may have both positive and negative effects on well-being. Therefore, it is interesting to see what other measures of well-being might indicate.

A growing literature investigates trends in reported happiness over time. Most of this evidence suggests that reported happiness has been largely unchanged over the past thirty years, with perhaps a very small downward trend.[7] Inequality in happiness has declined during this period, with groups that traditionally reported less happiness (black Americans or men) showing gains, and groups that traditionally reported more happiness (white Americans and women) showing losses. On the one hand, this suggests that Americans have not generally become worse off over the past three decades, based on their reported happiness levels. On the other hand, the growing income levels shown in the earlier tables should produce increases in happiness. Why hasn't this happened?

Luttmer (2005) suggests that reported happiness is affected by relative position in the economy. At the same income level, people who live in higher-income areas report themselves as less happy, all else equal, than people who live in lower-income areas. Rising income inequality could work to reduce reported happiness, as those in the middle and bottom of the income distribution observe that there are others who are markedly richer than themselves. This could offset the happiness-increasing effects of overall rising incomes. This suggests the need to study the impact of these changes in income inequality on individual perceptions of their own well-being relative to others'.

An alternative measure of satisfaction is perceived economic security. Several studies have shown that levels of self-reported economic security have been relatively flat since the late 1970s. But since unemployment rates have fallen over this time period, which should make people feel more economically secure.[8]

Why would people's sense of economic insecurity remain high even as unemployment falls? One possibility is growing income volatility. There are a variety of papers that suggest that income volatility has risen in the United States since the 1970s.[9] Income variability from year to year appears to have grown particularly among the self-employed and among married couples (whose earnings are correlated and tend to go up and down together).

Changes in economic insecurity may also reflect changes in job stability. If more people change jobs more frequently, this could increase the sense of economic risk that they are facing. Farber (2008) notes that there are large declines in mean tenure on a job among male private-sector workers between 1979 and 2006, although other groups of workers show stability in tenure or even increases in tenure. Stevens (2008) shows that the mean length of longest job held has declined between the mid-1970s and 2004.

These other measures of well-being suggest that the rising per person income described in this book has not translated into increases in other measures of well-being. Happiness levels and perceived economic insecurity appear to have changed little. In fact, adjusted for unemployment, perceived economic insecurity has risen, perhaps reflecting more job changes and a declining number of lifetime jobs.

There is clearly more research to be done on how shifts in income levels and income inequality translate into changes in well-being. Rising income among families could be offset by other factors, such as rising childcare expenses as women work longer hours in the labor force. More adults in the work force might make a family pay more attention to economic cycles as multiple adults are aware of the economic factors affecting their jobs and wages. Greater market work among women may create more economic independence and greater household "voice." But it could also create more time-related stress, particularly among parents who both work full-time. Finally, growing inequality in incomes may result in a reduced sense of well-being, even among those whose incomes have continued to grow, if relative income comparisons are important to family well-being. Although it is important to know that per person income has risen along with rising inequality over the past three decades, it is not easy to draw conclusions about whether this means gains or losses in the satisfaction that people express about their life.

PART II

Can Inequality Be Reduced?

FIVE

How Economic Shocks
Change Income Distribution

The results in part I indicate a long-term trend toward rising inequality over the past three decades. In this section, I step back from the data and discuss the events that might *change* such a trend and bring about a narrowing of the income distribution within the United States. I focus on the question, What changes might bring the recent period of rising inequality to an end? This question has particular salience given the economic crisis of 2008–09, in which the U.S. economy (and the global economy) was engulfed. Rapid declines in wealth, due to a collapse in financial markets, led to a deep recession, with high unemployment and declines in income.[1] In order to understand whether and how an economic shock like the deep recession of 2008–09 might affect the distribution of income, this chapter reviews historical evidence on how past economic disruptions have (or have not) led to changes in the distribution of economic resources.

This chapter looks at the ways that economic shocks can cause changes in economic inequality in a society. I use the term "economic shock" to refer to political, economic, or technological changes that alter the economic opportunities or constraints facing a nation. Of course, these events may have important non-economic implications as well, which I will leave largely undiscussed. I will refer to a catastrophic shock as a major economic shock that reduces economic possibilities and that typically occurs within a relatively short, well-defined period of time, although the long-term effects may unfold only gradually. This includes events such as wars, pandemics, deep recessions, and natural disasters. But a major economic shock need not be catastrophic. It may unfold more gradually over time, through the introduction of a new technology, the opening of a new frontier, or a policy change. For example, the invention of and improvement in personal computing technology is an economic shock, with long-term economic implications, that opens up new possibilities for greater efficiency in business and consumer transactions. Similarly, policy changes that reduce the cost of higher education can increase skills among lower-income populations and raise their wages and productivity.

In general, economic shocks shift the economic constraints in a society by affecting one of the three primary factors of production: labor (human capital), physical capital, or land. Let me discuss each of these factors in turn.

Economic shocks can change human capital and population immediately through catastrophic events that increase death rates. Or these changes can happen over time, following events that lead to a significant increase or decrease in population size or population skills. For instance, the invention of the birth-control pill appears to have reduced fertility rates (Bailey, 2010). This will affect population size and, if contraception is used at different rates by different groups in the population, can also change skill levels. A change in skill levels has both a direct compositional effect on inequality (for example, a society with more people clustered near the median educational level is likely to be more equal) and a (sometimes offsetting) indirect effect through the influence of labor-supply shifts on relative wages (for example, wages for highly skilled workers will be higher in a society with fewer workers at the top of the education distribution). If the wage elasticity of the labor supply is large at the bottom of the educational distribution or small at the top, then clustering more people near the median education level will generally be equalizing.

Economic shocks can directly affect the physical capital available to a society as well. This can happen quickly, through the destruction, in a war or natural disaster, of infrastructure, industrial plant and equipment, or other physical assets. This produces immediate effects on wealth and income, usually affecting those at the top of the income distribution more than those at the bottom. (Of course, there is an offsetting effect, since the price of capital rises as it becomes scarcer.) Capital destruction may also create opportunities for future wealth creation that may affect the long-run resources available to different groups in society. Economic shocks, such as shifts in technology, that gradually change the production possibility curve can also affect the long-term accumulation of physical capital. Increased capital accumulation can be equalizing if it democratizes the distribution of capital or drives down profit rates. However, high-income persons tend to hold the most capital, so it may be disequalizing if the new capital winds up in the hands of high-income persons who are already capital-rich.

Finally, economic shocks can change the land and resource constraints available to an economy. There can be abrupt gains or losses in nationally controlled territory in a war. Political bargains can open new frontier land that was previously unavailable, or the invention of new mining or processing technologies can create mineral wealth in land that was previously worth little.

Of course, these economic constraints interact with the political economy around them. As I will discuss later, in many cases the effects of such shocks on economic inequality are determined as much by how they affect social and political behavior as by their direct economic effects.

An extensive literature discusses the ways in which shifting economic constraints change the growth trajectories of nations. In fact, much of the development literature is focused on finding ways to generate economic growth by bringing new skills, technology, or other resources to less-developed nations. Although I recognize that everything I discuss here will have impacts on economic growth, I am not going to focus on growth but on the ways in which these shifting economic constraints might change the distribution of resources within a nation.

This chapter is divided into two sections. The first reviews the ways in which catastrophic events might shift economic inequality in a nation, while the second discusses economic shocks that unfold more gradually over time. I end the chapter with a summary of the key issues that appear to determine the effects of economic shocks on economic inequality.

CATASTROPHIC EVENTS
AND THEIR IMPACT ON INEQUALITY

All nations would prefer to avoid wars, natural disasters, plagues, and deep and sustained economic recessions. An optimistic rhetoric sometimes suggests that developed nations are immune from such disasters: Interlocking global trade effectively eliminates the possibilities of destructive war between developed nations. Modern medicine prevents plague. And the tools of modern economics will keep the inevitable downturn in the business cycle brief and mild.

Unfortunately, although such major disasters may be less likely in the developed world, their risks have not disappeared, as has been demonstrated by the deep worldwide economic recession that began at the end of 2007. Over the last decade, attacks in the United States, Spain, England, and other countries have indicated that all nations face the threat of terrorism, requiring substantial public resources for military and security defense, with death and destruction of property and infrastructure when those defenses prove inadequate. Many medical experts think that widespread death through pandemic flu remains frighteningly possible in the developed world, as indicated by concern over recent disease episodes such as SARS and the H1N1 flu. And the destruction wrought by Hurricane Katrina proved that the developing world remains vulnerable to catastrophic natural events.

Using language that describes catastrophic events as "shocks" may be misleading, since this suggests that these are exogenous events that "just happen." Though catastrophes may be caused at least in part by some unavoidable events, they are also affected by historical and current policies. Even if war, recession, disease, and natural disaster are not entirely avoidable, they can be contained, their effects can be minimized, or the distribution of costs across groups can be shifted. This is particularly true in richer, more developed countries through such mechanisms as diplomatic effort, effective government banking policy, good public health procedures, or strong levees and building codes. Both the sequence of actions that precede a catastrophic event and the effects of that event depend upon the individual and collective actions of the people and the nations involved.

The evidence on how catastrophic events affect economic inequality is scarce, and one typically must deduce these effects from evidence that focuses on other economic issues. Herewith I provide a sampling of the existing evidence, taking as examples the effects of war, economic recession, and pandemic disease. I emphasize that there are many serious and wrenching effects of these catastrophic shocks that are not mentioned in my discussion; I focus just on their distributional effect.

War

War causes the destruction of both physical and human capital. High death rates, particularly among young men in a war, create an enormous opportunity cost (to use the coldhearted language of economics) by eliminating the social and economic contributions these men would have made over their lifetimes. From an economic perspective, this includes everything from goods production to tax payments to future fertility. Wars often destroy physical capital as well, eliminating infrastructure and productive capacity. Private and public wealth is lost when homes, businesses, and public buildings are destroyed.[2]

World War II destroyed a substantial share of European wealth and infrastructure. In a recent book, Atkinson and Piketty (2007) investigate trends in inequality among those at the top of the income distribution in ten nations over the past century. All of these countries show a steep decline in inequality between 1940 and 1945 that is uniformly ascribed to the destruction of wealth and capital during the war. Interestingly, the decline in inequality in the early 1940s is also visible in the United States, even though the United States suffered no destruction of physical property on its own shores.[3] In a world where wealth is held internationally, war in one part of the world can destroy wealth held by individuals across the ocean. Rebuilding physical capital after a war often takes substantial private and public wealth and may create new opportunities for wealth creation and income mobility. In many cases, physical capital has been quickly rebuilt after war ends.[4]

There may also be long-term effects on human capital. These can have positive or negative effects on inequality. A study of Civil War veterans, a group that suffered high rates of injury and even higher rates of disease exposure, indicates that those who were wounded or who experienced serious illness while in the military had lower wealth accumulation in the years afterward.[5] This suggests that the "disabling" effects of war on veterans can create a larger group of poor individuals and widen income inequality. Similar negative effects of military service on earnings and health have been found in studies of veterans of World War II and Vietnam.[6] On the other hand, the areas in the United States that suffered more deaths in World War I appeared to experience greater wage growth due to decreased labor supply immediately after the war in jobs typically filled by less-skilled young men, which likely reduced inequality.[7] Wars also may cause substantial shifts in the land and resources under control of a government when national boundaries shift or far-flung colonial empires disappear. With modern methods of warfare, land may be lost to productive uses through everything from nuclear contamination to large-scale placement of land mines.

Wars shift political alliances and may lead to new policy choices. Atkinson and Piketty (2007) indicate that the long-term moderation in European income inequality following World

War II was due to the significantly more progressive tax and transfer systems adopted by European nations, designed to help rebuild these nations. In the United States, policies adopted following World War II altered educational levels. The United States implemented generous college subsidies to veterans through the GI Bill, as a way to repay them for their service. The effect was a surge in college graduation rates (and in wages) among World War II veterans, which raised income and reduced economic inequality.[8]

The overall impact of war on economic inequality is uncertain. Typically, the immediate destruction of capital will reduce wealth and equalize resources within a nation. But the longer-term effects are less clear. The speed and nature of physical capital rebuilding depends on the political and economic environment following a war. The long-term changes in human capital may be uncertain. If soldiers come from across society, increases or decreases in their future economic contribution may have little effect on overall inequality. If soldiers are disproportionately recruited from among poorer groups (as opposed to a national draft or required military service among all groups), any disabling effects of service can increase inequality, while future veterans' benefits might work in the opposite way to reduce inequality.

Deep Recession

As the world learned all over again in 2008 and 2009, a deep and prolonged recession is a catastrophic event. It is obvious that a prolonged economic slowdown has major economic consequences, with slower growth and high and sustained unemployment.

A recession need not have any effects on inequality if the costs of unemployment and slower growth are spread throughout society. Unemployment is almost always concentrated among less-skilled and lower-wage workers, however. Among workers who kept their jobs in the 1930s, the U.S. wage structure in the Great Depression was fairly stable. Wage equality rose in the earlier part of the century and during the 1940s, but not during the Depression.[9]

If a recession is initiated by or induces substantial financial-market failure, there may be wealth losses among those at the top of the income distribution, which would reduce inequality. The evidence from Piketty and Saez (2003, 2007) on income among persons at the very top of the income distribution suggests that there was a noticeable "1929" effect on income from wealth among those in the top 1 percent of the income distribution in the United States (although this decline was not nearly as large as that which occurred at the time of World War II, between 1940 and 1945). Below the top 1 percent, income was dominated by earnings, and because of rising relative wages, income shares among those in the ninetieth to ninety-ninth percentile rose between 1929 and 1932. The result was a relatively constant income share among the entire top decile over the 1930s. In general, inequality appears to have fallen a little during this time period.[10] Much bigger shifts in distribution appear to have occurred during the 1920s and the 1940s than during the 1930s.[11]

In the post–World War II era, the economy has experienced only one period of extremely deep recession prior to the current one. Between 1980 and 1982 there were two back-to-back recessions, and unemployment rose over 10 percent. During these recessions (and in the years following), income inequality in the United States rose steeply. This occurred because of disequalizing changes at both the bottom and the top of the income distribution.[12] Wages among less-skilled workers declined; rising unemployment in the early 1980s created further income declines. At the same time, incomes among more-skilled workers rose. Few people view these changes as closely related to the recession of the early 1980s, however, since they started prior to that event and continued at a rapid pace even through the brisk economic growth period of 1982 to 1989.

Perhaps surprisingly, the U.S. evidence from the twentieth century suggests that deep recessions did not have large effects on income inequality—or, perhaps stated more accurately, that other events had much stronger effects on inequality than did recessions.[13] Of course, the effects of a recession on inequality will depend on the nature of the recession and the amount and distribution of wealth destruction and income loss. Recessions can have larger long-run effects if they lead to policy changes that alter tax and transfer systems, such as the New Deal in the 1930s.

Disease

Epidemics occur when a significant portion of the population is affected by illness. The so-called Black Death of the mid-fourteenth century is estimated to have killed over a quarter of Europe's population in just a few years. A number of economic historians have attempted to determine the economic effects of this plague on wage rates, with somewhat mixed conclusions.[14] None of this work looks at inequality, since data on income distribution is unavailable from this time period. One might speculate, however, that inequality would have been reduced for some time following the plague years. If labor shortages increased wages following the Black Death, this would tend to reduce inequality. If deaths were most prevalent among those who were poorer, older, or in worse health, those who survived would be the healthier and more productive individuals.

Of course, even if the short-run effects of plague are to reduce income inequality by killing the less-healthy members of society, inequality might be widened in the long run if a number of survivors contract the disease but find their long-term health and productivity weakened. The 1918 flu pandemic appeared to strike a disproportionately high share of young adults. The reduced population within these cohorts appears to have resulted in higher wages for this group in the following decades.[15] But other evidence suggests that children who were in utero in 1918 displayed poorer health and lower incomes during their lifetimes.[16]

More recent work looks at the AIDS epidemic of past decades. Evidence from less-developed countries suggests that poorer individuals are more likely to contract AIDS and to die once infected.[17] This may lessen income inequality over time. The long-term effects of this, however, remain unclear, since the impoverishment and developmental effects on the large number of children who are left orphaned could lower their earnings ability in the long run.[18]

In the post–World War II era, although there have been significant and deadly diseases that struck unexpectedly within the more-developed world, the death rates from these have been quite low. AIDS is the most prominent incurable disease to have appeared in the developed world in recent decades. Yet, in the year immediately prior to the development of the drugs that largely prevent death from AIDS, only 0.016 percent of the U.S. population died of AIDS. Though the effects of these deaths were devastating on the communities in which they occurred, this death rate is low enough to have no aggregate economic effect, either on economic growth or on inequality.

We are fortunate to have no population-wide "plague events" in the modern economic era by which we can benchmark the economic effects of a major disease outbreak in the developed world. Epidemiologists warn, however, that the rapid spread of a virus that causes widespread death in both the developing and the developed world is more likely than we might wish.[19]

ECONOMIC SHOCKS THAT UNFOLD OVER A LONGER TIME PERIOD, AND THEIR IMPACT ON INEQUALITY

Catastrophes are visible. We know when they occur, and we can often date them quite precisely. Other economic shocks often unfold more slowly and may not be visible as important "events" until years after they actually occur. This is particularly true of such events as technological shifts, or skill and population shifts. Because many things are changing over time, it is typically harder to identify the effects of long-term economic shifts (unlike catastrophes, where many effects are immediately measurable). In fact, often it is the economic results of such events that are seen first, leading researchers to go back to look for the causal forces behind these changes.

This is not a bad description of how researchers have approached the most recent episode of rising inequality in the United States. In the late 1980s, when it first became clear that rapid increases in inequality were more than a short-term or cyclical phenomenon, researchers began to look for causes. It was almost a decade before widespread consensus was reached among economists that these changes were largely driven by skill-biased increases in demand, many of them probably the result of technological changes linked to a growing use of computer technologies.[20] Yet the link between these demand shifts and technological change continues to be debated,[21] largely because of the difficulties in measuring the nature and speed of technological change. It is possible that another decade from now, when hindsight is clearer, this conclusion will be amended.

This section discusses four types of economic shocks that occur over time and that might produce changes in economic inequality. I will discuss technological changes, changes in frontiers and land availability, changes in skill levels, and changes in economic policy. Long-term climate change, although not discussed here, may be another example of an economic shock that develops over time.

Technology

New technologies typically shift the production possibility frontier outward, allowing economies to produce more with the same amount of resources. Although we remember particular moments that come to symbolize specific technological breakthroughs, such as Alexander Graham Bell's first phone call, technological change is often more a process than a single event. The invention of a new technology can spawn a variety of closely related follow-on changes. For example, the harnessing of electricity became more and more effective over a period of years, allowing electrical generators to become more powerful while at the same time creating smaller and smaller electric motors that could be attached to individual machines (David, 1990). In a similar way, computer technologies have changed dramatically as microchip processors have become more powerful and smaller. Technological changes are not a single event but a series of linked events that follow one another.

Technologies that utilize capital and labor to produce output can shift economic inequality in two ways. First, new technologies are opportunities for wealth creation. Spurts of inventiveness are often followed by the creation of new fortunes as entrepreneurs see ways to use this knowledge to create new or improved products. Only a limited number of individuals may have the entrepreneurial or inventive skills or the available capital to take advantage of new technologies at the beginning. Or a limited number of individuals may have the political power to be able to create protected markets (by persuading the government to charter railroad monopolies, for instance) that reduce new entry into a growing market. In these cases, one would expect widening inequality driven by wealth accumulation at the top of the income distribution. This is often discussed as the reason for the very high levels of wealth and income inequality in the United States during the last part of the nineteenth century, as the industrial revolution created great fortunes among the so-called robber barons.

Second, new technologies may be skill-biased in their demand for labor. As these technologies spread, they will advantage one group of workers and disadvantage another. Skill-biased technological change appears to be the primary reason given for rising wages among highly skilled individuals in the United States over the past three decades. Since the mid-1990s, in fact, this bias seems to most strongly favor those whose educational credentials go beyond a four-year college degree.[22] Even though the supply of such individuals is slowly increasing over time, as more individuals pursue graduate or professional degrees, demand appears to have increased at an even faster rate than supply, steadily driving up wages. How long this situation might continue is unclear.

Of course, technological change may have different short-run versus long-run effects. Whereas new technologies may be initially disequalizing, increasing demand for only the most skilled workers, over time technologies may become more and more "user friendly," so that they increase the productivity and value of less-skilled workers as well. Some have argued that the current computer technologies that advantage more-skilled workers will, over time, lead to technologies that complement the abilities of lower-skilled workers, raising their productivity and value in the workplace (Davis and Wessell, 1998). In this case, these technologies, initially disequalizing, would have longer-term equalizing effects. In the end, predicting the long-run effects of technological change is difficult. It is also possible that ongoing changes in computer power and usage will advantage more-skilled workers even further and lead to additional growth in inequality over time.

In contrast to the skill bias of technological change in the workplace, which appears to have benefited workers with higher education, new technologies that eradicate disease or otherwise improve health may be particularly helpful to low-income groups. Poor health is much more common among those with lower incomes, so health improvements are often equalizing in their economic effects. For instance, Bleakley (2010) notes that malaria-eradication campaigns in the United States in the 1920s, aimed primarily at poor southern areas (where malaria was most prevalent), significantly raised the long-term incomes of the children in these areas. Health-related technological advances (immunization, disease eradication, new medications or treatments) are often highly beneficial to poorer communities.

Skills and Human Capital

Human capital and physical capital are often complements in the production process, so that skilled workers typically increase overall productivity. Of course, one should not think of people and machines as independent factors. There is endogeneity between human skill and technological change, so that a larger number of skilled workers in the economy may increase innovation over time and result in more effective processes to produce and deliver goods and services.

Substantial research in developing countries indicates that the basic skills acquired in elementary school (particularly literacy) are closely correlated with declines in poverty. Indeed, one of the policy lessons often cited in the development literature is the need to assure that girls as well as boys attend school, because of the economic benefits that arise when women are educated. Education raises income and productivity among these women, but also increases the health and education levels of their children.[23] A growing body of research in the United States indicates that early-childhood experiences, including high-quality preschool, can have lifelong impacts, suggesting that skills are acquired early and that policies to increase human capital should not focus only on adolescents or adults, but may start with very young children.[24]

Goldin and Katz (2008) provide an extended discussion of the value of increased education in the United States, first through the expansion of free public elementary schools and then through the expansion of public high schools throughout the country. They claim that the United States was able to move ahead of other countries as an economic power because it provided free public education before other countries and pioneered the expansion of public education to high school.

One group for whom educational opportunities were not so freely or equally provided was African-American children. The lower incomes and greater poverty of black Americans has raised American inequality for centuries. After public schools were integrated, incomes among those African-American students who benefited from more equitable public schooling rose noticeably, with a net equalizing effect.[25]

Although greater skills in the work force may clearly enhance economic growth, their effects on economic inequality could go in either direction. If educational improvements are available only to certain groups, or are confined to a small elite within the population, greater educational skills among this group can be disequalizing. When educational improvements are widespread, with expanded public schooling available throughout the population, such changes can be neutral or equalizing over time. Goldin and Katz argue that the widespread growth in education within the labor force was one of the reasons why inequality lessened for several decades in the post–World War II era in the United States. Only after educational levels stopped growing (in the mid-1970s) did the trend toward increasing equality reverse itself. Over the next two decades, the demand for more-skilled workers outstripped supply (indeed, the share of men going to college during this time period did not increase at all), leading to growing inequality.

Land, Frontiers, and the Discovery of New Mineral Resources

The discovery of new mineral resources or the opening of new frontier land within a nation is, like new technologies, an opportunity for new wealth creation. It expands the possibilities for economic growth.

As with technological change, the wealth-creation opportunities can lead to disequalizing growth if they are dominated by a small number of individuals with either the technical know-how or the political power to protect their ownership of these resources. The creation of the British Empire led to a number of great fortunes—in some cases, with business monopolies protected by royal charter.

The availability of new land resources need not always be disequalizing, however. García-Jimeno and Robinson (2011) find some evidence that countries that had larger frontiers in the mid-nineteenth century had less income inequality in modern times.[26] They hypothesize that this effect might depend on national political institutions, and they contrast the use of the frontier in nondemocratic South American countries to its use in the United States and Canada, arguing that the frontier may have decreased long-run income inequality more in countries with strong constraints on executive power. In the United States, for instance, the Homestead Act was designed to make frontier farmlands available to those without investment capital. Unfortunately, with only twenty-one examples, García-Jimeno and Robinson do not have decisive evidence on whether institutions determined the frontier's effect on inequality.

Of course, the degree to which the Homestead Act reduced economic inequality depends upon who homesteaded the land. Stewart (2006) shows that those who moved to the Great Plains between 1860 and 1870 were disproportionately those who were landless and had lower incomes in the East. His conclusion is that the frontier provided income mobility for low-income persons who otherwise might not have been able to improve their economic status.

The impact of changes in landholdings or mineral resources on economic inequality also depends heavily upon the group being studied. Most frontiers, colonies, or mineral wealth were once under the control of another group. Displacement of Native

Americans or the political dispossession of colonized natives had clearly impoverishing and disequalizing effects on their societies, even as it created new wealth opportunities for those who were moving in.

Policy Changes and Redistributional Programs

Much of the preceding discussion talks about economic shocks as if they were inevitable changes. In reality, changes in capital, land, and human skills are often facilitated by public policy. Policies that reward entrepreneurial skills and encourage innovation may create a society more likely to experience technological change. For instance, government subsidies for investments in "green technology" are an effort to increase experimentation and innovation in energy-saving technologies.

The most immediate effect of policy on equality, however, is through the resource redistribution that government policy enforces. Some of the largest government programs (Social Security and Medicare) redistribute income from current workers to current retirees. Since retirees typically have lower incomes, these programs reduce inequality. A variety of other means-tested programs are aimed at lower-income families and provide them with additional resources, further reducing inequality. This includes such programs as housing assistance, the Earned Income Tax Credit, and the Supplemental Nutrition Assistance Program (formerly known as the Food Stamp Program). But not all government policies reduce inequality. Other programs add more to the resources available to higher-income persons than lower-income persons, such as the mortgage tax deduction for homeowners or farm subsidy programs. In general, after-tax incomes are distributed much more equally than before-tax incomes. However, many state tax systems are regressive—that is, they tax lower-income persons at a higher rate than higher-income persons.

Changes in redistributional policy emerge out of a political process that is itself affected by economic shocks. Hence, the Great Depression created a political window of opportunity that resulted in the creation of a number of programs that greatly enhanced the federal safety net for workers and the elderly in the United States. Heclo (1986) notes that these policies were designed for near-term social stabilization and that not all of them survived the Depression. Those that did survive provided benefits to a broader array of people and were less means-tested (such as Social Security and unemployment insurance). In the long run, however, these surviving programs have narrowed U.S. inequality. Similarly, large changes in tax codes can shift wealth holdings and change economic inequality. This is apparent in the post–World War II period in most European nations.[27]

As I noted earlier, many skill-enhancing policies are the direct result of publicly funded educational opportunities. Free public schooling produced a literate population and was almost surely a force for greater equality in economic opportunity. Policies that improved educational opportunities for black students are associated with improved earnings among black adults in the following generations.[28] Similarly, expanded access to higher education can also raise incomes. The increases in college attendance due to the GI Bill, which subsidized college educations for veterans following World War II, had a noticeable effect in raising men's college-completion rates.[29]

The interaction between policy and the external environment can be reinforcing, creating long-term trends toward or away from greater economic equality. A society that provides more economic opportunities to its poorer members is likely to also provide them with more opportunities to be involved in political decision-making. This, in turn, will generate political support for ongoing or expanded redistribution. Or, alternatively, a society in which a small group holds substantial wealth may replicate itself, since these individuals are able to use their wealth to retain the political structure that supports their economic power and provides their children with the education, skills, and connections to retain their dominance.[30]

So, whereas policy change can sometimes be viewed as an economic shock that widens or narrows the distribution of income, these changes often emerge from a series of other economic and political events. Just as new economic shocks might create opportunities for new wealth creation, so they can also create the opportunities for new political alignments—upsetting, or at least rearranging, the existing social order.

SUMMING UP: WHAT DETERMINES THE EFFECTS OF ECONOMIC SHOCKS ON CHANGES OR TRENDS IN INEQUALITY?

It should be clear from the preceding discussion that the effect of economic shocks, whether catastrophic or more gradual, can be equalizing or disequalizing. This review suggests that there are some general lessons that one should take away in thinking about the potential economic ramifications of these events.

First, economic shocks almost always shift wealth-creation opportunities. Technological change and changes in land or mineral resources typically allow new wealth creation. Catastrophic events almost always destroy wealth and open opportunities for future rebuilding. If wealth is held primarily by those at the top of the income distribution, rapid wealth destruction is likely to be economically equalizing. But the effect of opportunities for new wealth creation is more difficult to predict. On the one hand, this may lead to disequalization if access to this new wealth creation is limited to those who already have wealth and political influence, and if this allows them to further consolidate their economic and political advantages. On the other hand, if economic shocks open up wealth-creation opportunities to new groups, the effect can be equalizing. This may occur because previously unempowered groups have access to unique information or entrepreneurial skills that this new wealth creation requires. Or the economic shocks could upset the existing political and economic order, allowing previously dispossessed groups to gain access to the new wealth.

I should note that population changes or changes in skill levels are another version of wealth creation or destruction, except that in this case the wealth is human capital rather than physical capital. Deaths from war or disease destroy economic resources as surely as the loss of property. Indeed, human losses often have more far-reaching and deep effects on a society than capital losses. Similarly, increased educational opportunities and new skill-enhancing technologies also create wealth by increasing the productive resources in a society.

Second, the long-term effects of economic shocks may be different than the short-term effects. This is because these events themselves initiate a new process of change in society. Opportunities for new wealth, even if initially beneficial to only a small number of people, may over time create new jobs and allow the wealth generated by these new opportunities to spread more widely. Economic catastrophes, such as civil wars, that destroy lives and wealth and equalize resources may lead to long-term political changes that advantage the winning side and create much greater inequalities over time between different ethnic or religious groups. The harnessing of electricity might originally have created an opportunity for a few industrialists to accumulate wealth (a short-term disequalizing effect), but as electricity became more broadly utilized among different groups over time, its benefits enhanced productivity among all workers and raised wages (long-run equalizing). Expanded educational levels among a dominant ethnic group (initially disequalizing) might lead to new social or political norms that value education more highly and insist that it be provided to all groups (long-run equalizing).

Third, the political economy in which these events occur is crucial to their effect on economic inequality. Indeed, one could argue that the long-term effects of an economic shock are almost entirely determined by the political institutions and culture in which that shock occurs. A political environment that values greater equity (or that at least values providing opportunities to those who are poorer) is more likely to create a set of institutions that make these events equalizing. Frontier land that is provided free to all who want to farm it will result in a more equalizing process than frontier land that is allocated to wealthy families or corporations through public charter. Expanded public schooling that is freely provided to all citizens will be more likely to result in equalizing growth than expanded schooling that is restricted to the children of the elite or to the children of particular racial or ethnic groups. A country that rewards war veterans with expanded educational and economic opportunities is more likely to experience equalizing long-term growth following that war.

Fourth, economic shocks often change the political economy

of a nation, by changing the attitudes of both leaders and citizens. Because context is very important in determining whether these events have disequalizing or equalizing effects, changes in political economy can be key to the long-term effects of these economic changes on inequality. If the effect of new frontiers is to create a national self-identity that assumes that economic mobility is available to everybody ("Everybody can make it in this society if they work hard. Look what my grandparents achieved on the prairie, starting with nothing!"), this may limit political willingness to provide generous safety-net programs long after the frontier is a distant memory, and may lead to future economic inequality. If past wealth creation was controlled by strong elite interests and this generates a public reaction against a government controlled by wealthy elites, this can produce a society with more democratic institutions and greater redistributional capacity.

All four of these "lessons" about the impact of economic shocks suggest that these shocks can have long-term effects on income distribution. These effects are more likely to change long-term trends in inequality when they lead to substantial changes in wealth (physical or human), either destroying previous wealth or creating new opportunities for future wealth creation. Shifts in long-term inequality are also more likely when economic shocks affect the political constraints within a country and change attitudes and institutions in ways that lead to greater (or less) future economic inequality. Ultimately, however, the effects of economic shocks are mediated by the political economy in which they occur.

SIX

Ways to Reduce Inequality (and Their Limits)

The last chapter discussed some of the historical economic events that have affected income levels and income inequality. This chapter provides some sense of the magnitude of change that is necessary to significantly reduce income inequality in the United States.

Just as many factors have led to rising inequality over the past thirty years, so there are many paths that could lead to reductions in inequality. I will discuss four different types of changes: changes in skills; changes in key economic variables, such as wages, labor-force participation, and investment income; changes in marital choices; and changes in redistributional policies. In each case, I assume a ten-year future horizon, simulating the effects of particular changes over the next ten years.

I will simulate changes that are highly optimistic in some cases, but not outside the range of past experience. They are changes of a magnitude that *could* occur in some state of the world over the next ten years. That said, I am not going to provide extensive background justifications for these proposed simulations. These simulations are not designed to model what I think is likely to happen, but to show what the effect would be if significant changes occurred in U.S. demographics, economics, or public policy.

I do not model scenarios in which top income recipients lose earnings. (The exception to this is the "reduced investment-income scenario" that is discussed later.) I focus instead on scenarios that impact the numbers or economic circumstances of lower-income individuals. I do this because it seems virtually impossible that highly skilled individuals will face serious economic problems in the United States over the next decade that would eliminate their wage gains over the past half century. In fact, an economic environment that eroded incomes among top income earners would almost surely have even worse effects among less-skilled workers.

Similarly, I also do not model any simulations that undo the economic progress made by women over the past three decades. As we have seen, expanded work and earnings by women are a major cause of rising inequality. We could reduce inequality by assigning highly educated women to lower-wage jobs and making market work less attractive or less available to all women, but this is not a change that most Americans would like to see. Hence, one perspective on this chapter is that it primarily investigates changes that could reduce inequality and that some (although not all) would argue are positive changes. This includes improvements in skills, increases in marriage, and increases in the social safety net.

IMPROVEMENTS IN SKILLS

In the first scenario, I assume that skills rise among the lower-skilled population. Over the past twenty-eight years, between

1979 and 2007, the population share of high school dropouts and high school graduates has declined markedly, while the population share of those with higher educational credentials has increased. I assume that the average annual change over the past three decades continues for the next ten years. The share of high school dropouts in the population fell, on average, 0.426 points per year between 1979 and 2007. Hence, I assume that it falls at the same rate over the next ten years (that is, it falls another 4.26 points, which is equal to the ten-year average decline over the past twenty-eight years). Details on how this and other simulations in this chapter are calculated are provided in appendix 4.

Part A in table 10 shows the effects of this simulation on population shares by skill level. The first two columns show the actual population shares in 1979 and 2007. The third column indicates the simulated population skills that would occur if we continued the average rate of change for another ten years. High school dropouts fall from 12.6 percent of the population to 8.4 percent under this simulation. High school graduates fall from 29.8 percent to 25.7 percent. Those with some college, a college degree, or more than a college degree all grow.

I should note that this simulation is very optimistic. Most of these skill shifts occurred in the first part of the period 1979–2007, and the change has been much slower in the last decade. This is because there was an acceleration in educational achievement following World War II. By the early 1980s, the older less-educated population was leaving the work force, and the skill distribution shifted upward rapidly.

In more recent years, skills have increased more slowly. Younger persons are not as markedly more educated than older persons. In part, this is because native males' education levels have not increased much in recent decades. In part, this is

TABLE 10

Simulating a Continued Upgrading in Population Skills

	Actual, 1979	Actual, 2007	Simulated
	(1)	(2)	(3)
PART A. SIMULATED POPULATION SHARES BY SKILL LEVEL (% OF POPULATION)			
Less than high school	24.6	12.6	8.4
Exactly high school	41.1	29.8	25.7
Some college	18.1	29.5	33.5
Exactly college degree	11.9	19.0	21.5
More than college degree	4.4	9.2	10.9
PART B. EFFECTS OF SIMULATION ON MEDIAN ANNUAL INCOME AND INEQUALITY MEASURES			
Median income	$29,753	$36,897	$39,840
Gini coefficient	0.35	0.43	0.42
90/50 ratio	2.02	2.41	2.36
50/10 ratio	2.97	3.69	3.52

NOTE: The sample includes all persons aged eighteen to sixty-four. Simulated skills change takes the average decline in population share between 1979 and 2007 and forecasts this same change for another ten years. See appendix 4 for details. Data in part B are per person income based on family-unit income adjusted for family size.

because of an increase in low-skilled immigrants into the United States in recent decades. Hence, for the average skill shifts from 1979 to 2007 to continue, there must be a very strong acceleration in the skills of younger persons. The simulation assumes that something happens in terms of policy and behavior that generates a strong increase in education among younger persons over the next decade.

Part B of table 10 shows what the effect of this skill change is on the level and distribution of income among eighteen- to sixty-four-year-olds. I assume that the income available to individuals at each skill level does not change, so the simulation shows only the effects of a shift in the skill mix. As in chapters 3 and 4, all of the income calculations show per person income based on family-unit income adjusted for family size.

This significant upward shift in the skills of the population raises median income by about $3,000. The effect on inequality is small, however. This change has a minor effect on the overall Gini coefficient, moving it from 0.43 to 0.42. There is also a small downward shift in the 90/50 ratio and the 50/10 ratio relative to their 2007 values. I conclude that a strong increase in the skills of the population will have small equalizing effects on income distribution and will shift the overall distribution farther to the right. For skill shifts to change the income distribution more rapidly over the next decade, we would have to see skill shifts far outside historical experience and reasonable expectation.

EQUALIZING CHANGES IN WAGES, LABOR-FORCE PARTICIPATION, AND INVESTMENT INCOME

I next investigate the potential effects of shifts in wages and investment income that provide relatively more income to lower-income individuals. I also look at shifts in labor-force participation that might occur if there was strong consistent wage growth in the bottom part of the wage distribution.

Although the most equalizing wage changes require substantially stronger wage growth at the bottom than at the top of the income distribution, all of the evidence we have about demand for greater skills in the modern U.S. economy suggests that this is unlikely to occur. I simulate a situation in which hourly wages grow by 8 percent among all workers in the bottom 80 percent of the hourly-wage distribution over the next ten years and by only

TABLE II

Simulating a Significant Shift in Economic Variables

	Actual 1979	Actual 2007	Wage Simulation	Labor-Force Participation (LFP) and Wage Simulation	Declining Investment-Income Simulation	Combining Wage, LFP, and Investment-Income Simulations	Combining Wage, LFP, Investment-Income, and Skill Simulations from Table 10
	(1)	(2)	(3)	(4)	(5)	(6)	(7)
Median income	$29,753	$36,897	$39,304	$40,834	$36,502	$40,500	$43,208
Gini coefficient	0.35	0.43	0.42	0.41	0.43	0.41	0.40
90/50 ratio	2.02	2.41	2.37	2.31	2.40	2.29	2.26
50/10 ratio	2.97	3.69	3.71	3.50	3.65	3.49	3.33

NOTE: The sample includes all persons aged eighteen to sixty-four. Data are per person income based on family-unit income adjusted for family size. The wage simulation assumes that wages increase by 8 percent among those in the bottom 80 percent of the wage distribution and increase by 4 percent among those in the top 20 percent of the wage distribution over the next ten years. The LFP simulation assumes that male labor-force participation by skill level returns to its 1979 levels over the next ten years. The declining investment income simulation assumes that investment income falls to 5 percent of total income (from its 2007 level of 6.3 percent). The sixth column simulates all of these changes together, and the final column simulates all of these changes and also includes the skill shifts simulated in table 10. See appendix 4 for details.

4 percent among workers in the top 20 percent of the hourly-wage distribution.

An 8 percent wage increase is the average annual increase in median hourly wages over the period 1979–2007, multiplied by ten. Wages did not increase steadily over this period, however, with weaker wage growth in the 1980s and 2000s, and very strong growth in the 1990s. Furthermore, this level of hourly-wage growth was not experienced by low-wage workers. So this is an optimistic scenario and assumes wage growth for low-wage workers that is well above recent experience. Although I view a lower rate of wage growth among the top 20 percent of the population as unlikely, this could occur if wage increases were modified at the top in response to the recent economic collapse, if demand in higher-wage industries (such as financial or business services) remains weak, or if the supply of less-skilled workers continues to decrease relative to the supply of highly skilled workers.

Table 11 shows the effects of this wage change on the level and distribution of income. Columns 1 and 2 of table 11 show the actual measures of inequality and median income in 1979 and 2007. Column 3 shows what these measures would look like with high wage growth among the bottom 80 percent of the population, lower wage growth at the top, and constant labor-force participation over the next ten years. The effect is a significant increase in median income, which grows by just under $2,500, but relatively small changes in the distribution. The 90/50 ratio and the Gini coefficient decline a little, whereas the 50/10 ratio slightly increases because families with no workers or only part-time workers at the bottom of the income distribution fall relative to the median.

One might hope that sustained wage growth would stimulate

greater labor-force participation, especially among less-skilled male workers, who have been working less in recent decades. The next simulation assumes that these wage increases lead to a strong increase in male labor-force participation. In particular, I assume that growing wages (perhaps with other changes) lead male labor-force participation rates at each skill level to return to their 1979 levels. This means a ten-point rise in labor-force participation among male high school dropouts, an eight-point rise among male high school graduates, a six-point rise among men with some college, and a two-point rise among men with a college education or more. Given the steep rises in labor-force participation among women over the past several decades, I do not assume further increases for them. These are highly optimistic labor-force changes, but they show what a sustained increase in work effort, particularly among less-skilled men, would accomplish.

Column 4 of table 11 shows the effects of simulating the wage increase and the labor-force participation increase together. Of course, median income increases even more (by almost $4,000) when male labor-force participation rises with wages. The effects on inequality are noticeable. The Gini coefficient declines a little more than with only a wage increase, the 90/50 ratio declines somewhat, and the 50/10 ratio falls by quite a bit. This simulation represents quite dramatic changes in wage and labor-force outcomes and leaves inequality in the income distribution well below its 2007 levels, although it does not approach the 1979 levels of inequality.

For comparison, I also simulate the effect of long-term reductions in investment income. In 2007 investment income was 6.3 percent of total income. I simulate the effect if it should be reduced from 6.3 percent to 5.0 percent. This would require long-term reductions in wealth holdings or their returns. I reduce investment income among all families with such income, which disproportionately affects income among higher-income families.

Column 5 of table 11 shows the effect of this lower investment-income simulation. Because relatively few persons have significant amounts of investment income, the effects are small, but they are equalizing.

Column 6 of table 11 combines the effects of reduced investment income, wage growth that is lower among workers in the top 20 percent of the income distribution, and substantially increased labor-force participation among lower-wage workers. The result is a significant increase in median income of almost $4,000, due to the wage and labor-force participation changes. As expected, inequality falls by a noticeable amount, but the combined effect of all of these changes still leaves the measures of inequality reasonably close to their 2007 levels and far above their 1979 levels.

The final column of table 11 combines all of these economic effects and also includes the upward skill shift simulated in table 10. In this simulation, skills levels and labor-force participation have increased, along with equalizing changes in wages and investment income. These are substantial economic changes, almost surely more equalizing and much larger than any that are likely to occur over the next decade. Median income grows strongly in this simulation—from almost $37,000 to over $43,000. All measures of income inequality fall, with the Gini coefficient declining from 0.43 to 0.40—a significant reduction—and significant declines in the 90/50 and 50/10 ratios. But even with these substantial changes, income inequality is closer to its 2007 level than to its level in 1979.

The conclusion to be drawn from this section is that even fairly drastic shifts in behavior, skills, and wages that favor lower-income populations would not bring income inequality anywhere near its 1979 levels. In part, this is because of the selectivity in household composition, in which higher-earning people are more likely to be living in households with other higher-earning people. In part, this reflects the very strong wage increases among the top earners over the past twenty-eight years, which none of these simulations reverse. (I do not simulate such a reversal because I view it as outside the bounds of any reasonable expectations.) Although these simulations increase earnings among lower-income populations, these increased earnings do not begin to catch up with the earnings gains among higher-income persons.

On the other hand, these changes would continue shifting the income distribution upward, with very substantial increases in median income. Many more people would have substantially higher incomes.

INCREASES IN MARRIAGE

More conservative social commentators have regularly called for a greater rate of marriage, as a way to reduce poverty and to improve the long-term prospects for low-income children. Marriage also increases the number of workers in a household and reduces the number of lower-income single-individual and single-headed family units.[1]

To simulate a change in marriage behavior, I substantially reduce the number of single-headed family units and single-person family units while increasing the number of married-couple family units. Throughout, I focus on lower-income households among each family type. Specifically, I assume that 20 percent of single persons who both head families and are in the bottom half of the income distribution of single-headed family units become married. This reduces the overall number of single-headed family units by 10 percent but targets all of that reduction among the poorest half. For each single-headed family unit that I "marry off," I also eliminate a single individual of the opposite sex. At the same time, I increase married-couple families in the bottom half of the income distribution of married couples. Note that married couples in the bottom half of their income distribution have substantially higher incomes than single-headed families in the bottom half of their income distribution. So the net effect is to increase (wealthier) married-couple family units and to decrease (poorer) single-person and single-headed family units. (Details of the specific calculations involved in this simulation are available in appendix 4.)

A 20 percent decline in the number of families in the bottom half of the single-headed family unit income distribution (a 10 percent decline in the number of all single-headed family units) is a substantial change. Over the past three decades, we have seen steady increases in the share of the population in single-person and single-headed family units, and steady declines in the share of the population in married-couple families. If we could reverse this trend and move the population shares of married-couple families upward, it would be a very significant social change.

Table 12 shows the effects of this simulation. Part A shows how these changes affect the share of the population in each type of family unit. Single-headed family units decline from 17 to 15 percent of the population. Single individuals decline from 21 to 20 percent of the population. And married couples rise from 62 to 65 percent of the population.

Part B of table 12 shows the effects of this simulation on the level and distribution of income. This simulation increases

TABLE 12

Simulating a Shift toward Marriage

	Actual, 1979	Actual, 2007	Simulated
	(1)	(2)	(3)
PART A. SIMULATED POPULATION SHARES BY FAMILY TYPE (% OF POPULATION)			
Single Individuals	13.4	21.0	19.9
Single-headed family units	11.9	16.9	15.2
Married-couple family units	74.7	62.2	64.9
PART B. EFFECTS OF SIMULATION ON MEDIAN ANNUAL INCOME AND INEQUALITY MEASURES			
Median income	$29,753	$36,897	$37,342
Gini coefficient	0.35	0.43	0.42
90/50 ratio	2.02	2.41	2.39
50/10 ratio	2.97	3.69	3.53

NOTE: The sample includes all persons aged eighteen to sixty-four. Simulated changes reduce the number of single-headed family units in the bottom half of their income distribution by 20 percent. (This is a 10 percent reduction among all single-headed family units.) The number of single individuals in the bottom half of their income distribution is also reduced, removing one individual of the opposite gender for each head of a single-headed family who is removed from the single-headed family unit distribution. The simulation increases the number in the bottom half of the income distribution of married couples by an equivalent number that keeps total population unchanged. See appendix 4 for more details. Data in part B are per person income based on family-unit income adjusted for family size.

median incomes by a little under $500 and reduces inequality. Almost one-quarter of the 1979–2007 increase in the 50/10 ratio is reversed with this increase in marriage. These changes in marital behavior would reduce inequality at the bottom of the distribution and would be socially significant, with increases in marriage for the first time in the past three decades; but they only partially reverse the rising inequality since 1979.

The conclusion to this section is that significant changes in family composition will have only small effects, even if those changes result in higher marriage rates. This is consistent with the results in chapter 4, where I indicated that changes in family formation since 1979 explain only a minority of the change in overall inequality. For household-formation changes to really affect the distribution of income, they would have to be extremely large over the next decade, reversing the long-term trend away from marriage at a much faster rate than I simulate here. This seems unlikely to occur.

AN INCREASED SAFETY NET

One of the most powerful tools for resource redistribution is through government programs. I focus here on antipoverty programs designed to increase the resources available to very low income families. In reality, of course, government programs redistribute to many groups, such as homeowners (through mortgage interest deductions), nature lovers (through the National Park Service), and college goers (through state and federal subsidies to higher education).

As discussed in chapter 4, some of our major antipoverty programs are implemented through the tax system or through noncash in-kind benefits. Because my data are based on cash income, it is difficult to simulate changes in these programs. You could imagine the simulation outcomes discussed here coming through in-kind or tax-based programs where the effects of the program are shown in terms of cash income.

The United States has relatively high rates of poverty compared with other developed nations, largely because we provide a less extensive safety net of public assistance. Other countries, particularly European countries, typically provide greater amounts of employment support (through higher wages for low-skilled work, often the result of centralized wage-bargaining systems, or through more extensive unemployment support payments) and/or greater levels of public assistance to those who do not work.[2] My goal in this section is to show how much of the inequality in the U.S. income distribution is due to the larger share of the U.S. population at very low levels of income.

To demonstrate this, I create a somewhat unreasonable simulation: I assume that families with income below the poverty line are brought up to the poverty line.[3] One could do this through a cash public-assistance program, through expanded food and housing subsidies, through greater wage subsidies (such as an expanded EITC for families without children), or through other mechanisms that provide income or subsidize earnings. I am less concerned with how this is done than with showing what the effects of eliminating poverty are on the income distribution.

Table 13 shows the results of several simulations that assume greater redistribution. Columns 1 and 2 show the 1979 and 2007 statistics on the distribution of income. Column 3 shows the simulated distribution if I were to raise all families with a worker to a level above the poverty line (perhaps through expanded wage subsidies). Column 4 shows the simulated distribution if I raise all families with children under the age of eighteen to a level above the poverty line (perhaps through an expanded safety-net program). Column 5 shows the simulated distribution if I eliminate all poverty by raising the income of all families originally below the poverty line. In all of these simulations I assume that funding for greater redistribution is created without negative consequences. I do not model any reductions in income among higher-income families to offset this new spending.

TABLE 13

Simulating a Shift toward Greater Redistribution

	Actual, 1979	Actual, 2007	Simulating No Poverty among Family Units with Workers	Simulating No Poverty among Family Units with Children	Simulating No Poverty among Any Family Unit
	(1)	(2)	(3)	(4)	(5)
Median income	$29,753	$36,897	$36,897	$36,897	$36,897
Gini coefficient	0.35	0.43	0.42	0.42	0.41
90/50 ratio	2.02	2.41	2.41	2.41	2.41
50/10 ratio	2.97	3.69	3.40	3.33	3.33

NOTE: The sample includes all persons aged eighteen to sixty-four. The simulations assume that redistributional programs entirely fill the poverty gap for the indicated group of families. The "No poverty among family units w/ workers" simulation indicates what would happen if a combination of public-assistance and work-subsidy programs brought all families with workers who are currently below the poverty line up to the poverty line. The "No poverty among family units with children" simulation indicates what would happen if program changes brought all families with children who are currently below the poverty line up to the poverty line. The "No poverty among any family unit" simulation indicates what would happen if all family units below the poverty line are brought up to the poverty line. See appendix 4 for details. Data are per person income based on family-unit income adjusted for family size.

The results in table 13 are quite striking. Because these changes affect only people at the very bottom of the distribution, there is no change in median income with these simulations, and no change in the 90/50 ratio. In all cases, the 50/10 ratio is reduced, as expected. But the effect on the Gini coefficient is not large. In columns 3 and 4, the Gini is only slightly reduced. In column 5, where I eliminate poverty entirely, the Gini goes from 0.43 to 0.41, with a 3.7 percent reduction in inequality.[4] On the other hand, the 50/10 ratio goes down markedly. Eliminating poverty closes 50 percent of the rise in the 50/10 ratio since 1979.

The primary conclusion from this exercise is that it is not the presence of poor Americans that explains the high 2007 levels of inequality. Entirely eliminating poverty reduces inequality at the bottom but leaves overall inequality far above its 1979 levels. This does not mean that the United States should not expand its safety net and improve economic outcomes for poor and near-poor families. There are many reasons to think about such policies, particularly if one cares about the well-being of the worst-off in society. In fact, one might believe that antipoverty policies have greater social value than other policies that do more to equalize the entire income distribution. But these antipoverty policies are not likely to substantially reduce overall economic inequality.

CONCLUSIONS

This chapter has focused on the potential effects on the income distribution of substantial economic and demographic changes. I have tried to simulate changes that, although not outrageous in their assumptions, are nonetheless highly optimistic in what they assume might happen over the next ten years. These simulated changes were focused on improving incomes among lower-income populations. Yet, the results indicate that even rather substantial changes in economic behavior and outcomes would have surprisingly small effects on the distribution of income, narrowing it only a little. In this chapter, I have looked at the effects of relatively large changes in economic opportunities and social safety-net policies, increases in skills or marriage, or greater labor-force participation among men. Though all of these changes help to reduce inequality, especially at the bottom of the income distribution, these reductions are small relative to the large increases in inequality since 1979. None of these changes reduce overall inequality in the United States to a level near where it was in 1979.

Why is this so? As we saw in earlier chapters, the large shifts in the distribution of wages and the increases in female labor-force participation (particularly among women married to higher-income men) have resulted in large increases in measured inequality over the past three decades. These changes are large enough that even significant alterations in policy, behavior, or economic opportunity will not undo them. This suggests that the United States will have higher inequality for the foreseeable future. It will take a long-term and sustained trend toward greater equality—one that probably will need to last for more than a decade—before inequality in the United States moves substantially closer to its 1979 levels. Of course, whether or not this is desirable is an open question. Reversing inequality could also mean reversing some of the significant income gains of the past thirty years. The general lack of support for substantial wealth redistribution in the United States might suggest that many Americans would rather live in the current world, with higher incomes, greater labor-force participation, and higher inequality, than take the risk of shifting to a lower-inequality world that may or may not also produce slower income growth.

SEVEN

Changing Inequality in the United States Today

This last chapter speculates about possible changes in inequality in the United States within the next few decades. Like all prognostication, this is highly risky, since we are all constantly surprised as our personal and national histories unfold.

The United States has been experiencing an extended period of rising inequality since the mid-1970s, following an extended period of downward-trending inequality that began sometime after 1910, including sharp reductions in inequality in the 1920s and the early 1940s. What are the factors that might lead inequality to stabilize or even reverse itself in the near future? What opposing factors might lead to continuing growth in inequality?

On the one hand, the best prediction of a long-term trend is that it will continue. Among the factors that are likely to continue the current trend toward increasing inequality are the following:

- Ongoing technological changes that will continue to advantage more-skilled workers in the United States. There is little evidence that skill-biased technological change has reached an end. Indeed, as markets become increasingly international, the biggest returns will be to persons who can work in a global marketplace. This requires people with high degrees of managerial, technical, and interpersonal skills. The growth in the share of highly educated workers in the United States over the past two decades has been slow. Should demand continue to rise faster than supply, the returns to skill in the marketplace will continue to increase, generating ongoing widening in inequality.

· Greater competition from the developing world may also reduce economic opportunity for U.S. workers who are not among the most highly skilled. The large economies of China and India have grown rapidly in the last decade. They will continue to develop more-sophisticated economies, competing with the United States to produce exportable goods and services. This may affect the demand for and the wages of middle- and lower-wage workers. Of course, the rising incomes in these countries will also create new markets for U.S.-produced goods, and the rising output of these countries will reduce the prices faced by U.S. consumers at all income levels.

· Since Ronald Reagan's presidency in the 1980s, the U.S. political environment has generally favored lower taxes and has been wary of expanding redistributional programs. For instance, there have been substantial cuts in taxes, with the largest cuts for higher-income families. Benefits in cash assistance programs have declined markedly. Despite minimum-wage increases, the value of the minimum wage is far below its historical high point in the 1970s. In contrast, the income subsidies through the Earned Income Tax Credit have grown markedly, but this is a conditional transfer that occurs only if a low-income individual is employed, and it provides less of a safety net than do more-traditional public-assistance programs.[1] If Americans feel economically insecure in the years ahead, the demand for even lower taxes and less redistribution could dominate the political environment.

On the other hand, the deep recession of 2008–09 was an economic shock that changed the economic environment. Certain factors may cause economic inequality to cease rising and even reverse itself.

· The collapse of the financial sector, with a sharp decline in the stock market, created a steep wealth loss in 2008. If the stock market does not recover its previous highs, this will result in a more equal wealth distribution and a somewhat more equal income distribution.

· The economic recession of 2008–09 led companies throughout the private sector to rethink their business plans, including salary structure. The financial sector was a poster child for high executive salaries over the 1990s and 2000s. The symbolic enforced reductions in the salaries of executives of companies that took federal bailout money may translate into lower executive salaries throughout the private sector, and this more equal structure might remain in place for some time. An examples is the pay cut taken in 2009 by Lloyd C. Blankfein, CEO of Goldman Sachs. Blankfein received just $9 million in bonuses, an 87 percent cut from his record $68-million bonus just three years earlier.

· High and sustained unemployment may lead many Americans to feel greater empathy with those facing economic difficulties, and to perceive a greater risk of becoming low-income themselves. This can shift the political environment as it did in the 1930s, resulting in a greater willingness to provide redistributive programs through the government.

· The acceptance of somewhat higher tax rates or new taxes may grow in the years ahead. Higher taxes may be needed to reduce the growing government deficit that was in place before the recession and that has been exacerbated by large expenditures on fiscal stimulus. Higher taxes could also be needed at the state level, to address serious state deficits and to fund public-sector pension payments. It is likely that the burden of any tax reform is going to fall more heavily on higher-income families.

Which of these scenarios is most likely to occur is uncertain. Political leadership will matter a great deal. For instance, the health-care reform legislation passed in 2010 provides insurance options to uninsured persons and could make reductions in inequality more likely. Congressional reluctance to raise taxes on higher-income families could make declines in inequality less likely.

Of course, as the discussion in the earlier part of this chapter made clear, there are other, less foreseeable future events that could also affect economic inequality. A major global catastrophe, such as a deadly pandemic flu or the explosion of a nuclear bomb in an unstable part of the world, could shift inequality in ways that are hard to predict. More optimistically, new and yet unknown technological changes (such as new and cleaner energy options) could create great opportunities for new wealth creation as well as new job and earnings opportunities.

A major political push to fund the programs that would substantially increase attendance and completion of postsecondary education by American youth could change the skill mix in our nation. This not only would raise incomes for American families, but could increase productivity and innovation in the entire economy, leading to greater long-term growth that in turn leads to higher wage and income increases. Skill improvements have the promise of creating a "virtuous cycle" of change. The slowing rate of skill gains in the U.S. workforce threatens long-term economic growth in this country relative to other countries that are either catching up with or exceeding the United States in the share of their population with college and postcollege training.

All of these possibilities could change the distribution of economic resources in this nation. Whatever does occur, however, is unlikely to have "just happened." The discussion of past economic shocks in chapter 5 suggests that their effects are very much determined by the specific nature of when and how they happen and how the policy environment responds. There is little in any economic shock—deep recession or major technological improvement—that inherently mandates that its effects on inequality will be positive or negative.

The review in chapter 6 of possible policies that might reverse the trend toward rising inequality indicated that even substantial changes in behavior or economic opportunities will go only partway toward reversing the long-term rise in inequality. Indeed, it is not clear that it is desirable to return to the same level of inequality as in some arbitrary past year. While ongoing increases in inequality may lead to increasing social and economic problems, an abatement of this trend or a partial reversal may be sufficient, particularly if these changes come along with increases in income among all groups in society. Many of the changes simulated in chapter 6 produced substantial income gains that were focused among lower-income families. As this book has repeatedly noted, inequality levels may matter less in an economic environment in which income levels are rising for all groups.

Particularly in a nation with the resources and the governmental expertise of the United States, the long-term effects of economic change will depend upon the actions of the public and the private sectors. If the rising inequality of the past three decades is of concern, this nation can take steps that make it more likely that this trend will be reversed. These steps could include expanding the skills and educational opportunities of all American children. Skill increases should go along with policies that assure that less-skilled workers have the incentives to work and can earn enough to escape poverty. This in turn will encourage greater labor-force participation. Over time, a greater public willingness to enact progressive taxes or to expand redistributional programs will also mean less inequality.

We can select policies that are likely to produce economic gains among lower-income families, which will over time reduce inequality. Or we can ignore these issues and act in ways that further long-term growth in inequality. These are real choices, and they will matter.

DETAILS OF THE CHAPTER 2 SIMULATION AND APPENDIX FIGURES

The simulation presented in table 3 indicates how much of the change in the level and the distribution of earnings is due to changes in the distribution of wages by itself, with no shift in hours or labor-force shares among men and women by education level. I calculate this simulation by dividing the workers in each year into four samples, defined by gender and educational level. I distinguish two educational levels: those with a high school degree or less, and those with more than a high school degree. Within each of these four samples in 1979 and 2007, I rank every individual based on the number of hours he or she worked. I then divide each sample into a thousand equal-sized groups, each of which I will refer to as a *permillage*.[1] For example, the first permillage of male, less-skilled workers in 1979 includes the workers in this category who worked the *fewest* hours over the course of that year. I calculate the mean annual work hours for each of these permillages in the 1979 distribution. For the persons in each permillage in the 2007 distribution, I assign them mean work hours from the equivalent 1979 permillage among workers of their gender and educational level.

Said another way, I place each person in 2007 in a ranking from one to one thousand, based on their location in the distribution of annual hours of work among workers of their gender and educational level, and assign them the work hours that someone at an equivalent rank in the 1979 distribution would have received. This essentially provides a level and distribution of work for everyone in the 2007 sample that imitates the level and distribution of work in 1979. I make these calculations separately for both men and women and by education level, because the distribution of work hours is so different (and changes differentially) within each of these four groups. I then calculate simulated 2007 earnings, multiplying the simulated work hours by actual wages in 2007.[2]

This provides an earnings simulation for 2007 workers based on the 1979 hours of work distribution by gender and education level. But since this calculation of simulated earnings is based only on workers in 2007, it does not control for changes in the relative share of the labor force among men and women by education level. I deal with this by reweighting the 2007 simulated sample with the 1979 labor-force weights. For individual observations within each gender and skill category in 2007, I multiply the individual person-weight by the ratio of their category's share of the workforce in 1979 to their category's share of the workforce in 2007. This weights the 2007 data to approximate the 1979 shares in the labor force within each gender and skill group and holds workforce shares constant between these two years. The result is substantially fewer women and more people with just a high school degree or less in the simulated 2007 labor force.[3]

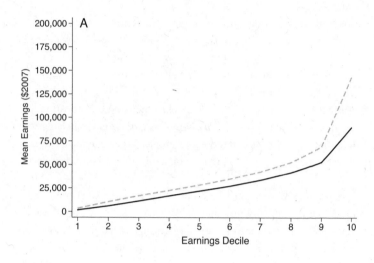

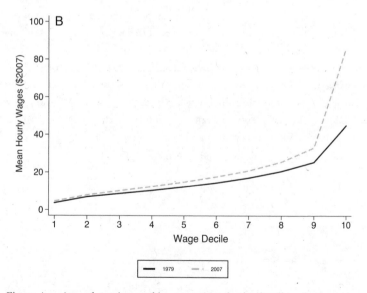

Figure A-1. Annual earnings and its components by decile, all workers: A. Mean annual earnings by decile in 1979 and in 2007; B. Mean wages by decile in 1979 and in 2007; C. Mean hours worked per week by decile in 1979 and in 2007; D. Mean weeks worked by decile in 1979 and in 2007. Each graph includes all civilian workers aged eighteen to sixty-four.

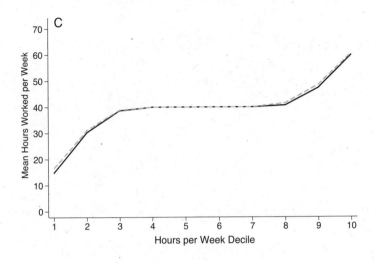

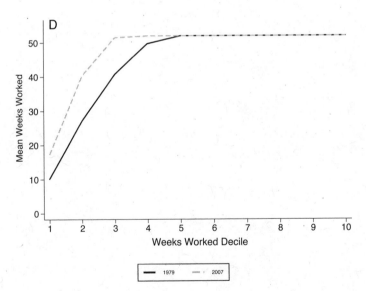

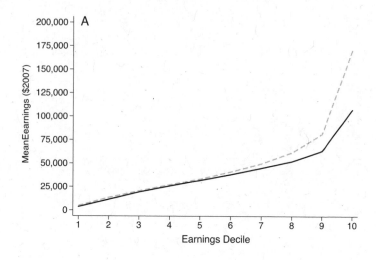

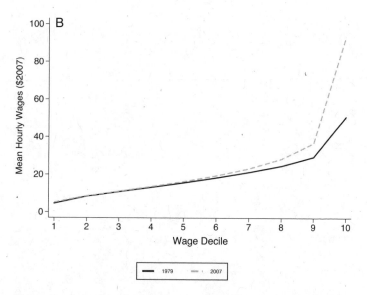

Figure A-2. Annual earnings and its components by decile, male workers:
A. Mean annual earnings by decile in 1979 and in 2007; B. Mean wages by
decile in 1979 and in 2007; C. Mean hours worked per week by decile in 1979
and in 2007; D. Mean weeks worked by decile in 1979 and in 2007. Each graph
includes all civilian male workers aged eighteen to sixty-four.

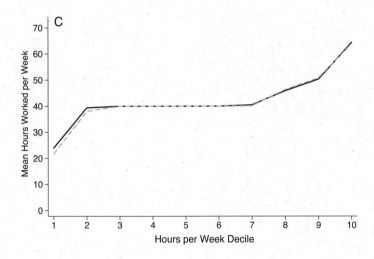

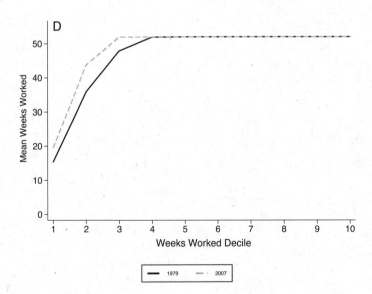

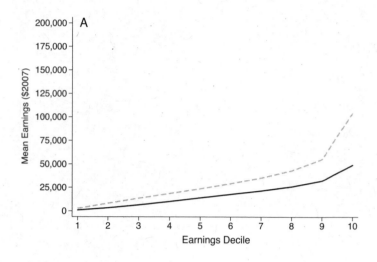

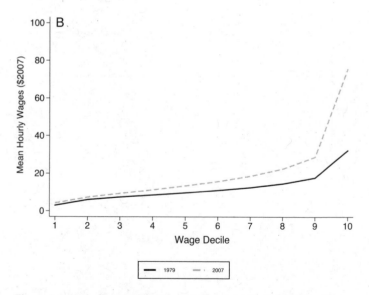

Figure A-3. Annual earnings and its components by decile, female workers: A. Mean annual earnings by decile in 1979 and in 2007; B. Mean wages by decile in 1979 and in 2007; C. Mean hours worked per week by decile in 1979 and in 2007; D. Mean weeks worked by decile in 1979 and in 2007. Each graph includes all civilian female workers aged eighteen to sixty-four.

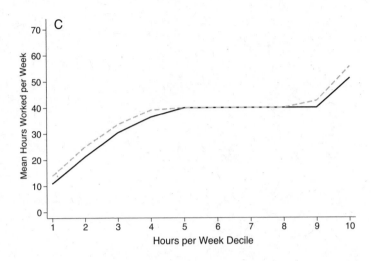

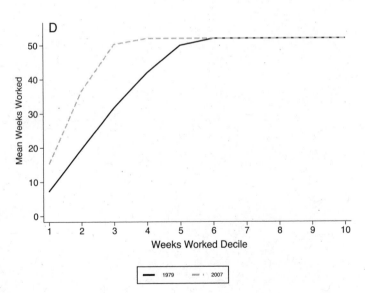

APPENDIX TWO

FIGURES SHOWING INCOME COMPONENTS
BY DECILE, 1979 AND 2007

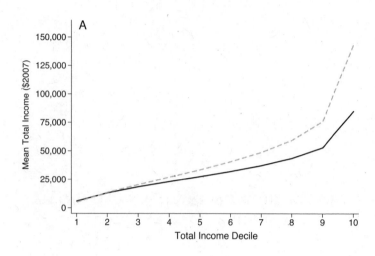

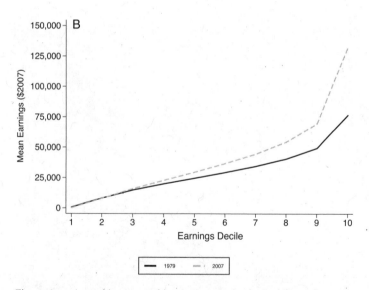

Figure A-4. Annual income and its components by decile, all people:
A. Mean total income by decile in 1979 and in 2007; B. Mean earnings by
decile in 1979 and in 2007; C. Mean government income by decile in 1979
and in 2007; D. Mean other income by decile in 1979 and in 2007. Each graph
includes people aged eighteen to sixty-four. Annual income for each person
is per person family-unit income adjusted for family size.

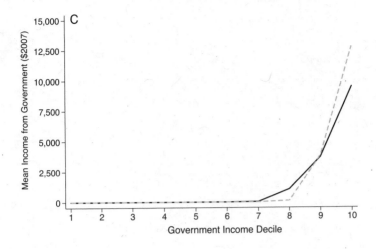

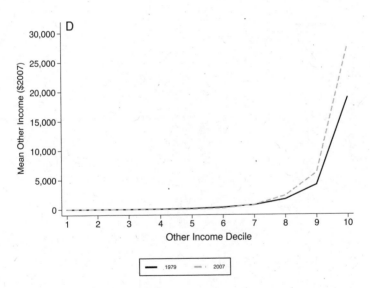

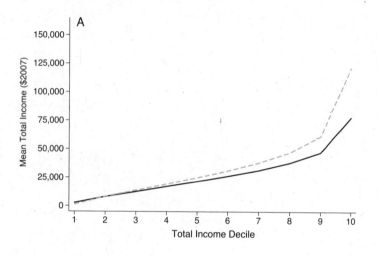

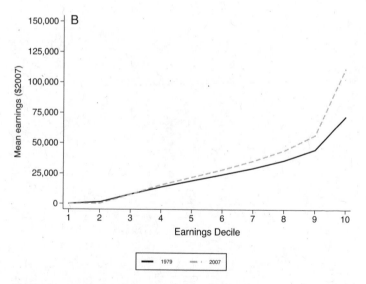

Figure A-5. Annual income and its components by decile, single individuals:
A. Mean total income by decile in 1979 and in 2007; B. Mean earnings by
decile in 1979 and in 2007; C. Mean government income by decile in 1979
and in 2007; D. Mean other income by decile in 1979 and in 2007. Each graph
includes all single individuals aged eighteen to sixty-four. Annual income
for each person is per person family-unit income adjusted for family size.

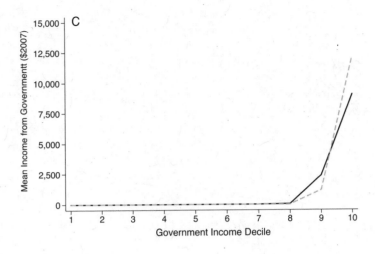

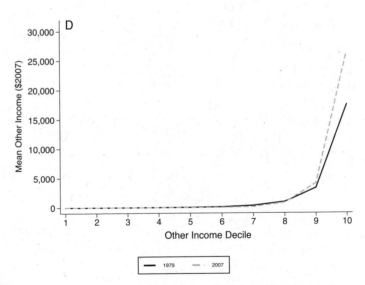

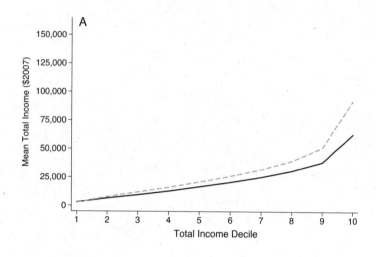

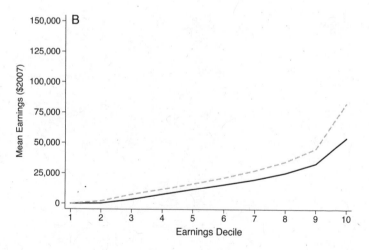

Figure A-6. Annual income and its components by decile, persons in single-headed family units: A. Mean total income by decile in 1979 and in 2007; B. Mean earnings by decile in 1979 and in 2007; C. Mean government income by decile in 1979 and in 2007; D. Mean other income by decile in 1979 and in 2007. Each graph includes members of single-headed families aged eighteen to sixty-four. Annual income for each person is per person family-unit income adjusted for family size.

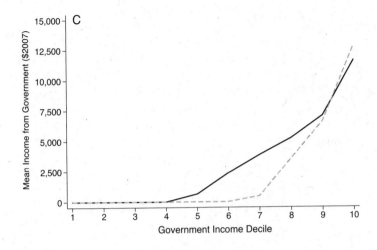

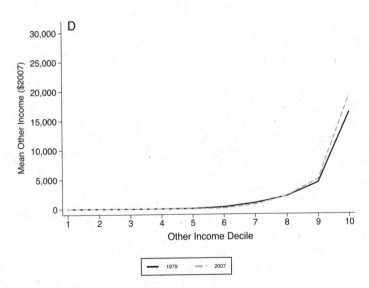

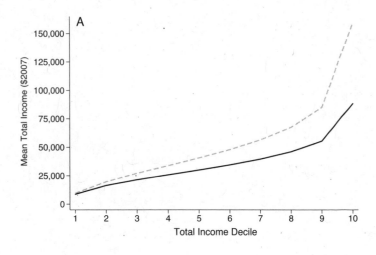

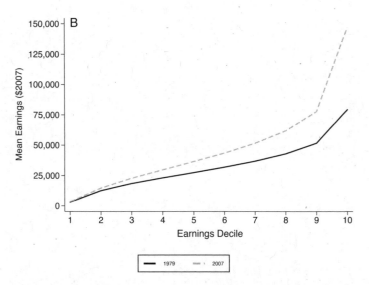

Figure A-7. Annual income and its components by decile, persons in
married-couple family units: A. Mean total income by decile in 1979 and in
2007; B. Mean earnings by decile in 1979 and in 2007; C. Mean government
income by decile in 1979 and in 2007; D. Mean other income by decile in
1979 and in 2007. Each graph includes members of married-couple-headed
families aged eighteen to sixty-four. Annual income for each person is per
person family-unit income adjusted for family size.

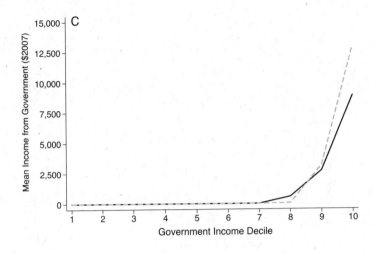

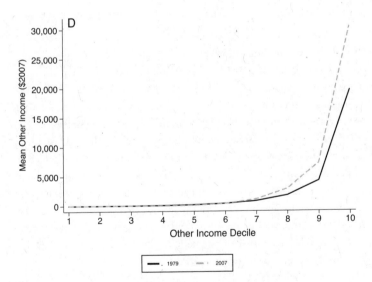

DETAILS OF THE CHAPTER 4 SIMULATIONS

A. SIMULATING A CONSTANT FAMILY SIZE WITHIN FAMILY TYPE (TABLE 6)

To implement the simulation reported in table 6, I divide my data into three samples composed of those individuals in each of the three family types. Because family size does not change among persons in single-person family units (which always contain only one individual), I work only with the two samples containing persons in single-headed family types and in married-couple family types. Within each of these family types, I rank all persons by family-size centiles in 1979 and 2007. This means dividing the persons within each family type into one hundred equal-sized groups, ranked by total family size. Of course, there are many persons who live in families of the same size and who need to be allocated among different centile groups. In cases where there are a large number of people with the same family-size level, I randomly assign people into a centile.

Within each 1979 centile, I calculate the mean family size. I then assign the mean family size from the 1979 centile to each person in the equivalent 2007 centile. So, the lowest-ranked centile in 2007 would be assigned the family size of the lowest-ranked centile from 1979; the second-lowest centile in 2007 would be assigned the family size of the second-lowest centile from 1979, and so on. I then recalculate per person income in 2007 using 2007 income levels but using the simulated 1979 family size for each individual rather than their actual 2007 family sizes. The simulated family-size distribution of all individuals in 2007 now mimics that of 1979 within each of these family types.

B. SIMULATING A CONSTANT SHARE OF PERSONS ACROSS FAMILY TYPES AND THEN SIMULATING CONSTANT SHARES AND CONSTANT FAMILY SIZES (TABLE 7)

I simulate the effect of changes in the relative share of family types by reweighting the 2007 data so that the share of eighteen- to sixty-four-year-olds in each family type is identically equal to its share in 1979. For each person in each of the three family types in the 2007 data, I multiply their person-weight by the ratio of the share of their family type in the eighteen- to sixty-four-year-old population in 1979 divided by the share of their family type in the eighteen- to sixty-four-year-old population in 2007. The result is to increase the weights on persons in married-couple families (which were more populous in 1979) and decrease the weights on persons in single-individual and single-headed family types (which were less populous in 1979). This data is used for the results in column 3 of table 7.

When simulating the effects of constant shares across family types as well as constant family size (column 4 of table 7), I use the reweighted population described in the previous paragraph and adjust it for family-size changes within each family type, using the technique described in section A of this appendix to hold family size constant. This both holds the population weights constant across family types and holds family size constant within family type.

C. SIMULATING A CONSTANT DISTRIBUTION OF EARNINGS, GOVERNMENT INCOME, AND OTHER UNEARNED INCOME (TABLE 8)

The technique I use here is based on that used in Reed and Cancian (2001). Let me first explain the simulation in part A of table 8. holding the earnings distribution constant at its 1979 levels. I divide the 2007 data into three samples, each containing all eighteen- to sixty-four-year-old individuals in each of the three family types. All of my analysis is then done within each sample by family type. For each family-type sample, I rank all persons in the 1979 sample by their family unit's total earnings and divide them into one thousand equal-sized groups; I refer to each of these as a *permillage*. Because I do not want to hold family size constant in this simulation, I do this ranking on the basis of each person's total family earnings (not per person income based on family earnings adjusted for family size). There are often many people with the same total family earnings who need to be assigned to different permillages in order to keep the number of people in each group equal. When there are a number of people tied at the same total family-earnings level, I randomly assign these people to an appropriate permillage. This is the same method I used to break family-size ties in section A of this appendix.

I calculate the mean total family earnings for each permillage in the 1979 distribution. I then divide the 2007 family-type samples into permillages as well. For the persons in each permillage in the 2007 distribution, I assign them mean total family earnings from their equivalent 1979 permillage. Said another way, I rank each person in 2007 from one to one thousand, based on their location in the total family-earnings distribution of their family type, and assign them the total family earnings that someone at an equivalent rank in the 1979 distribution of their family type would have received. This essentially provides a simulated level and distribution of total family earnings for everyone in the 2007 sample that imitates the level and distribution of total family earnings in 1979 by family type.

I simulate total 2007 per person income levels by adding actual family government income and other unearned income for each person to their simulated total family earnings and then adjusting for family size using persons' actual 2007 family sizes. This provides a measure of 2007 income among all persons, holding the distribution of earnings at its 1979 pattern within each family type while allowing the distribution of government and other unearned income, and family size and family-type composition, to change.

For part B of table 8, I simulate the distribution of total income. I again divide the 1997 and 2007 data into three samples, each containing all eighteen- to sixty-four-year-olds within a given family type. Within each family-type sample, I create permillages ordered by total income in 1979 and 2007. Following my treatment of family earnings, I do this ranking on the basis of each person's total family income (not per person family income adjusted for family size). Within each family-type sample, persons in each 2007 permillage of total income were assigned the total income level of the equivalent permillage in 1979. Hence, my simulation re-creates the 1979 distribution of total income within the 2007 sample for each family type. By working with total income, I take account of all of the correlations between different income components, which change together over time.

Once a simulated 2007 total family income is assigned to each person, I then define simulated per person income by using actual 2007 family size to adjust total family income to per person income for each individual. This allows the distribution of family size to change as it actually does between 1979 and 2007. Hence, I allow family size and family-type composition to change but hold the distribution of income constant.

D. SIMULATING CONSTANT INCOME AND CONSTANT FAMILY TYPE TOGETHER (TABLE 9)

The final simulations, shown in table 9, use the simulation techniques described earlier. In part A, I simulate a constant income distribution as described in section C of this appendix. These are the results reported in the first row of part A. Then, using this simulated data, I follow the techniques described in section B of this appendix to hold family size and composition constant in the second row of part A.

Part B reverses these simulations. I first do the simulation described in section B of this appendix to hold family size and composition constant (reported in the second row of part B), and then I use this simulated data to follow the techniques described in section C of this appendix to further hold income distribution and level constant (reported in the first row of part B).

The residuals from both of these two-part simulations are identical and reflect the further effect of the correlation between changes in income and changes in family composition and family size.

DETAILS OF THE CHAPTER 6 SIMULATIONS

A. SKILL SIMULATION (TABLE 10)

I first divide my sample of individuals in 1979 and 2007 into five educational categories based on their total education level: less than high school, exactly high school, some college (more than high school but less than a four-year college degree), exactly a four-year college degree, and more than a college degree. I calculate the share of eighteen- to sixty-four-year-olds in each category in 1979 and 2007, and then estimate the average per-year change in the population share within each educational category over this twenty-eight-year period. Using this, I calculate an "average ten-year change" by multiplying the average one-year change by ten. This calculation indicates that over the past twenty-eight years, the average ten-year change in population share for those with less than high school is −4.26; it is −4.05 for the exactly high school group; +4.06 for the some-college group; +2.52 for the exactly college group; and +1.72 for the more-than-college group. (These numbers are the difference between columns 2 and 3 in part A of table 10.)

I assume that these average skill shifts in the population continue post-2007 for the next ten years. This means that in the simulation, the share of eighteen- to sixty-four-year-olds with less than a high school education or exactly a high school education will be greatly decreased, and the share who attended some college will be greatly increased. There will be somewhat more modest increases in the share of the sample that has a college degree or more than a college degree. In order to simulate these educational gains in the U.S. workforce, I must make some assumptions about how people will sort themselves into family units after these changes. To do this, I split my sample into five groups, defined by the educational category of the head of each person's family unit. I assume that there are no changes in the characteristics of families (based on family size, composition, and income) within these categories. For instance, suppose 5 percent of family units headed by a person with exactly a college degree are married-couple family units with no children, a spouse who also has a college degree, and a per person income of $75,000. This will still be true after I simulate an increase in educational attainment.

To simulate this increase, I take advantage of the fact that most adult members of a family unit have the same educational attainment as the head of the family unit. I can therefore simulate an increase in educational attainment among all eighteen- to sixty-four-year-olds by deflating the weights of persons in families with heads who dropped out of high school or have exactly a high school degree, and inflating the weights of persons in family units whose heads attended some college, acquired a college degree, or had some postgraduate schooling. The factors by which I multiply persons' weights were found by solving for B in the linear equation $AB = C$, where A is a five-by-five matrix and each element a_{ij} is the share of eighteen- to sixty-four-year-olds who are in educational category i and whose family-unit head is in educational category j; B is a five-by-one matrix, and each element b_i is the factor by which I multiply the weights of persons whose family-unit head is in educational category i; and C is a five-by-one matrix where each element c_i is the share of eighteen- to sixty-four-year-olds in educational category i that I wish to simulate.

B. WAGE SIMULATION (TABLE 11, COLUMN 3)

I first categorize all workers by their location in the 2007 distribution of real hourly wages.[1] Next, I multiply their real earnings by 1.08 if they are in the bottom four quintiles and by 1.04 if they are in the top quintile. I then recombine these workers into their family units and add actual other unearned income and government income to the simulated earnings. I calculate simulated per person income based on simulated family-unit income adjusted for family size.

C. WAGE AND LABOR-FORCE PARTICIPATION SIMULATION (TABLE 11, COLUMN 4)

As described in the previous section, I first simulate an 8 percent wage increase for the bottom four wage quintiles and a 4 percent wage increase for the top quintile, using the 2007 data. Call this wage-simulated earnings. I then add together all of the members of each family unit and calculate their new simulated income levels with these wage-simulated earnings. I calculate simulated per person income based on simulated family-unit income adjusted for family size.

Next, I take both my 1979 and 2007 samples and divide males into five education groups.[2] For both 1979 and 2007, I calculate average labor-force participation rates for men in each education level. Using the 2007 wage-simulated data, I also calculate median earnings among male workers in each education group based on their wage-simulated earnings.

My goal is to re-create the 1979 labor-force participation rates in the 2007 data. Within each education group, I randomly select males who did not work at all in 2007 and make them workers by assigning them the median 2007 simulated earnings among workers in their education group. I continue to turn nonworkers into workers until the simulated 2007 labor-force participation rate among males in each educational group is equal to the 1979 labor-force participation rate among men in that educational group. I then recombine the men into their family units and calculate simulated family income with the higher labor-force participation rates and earnings among men, as well as the wage-simulated earnings from any women in the household, government income, and other unearned income. I calculate simulated per person income based on simulated family income adjusted for family size.

D. INVESTMENT SIMULATION (TABLE 11, COLUMN 5)

I define investment income as income from retirement, rent, dividends, or interest. In 2007, the ratio of the mean of family-size-adjusted family investment income to the mean of family-size-adjusted total income was 0.0629. In the simulations, I reduce this ratio to 0.05, by multiplying family-size-adjusted investment income by 0.7841. I create simulated total family income by adding the simulated lower-investment income to actual other unearned income, government income, and earnings in the family in 2007. I calculate simulated per person income based on simulated family income adjusted for family size.

E. MARRIAGE-INCREASE SIMULATION (TABLE 12)

In this simulation, I decrease the number of people in single-headed families in the bottom half of the income distribution of single-headed families by 20 percent. I assume that the heads of these single-headed families each marry a person from the sample of single individuals. For every "newly married" female head of a single-headed family, I decrease the number of male single individuals in the bottom half of the single-individual income distribution by one (and vice versa for single-male-headed family heads). I increase the number of persons in married couples in the bottom half of the married-couple income distribution by enough to keep the population constant

To do this, I first take the 2007 sample of all eighteen- to sixty-four-year-old persons and separate them into three family types: those living in single-person family units, single-headed family units, and married-couple family units. Using the family-size adjusted family income distribution within each family type, I separate the three samples into the top and bottom half of the distribution. I do not disturb the weights on people in the top half of the income distribution within any family type. I multiply the weights on people in the bottom half of the distribution of income among single-headed families by 0.8 to decrease the number of people in these families by 20 percent.

I then need to reduce the number of single individuals by an equivalent amount to adjust for the fact that the reduction in single-family heads occurs because each of these heads marries a single individual. Among all eighteen- to sixty-four-year-olds, I calculate the proportion who are male heads of single-headed family units and are in the bottom half of the single-headed family unit income distribution. Call this proportion *SHM*. Next, I calculate, among all eighteen- to sixty-four-year-olds, the proportion of persons who are female heads of single-headed families and in the bottom half of the single-headed family income distribution in 2007. Call this proportion *SHF*. Among all eighteen- to sixty-four-year-olds, I then calculate the proportion who are male single individuals and in the bottom half of the single individual income distribution. Call this proportion *SIM*. The share who are female single individuals in the bottom half of the single-person income distribution is *SIF*. I multiply the weights of all male single individuals by *(SIM − SHF /5) / SIM*. This decreases the number of male single individuals in the bottom half of the income distribution by one for every female head of a single-headed family that was removed into the married category. (The division by five reflects the fact that only one-fifth of these individuals are moved into the married category.) I do a symmetric procedure to deflate the weights of female single individuals, estimating *(SIF − SHM / 5) / SIF*.

Finally, I need to increase the population in married-couple families. Among all eighteen- to sixty-four-year-olds, I calculate the proportion who live in married-couple families and are in the bottom half of the married-couple family income distribution. Among all eighteen- to sixty-four-year-olds, I also calculate the proportion who live in single-headed families and are in the bottom half of the single-headed family income distribution. Let's call these proportions *MCP* and *SHP*. Realize that *SHM + SHF* is the proportion of the population that heads a single-headed family in the bottom 50 percent of the single-headed family income distribution; that is, it is the proportion of *heads* within these families rather than the proportion of all persons. By design, *(SHM + SHF) / 5* is the proportion of the population that is "married off" from among the sample of single individuals, since I eliminate one single individual for each single-family head who is eliminated, and I eliminate one-fifth of all single-family heads. In order to inflate the weight of all people in married-couple families in the bottom half of the married-couple family distribution, I multiply their weights by $[(MCP + SHM + SHF) / 5 + SHP / 5] / MCP$. This increases the population weights on persons in married-couple families in the bottom half of the distribution by the population weights of those whom I am "marrying off" from among the population of single individuals and persons in single-headed families. The result is an increase in the population in the bottom half of the married-couple distribution that is identically equal to the decline in the population among single individuals and single-headed families.

F. EXPANDED REDISTRIBUTION SIMULATIONS (TABLE 13)

In the first simulation (column 3 of table 13), I define all poor families with at least one person who worked one thousand hours or more as a working poor family. I increase the income of all these working poor families up to the poverty line to provide a simulated family income level. (Poverty lines are defined by family size and number of children, so the amount of additional income needed will depend upon each family's size and composition.) I calculate simulated per person income based on simulated family income adjusted for family size.

In the second simulation (column 4 of table 13), I increase the income of all poor families with at least one child under the age of eighteen up to their poverty line to provide a simulated family income level. I then calculate simulated per person income based on simulated family income adjusted for family size.

In the third simulation (column 5 of table 13), I increase the income of all families whose total family income is below the poverty line up to their poverty line to provide a simulated family income level. I then calculate simulated per person income based on simulated family income adjusted for family size.

NOTES

1. Alesina, Di Tella, and McCulloch (2004); but see Page and Jacobs (2009), who argue that Americans are upset by current large economic inequities.

2. For a summary of this research, see Aghion, Caroli, and García-Peñalosa (1999).

3. Indeed, the Kuznets hypothesis does not hold for all developing countries, either. Acemoglu and Robinson (2002) and Lundberg and Squire (2003) provide two recent explorations of this issue.

CHAPTER ONE

1. For the most recent contributions to this literature, see Autor, Katz, and Kearney (2008) and Lemieux (2008). Goldin and Katz (2008) summarize the conclusions of the last three decades of work on the causes and consequences of growing wage inequality.

2. Aslaksen, Wennemo, and Aaberge (2005) do a nice job of this type of analysis using Norwegian data.

3. Cancian and Reed (1999) provide an earlier look at this question.

4. Daly and Valletta (2006); Burtless (1999); Martin (2006); Thomas and Sawhill (2005).

5. In 1979, this was known as the Annual Demographic Survey.

6. Heathcote, Perri and Violante (2010) compare data over time on income and income inequality from the CPS and from the Panel Study of Income Dynamics (PSID), and find that the results are similar.

7. Although eighteen- to sixty-four-year-old persons compose my sample, when I calculate family income for these persons, I include income received by elderly members of the family unit because I expect this income to be shared among all family members. Similarly, children and the elderly are included when I calculate a family unit's size.

8. With this analysis, I ignore cohabitation and consider cohabitants to be in separate family units. Although the CPS makes it relatively easy to identify cohabitants in 2007, it is not possible to do this in 1979. Cohabitants share income, but to a lesser degree than do married couples (Kenney, 2003; Oropesa, Landale, and Kenkre, 2003; DeLeire and Kalil 2005; Treas and De Ruijter, 2008).

9. In order to protect the confidentiality of CPS respondents, the Census Bureau "top-codes" the income of persons at the very top of the distribution of each type of income. Prior to the 1996 survey, this meant that all individuals with an income above a certain censoring point would be assigned an income equal to the value of that point. For example, the censoring point for income from interest in the 1980 survey was $50,000. There were only fourteen CPS respondents who made $50,000 or more in interest in 1979, so these individuals could conceivably be identified by researchers if their actual income from interest was published. Therefore, in public-use files, each of these individuals was assigned an income of $50,000. In surveys that took place in 1996 or later, the Census Bureau instead assigned all top-coded individuals the mean income among those who were top-coded. This change improved the accuracy of income data, but it introduced a discontinuity that affects the measurement of inequality if not addressed.

10. An appendix indicating the specific variables that have been adjusted for top-coding and how this adjustment was done is available from the author upon request.

11. Specifically, we first calculate each individual's total earnings.

If total earnings are less than zero, we set earnings to zero. In 1979, the CPS reports the sum of net rental income and income from dividends. If this total is less than zero, then we set it to zero. In 2007, the CPS codes net rental income as its own variable. If net rental income is less than zero in 2007, we set it to zero. In all, 1.6 percent (0.7 percent) of adults above the age of seventeen had either negative earnings or negative rental income in 1979 (2007). In both years, negative net rental income was more common than negative earnings. In all, 3.6 percent (1.4 percent) of persons lived in a family where at least one person had negative earnings or negative net rental income in 1979 (2007). The conclusions in this book are not affected by these calculations.

12. For others who use this type of adjustment, see Atkinson (2003) and Daly and Valetta (2006). The alternative family-size adjustment used most commonly in the U.S. is the equivalence scales embedded in the official U.S. measure of poverty. These are problematic, however (Ruggles, 1990), and I prefer the simpler adjustment of dividing by the square root of family size. Fernández-Villaverde and Krueger (2007) compare six equivalence scales. They suggest using the mean of these six scales, which is very close to the equivalence scale used in this analysis.

13. Gottschalk and Smeeding (2000).

CHAPTER TWO

1. Defined as the percent of civilian women ages eighteen to sixty-four who worked for at least one hour over the course of the year.

2. Appendix 1 contains appendix figures A-1 through A-3. These present the information in figures 1 through 3 in a different way, showing mean earnings and earnings components at each decile in their distribution. These appendix figures make it clearer whether changes in the 50/10 ratio are the result of changes in the median or changes at the tenth percentile. Similarly, they also help to interpret changes in the 90/50 ratio.

3. Of course, this share has not declined as much as one might have expected it would in 1979. The trend toward increased college attendance slowed markedly after the mid-1970s, and increased immigra-

tion has renewed the pool of less-skilled workers. Nonetheless, the share of less-skilled workers in the labor market has declined, particularly among females.

4. For instance, see Goldin and Katz (2008) for a review of the research on skill-biased technological change. See Krugman (2008) for an argument about the effects of trade. See Freeman (2007) for a discussion of related institutional changes in the labor market.

5. Borjas (2006) shows the rise in the share of immigrants among lower-wage workers. However, Card (2009) indicates that immigration accounts for only 5 percent of the rise in U.S. wage inequality between 1980 and 2000.

6. Because both the ninetieth percentile and the median of reported weeks of work is fifty-two for men and women, the 90/50 ratio is one for all groups.

7. For instance, Juhn (1992) suggests that much of the decline in labor-force participation among less-educated men from the early 1970s to the late 1980s was due to their declining wages. On the other hand, there is remarkably little evidence that changes in female labor supply have resulted in noticeable changes in the distribution of male wages (Blank and Gelbach, 2006).

8. This is consistent with the results in Heathcote, Perri, and Violante (2010), who emphasize the importance of labor-force participation changes to changes in earnings.

CHAPTER THREE

1. The complete set of government income sources includes Social Security, Supplemental Security Income, public assistance or welfare, unemployment benefits (which include unemployment compensation, Supplemental Unemployment Benefits, and union unemployment or strike benefits), payments from the Veterans Administration, and workers' compensation payments. The CPS does not measure unemployment and worker's compensation payments that come from the government separately from those that come from unions or employers, so small amounts of nongovernment income may be included in the measure of income from government programs.

2. The complete set of other income sources includes income from interest, dividends, net from rent (including estates, trusts, and royalties), pension or retirement income other than Social Security and VA benefits, child support and alimony payments, regular financial assistance from friends and relatives outside the household, and other income not covered by specific CPS questions. In 2007, the set of other income sources also includes educational assistance (other than Pell Grants) and disability income and survivors' income (other than Social Security and VA benefits). Capital gains (or losses) are not included in this income definition.

3. There is one exception to this. If a cohabitant lives with the parent of his/her own children, the household will consist of a single-parent household and a single individual. In this case, the single individual would actually be living with related children. Unfortunately, I cannot identify this situation in the 1979 data.

4. For each figure, deciles are calculated using the *overall* income distribution, so someone in the second decile of income in the graph of single individuals has an amount of income available to her that is similar to that of someone in the second decile of income in the graph of married-couple families.

5. For a discussion of the effects of welfare reform on public assistance receipt, work, and earnings, see Blank (2002).

6. The figures in appendix 2 (figures A-4, A-5, A-6, and A-7) present the information in figures 6, 7, 8, and 10 in a different way, showing mean income and income components at each decile in their distribution. These appendix figures make it clearer whether changes in the 50/10 ratio are the result of changes in the median or changes at the tenth percentile. Similarly, they also help to interpret changes in the 90/50 ratio.

7. Whereas table 5 shows the overall change in inequality over the 1979–2007 period, Burkhauser et al. (2008) look at time trends in inequality from 1973 through 2004. (However, estimated inequality in their study is based on household income, not individual income.) Though the increase in inequality slows after 1993, they document a trend toward increasing inequality throughout the period.

8. In 1979, single mothers with children made up 66 percent of sin-

gle-headed family units; by 2007 they made up only 56 percent. This reflects both a small increase in male single-headed families with children and a larger increase in single-headed family units (headed by both men and women) without children under age eighteen.

9. The number of persons in single-headed family units with very low incomes (less than $5,000 per year) did not fall as much as did the number in such units with slightly higher incomes. This is consistent with other evidence that shows a group of "disconnected mothers" following welfare reform who have left welfare but who are not working steadily. While incomes increased on average for single-mother families following welfare reform, this group was worse off (Blank and Kovak, 2009).

10. For instance, see Juhn and Murphy (1997); Pencavel (2006); Aslaksen, Wennemo, and Aaberge (2005); Ahituv and Lerman (2007).

11. The data in figure 9 are based only on the husbands and wives who head married-couple family units and exclude any other adults in these family units. The graphs in figure 9 are updated versions of the graphs shown in Juhn and Murphy (1997).

12. In both years, note that women's labor-force participation has an overall equalizing effect on income distribution, since the difference in earnings among women with high- and low-earning husbands is less than the difference in their husbands' earnings. This is particularly true in 1979, when wives of high-earning husbands were less likely to work than wives of low-earning husbands. One message from figure 9 is that the equalizing effect of wives' labor supply has been declining over time, pushing up inequality.

13. These statistics are calculated for my sample of eighteen- to sixty-four-year-old adults and refer only to education levels among married couples in which one spouse is the head of the household. They exclude the small number of married couples who live in households headed by some other individual (often an older relative).

CHAPTER FOUR

1. The family-size simulation is not precise; there is a very small difference in simulated family size relative to the actual 1979 number.

As appendix 3 indicates, we approximate the 1979 family-size distribution. There is a small residual change in family size after this simulation, but it rounds to zero.

2. Blank (2009).

3. Edin and Reed (2005).

4. In this discussion, I ignore any behavioral shifts created by these tax changes. Alm, Lee, and Wallace (2005) find that tax changes between 1978 and 1998 increased inequality; Leiserson and Rohaly (2008) find a further increase in inequality due to tax changes between 2001 and 2008. Strudler, Petska, and Petska (2005) find that federal taxes become less progressive between 1979 and 2002. There is much less research on the long-term distributional trends in state and local taxes. McIntyre et. al. (2003) find that state and local taxes became more regressive between 1989 and 2002.

5. Medicaid, the public health-care program for low-income families, is also an in-kind program. I do not deal with it in this discussion because it is very difficult to monetize the value of public health care and add it to income as if it provided equivalent dollars.

6. Over the last decade, Kim and Lambert (2009) show that government benefits (both cash and noncash) have about the same redistributive effects in 2004 as in 1994.

7. See Blanchflower and Oswald (2004); Stevenson and Wolfers (2008).

8. Jacobs and Newman (2008); Fullerton and Wallace (2007).

9. Dynan, Elmendorf, and Sichel (2008), Hacker and Jacobs (2008), Nichols and Zimmerman (2008), and Jensen and Shore (2008). For an exception, see Congressional Budget Office (2008). Nichols and Zimmerman do a particularly nice job of reconciling different estimates across these research papers, showing that the magnitude by which volatility has risen is dependent upon the data sample and the measure of volatility.

CHAPTER FIVE

1. For a description of the events leading to this economic collapse, see Baily, Litan, and Johnson (2008).

2. For an excellent discussion of the potential effects of civil war on

human and physical capital and on institutional changes, see Blattman and Miguel (2010). Much of their discussion focuses on civil wars in developing countries, however.

3. Piketty and Saez (2003).

4. Blattman and Miguel (2010).

5. Lee (2005).

6. Hearst, Newman, and Hulley (1986); Angrist (1990); Angrist and Krueger (1994); Angrist (1998).

7. Garrett (2009).

8. Goldin and Katz (2008).

9. Goldin and Katz (2008).

10. Williamson and Lindert (1980).

11. Goldin and Margo (1992); Goldin and Katz (2008).

12. Danziger and Gottschalk (1993).

13. Heathcote, Perri, and Violante (2010) indicate that inequality rose slightly in recessions in the post–World War II period in the United States, but the effect is small.

14. For instance, see Munro (2009), who argues that past claims that the Black Death raised wages are wrong. Bell and Lewis (2005) summarize other research on the economic effects of the plague.

15. Garrett (2009).

16. Almond (2006).

17. Basu, Gupta, and Krishna (1997); Bloom and Mahal (1997).

18. Bell and Lewis (2005). The only research I could find on the distributional impact of AIDS is Cogneau and Grimm (2008) who claim that AIDS has had few distributional effects in Côte d'Ivoire.

19. The World Health Organization, on their website "Epidemic and Pandemic Alert and Response," notes evidence that the risks of a global flu epidemic have increased (accessed February 2009, http://www.who.int/csr/disease/avian_influenza/avian_faqs/en/#areall).

20. Katz and Autor (1999).

21. Card and DiNardo (2006).

22. Autor, Katz, and Kearney (2008).

23. Schultz (2002).

24. Heckman and Masterov (2007).

25. Card and Krueger (1992).

26. The authors note, however, that frontier size and strength of political institutions do not appear to be independent.

27. Atkinson and Piketty (2007).

28. Card and Krueger (1992); Aaronson and Bhashkar (2009).

29. Bound and Turner (2002).

30. Mancur Olsen (1982) notes that self-interested coalitions, once they are formed, seek to manipulate the political process to increase their share of the economic rewards, often in ways that may be costly to society as a whole.

CHAPTER SIX

1. For a statement of the argument for increased marriage as a way to improve economic opportunities for lower-income families, see Haskins (2005).

2. Smeeding (2006).

3. Note that the poverty line varies with family size and composition. Poverty is determined at the family level, based on the income shared among all family members. Except for its treatment of foster children, my definition of family is identical to that used to calculate poverty. In these simulations, I raise all families below the poverty line to an income level equal to the poverty line and then recalculate per person income. See appendix 4 for more details.

4. Of course, if one provided greater support to poor families, there would be an incentive for near-poor families to reduce their work effort and receive more public assistance. I do not take account of this effect in these simulations. This would increase the number of relatively lower-income families and offset some of the equalizing gains shown in this simulation.

CHAPTER SEVEN

1. The largest growth in redistributive programs has occurred in Medicaid, providing health insurance for a subset of persons in low-income families. Most of the growth in spending in Medicaid, however, has occurred not because of legislated expansions in the program

(although Medicaid coverage for children has expanded) but because of unforeseen changes in the cost and type of medical services provided. Indeed, several legislative efforts have tried (with only some success) to control costs in Medicaid.

APPENDIX ONE

1. According to Wikipedia, *permillage* is the appropriate word to use to reference one one-thousandth of the distribution, just as *percentile* references one one-hundredth of a distribution.

2. Realize that this simulation does not hold the interaction between wages and hours constant within each gender and education group. If the correlation between the distribution of wages and hours has shifted over time within these groups, this simulation allows this shift to occur. So, if higher-wage workers work more hours relative to lower-wage workers in 2007 than they did in 1979, more of them will be matched with the high-hour 1979 permillages. For this reason, this simulation cannot be interpreted strictly as showing what happens if only the distribution of wages shifts; it allows certain wage/hours interactions to shift as well.

3. I do this calculation by skill level because there are quite different patterns of change in female labor supply among more- and less-educated women over this period. Specifically, the rate of increase in labor-force participation was greater among more-educated women, and I want my simulation of the 1979 hours distribution to restore the relationship between education and labor-force participation to its 1979 pattern.

APPENDIX FOUR

1. When calculating these quintiles, I exclude nonworkers.

2. These categories are the same shown in part A of table 10 and include education levels that are less than high school, exactly high school, some college (i.e., some post–high school training, but less than a four-year degree), a four-year college degree, and more than a four-year college degree.

REFERENCES

Aaronson, Daniel, and Bhashkar Mazumder. 2009. "The Impact of Rosenwald Schools on Black Achievement." Federal Reserve Bank of Chicago Working Paper WP 2009-26. Chicago, IL: Federal Reserve Bank of Chicago.

Acemoglu, Daron, and James A. Robinson. 2002. "The Political Economy of the Kuznets Curve." *Review of Development Economics* 6 (2): 183–203.

Aghion, Philippe, Eve Cároli, and Cecilia García-Peñalosa. 1999. "Inequality and Economic Growth: The Perspective of the New Growth Theories." *Journal of Economic Literature* 37 (4) :1615–1660.

Aguiar, Mark, and Eric Hurst. 2007. "Measuring Trends in Leisure: The Allocation of Time over Five Decades." *Quarterly Journal of Economics* 122 (3): 969–1006.

———. 2009. *The Increase in Leisure Inequality: 1965–2005.* Washington, DC: AEI Press.

Ahituv, Avner, and Robert I. Lerman. 2007. "How Do Marital Status, Work Effort and Wage Rates Interact?" *Demography* 44 (3): 623–647.

Alesina, Alberto, Rafael Di Tella, and Robert McCulloch. 2004. "Inequality and Happiness: Are Europeans and American Different?" *Journal of Public Economics* 88 (9–10): 2009–2042.

Alm, James, Fitzroy Lee, and Sally Wallace. 2005. "How Fair? Changes in Federal Income Taxation and the Distribution of Income, 1978 to 1998." *Journal of Policy Analysis and Management* 24 (1): 5–22.

Almond, Douglas, Jr. 2006. "Is the 1918 Influenza Pandemic Over? Long-Term Effects of *In Utero* Influenza Exposure in the Post-1940 U.S. Population." *Journal of Political Economy* 114 (4): 672–712.

Angrist, Joshua D. 1990. "Lifetime Earnings and the Vietnam Era Draft Lottery: Evidence from Social Security Administrative Records." *American Economic Review* 80 (3): 313–336.

———. 1998. "Estimating the Labor Market Impact of Voluntary Military Service Using Social Security Data on Military Applicants." *Econometrica* 66 (20): 249–288.

Angrist, Joshua D., and Alan B. Krueger. 1994. "Why Do World War II Veterans Earn More than Nonveterans?" *Journal of Labor Economics* 12 (1): 74–97.

Aslaksen, Iulie, Tom Wennemo, and Rolf Aaberge. 2005. "'Birds of a Feather Flock Together': The Impact of Choice of Spouse on Family Labor Income Inequality." *LABOUR* 19 (3): 491–515.

Atkinson, A. B. 2003. "Income Inequality in OECD Countries: Data and Explanations." *CESifo Economic Studies* 49 (4): 479–515.

Atkinson, A. B., and Thomas Piketty, eds. 2007. *Top Incomes over the Twentieth Century: A Contrast between European and English Speaking Countries.* Oxford: Oxford University Press.

Autor, David H., Lawrence F. Katz, and Melissa S. Kearney. 2008. "Trends in U.S. Wage Inequality: Revising the Revisionists." *Review of Economics and Statistics* 90 (2): 300–323.

Bailey, Martha J. 2010. "'Momma's Got the Pill': How Anthony Comstock and *Griswold v. Connecticut* Shaped U.S. Childbearing." *American Economic Review* 100 (1): 98–129.

Baily, Martin Neil, Robert E. Litan, and Matthew S. Johnson. 2008. "The Origins of the Financial Crisis." Initiative on Business and Public Policy, Fixing Finance Series, Paper 3. Washington, DC: Brookings Institution. www.brookings.edu/~/media/Files/rc/papers/2008/11_origins_crisis_baily_litan/11_origins_crisis_baily_litan.pdf.

Barro, Robert J. 2000. "Inequality and Growth in a Panel of Countries." *Journal of Economic Growth* 5 (1): 5–32.

Basu, Alaka M., Devendra B. Gupta, and Geetanjali Krishna. 1997. "The Household Impact of Adult Morbidity and Mortality: Some Implications of the Potential Epidemic of AIDS in India." In *The Economics of HIV and AIDS: The Case of South and South East Asia*, ed. David E. Bloom and Peter Godwin, 102–154. Oxford: Oxford University Press.

Bell, Clive, and Maureen Lewis. 2004. "The Economic Implications of Epidemics Old and New." *World Economics* 5 (4): 137–174.

Blanchflower, David G., and Andrew J. Oswald. 2004. "Well-Being over Time in Britain and the U.S.A." *Journal of Public Economics* 88 (7–8): 1359–1386.

Blank, Rebecca M. 2002. "Evaluating Welfare Reform in the U.S." *Journal of Economic Literature*, 40 (4): 1105–1166.

———. 2006. "What Did the 1990s Welfare Reforms Accomplish?" In *Public Policy and the Income Distribution*, ed. Alan J. Auerbach, David Card, and John M. Quigley, 33–79. New York: Russell Sage Foundation.

———. 2009. "What We Know, What We Don't Know, and What We Need to Know about Welfare Reform." In *Welfare Reform and Its Long-Term Consequences for America's Poor*, ed. James Ziliak. Cambridge: Cambridge University Press.

Blank, Rebecca M., and Jonah Gelbach. 2006. "Are Less-Educated Women Crowding Less-Educated Men Out of the Labor Market?" In *Black Males Left Behind*, ed. Ronald B. Mincy, 87–120. Washington, DC: Urban Institute Press.

Blank, Rebecca M., and Brian Kovak. 2009. "The Growing Problem of Disconnected Single Mothers." In *Making the Work-Based Safety Net Work Better: Forward Looking Policies to Help Low-Income Families*, ed. Carolyn J. Heinrich and John Karl Scholz, 227–258. New York: Russell Sage Foundation.

Blank, Rebecca M., and Heidi Shierholz. 2006. "Exploring Gender Differences in Employment and Wage Trends among Less-Skilled Workers." In *Working and Poor: How Economic and Policy Changes Are Affecting Low-Wage Workers*, ed. Rebecca M. Blank, Sheldon H. Danziger, and Robert F. Schoeni, 1–20. New York: Russell Sage Foundation.

Blattman, Christopher, and Edward Miguel. 2010. "Civil War." *Journal of Economic Literature* 48 (1): 3–57.

Blau, Francine D., and Lawrence M. Kahn. 1997. "Swimming Upstream: Trends in the Gender Wage Differential in the 1980s." *Journal of Labor Economics* 15 (1, pt. 1): 1–42.

———. 2006. "The U.S. Gender Pay Gap in the 1990s: Slowing Convergence." *Industrial and Labor Relations Review* 60 (1): 45–66.

Bleakley, Hoyt. 2010. "Malaria Eradication in the Americas: A Retrospective Analysis of Childhood Exposure." *American Economic Journal: Applied Economics* 2 (2): 1–45.

Bloom, David E., and Ajay S. Mahal. 1997. "AIDS, Flu, and the Black Death: Impacts on Economic Growth and Well-Being." In *The Economics of HIV and AIDS*, ed. David E. Bloom and Peter Godwin, 22–52. Oxford: Oxford University Press.

Borjas, George J. 2006. "Wage Trends among Disadvantaged Minorities." In *Working and Poor: How Economic and Policy Changes Are Affecting Low-Wage Workers*, ed. Rebecca M. Blank, Sheldon H. Danziger, and Robert F. Schoeni, 59–86. New York: Russell Sage Foundation.

Bound, John, and Sarah Turner. 2002. "Going to War and Going to College: Did World War II and the G.I. Bill Increase Educational Attainment for Returning Veterans?" *Journal of Labor Economics* 20 (4): 784–815.

Burkhauser, Richard V., Shuaizhang Feng, Stephen P. Jenkins, and Jeff Larrimore. 2008. "Estimating Trends in U.S. Income Inequality Using the Current Population Survey: The Importance of Controlling for Censoring." NBER Working Paper 14247. Cambridge, MA: National Bureau of Economic Research.

Burtless, Gary. 1999. "Effects of Growing Wage Disparities and Changing Family Composition on the U.S. Income Distribution." *European Economic Review* 43 (4–6): 853–865.

Cancian, Maria, and Deborah Reed. 1999. "The Impact of Wives' Earnings on Income Inequality: Issues and Estimates." *Demography* 36 (2): 173–184.

Card, David. 2009. "Immigration and Inequality." *American Economic Review* 99 (2): 1–21.

Card, David, and John DiNardo. 2006. "The Impact of Technological Change on Low-Wage Workers: A Review." In *Working and Poor*, ed. Rebecca M. Blank, Sheldon H. Danziger, and Robert F. Schoeni, 113–140. New York: Russell Sage Foundation.

Card, David, and Alan B. Krueger. 1992. "School Quality and Black-White Relative Earnings: A Direct Assessment." *Quarterly Journal of Economics* 107 (1): 151–200.

Cogneau, Denis, and Michael Grimm. 2008. "The Impact of AIDS Mortality on the Distribution of Income in Côte d'Ivoire." *Journal of African Economies* 17 (5): 688–728.

Congressional Budget Office. 2008. "Recent Trends in the Variability of Individual Earnings and Household Income." CBO Paper. Washington, DC: CBO.

Daly, Mary C., and Robert G. Valletta. 2006. "Inequality and Poverty in the United States: The Effects of Rising Dispersion of Men's Earnings and Changing Family Behaviour." *Economica* 73 (289): 75–98.

Danziger, Sheldon, and Peter Gottschalk, eds. 1993. *Uneven Tides: Rising Inequality in America.* New York: Russell Sage Foundation.

David, Paul A. 1990. "The Dynamo and the Computer: An Historical Perspective on the Modern Productivity Paradox." *American Economic Review* 80 (2): 355–361.

Davis, Bob, and David Wessell. 1998. *Prosperity: The Coming 20-Year Boom and What It Means to You.* New York: Random House.

DeLeire, Thomas, and Ariel Kalil. 2005. "How Do Cohabiting Couples with Children Spend Their Money?" *Journal of Marriage and Family* 67 (2): 286–295.

Dynan, Karen E., Douglas W. Elmendorf, and Daniel E. Sichel. 2008. "The Evolution of Household Income Volatility." Working paper. Washington, DC: Brookings Institution. www.brookings.edu/~/media/Files/rc/papers/2008/02_useconomics_elmendorf/02_useconomics_elmendorf.pdf.

Edin, Kathryn, and Joanna M. Reed. 2005. "Why Don't They Just Get Married? Barriers to Marriage among the Disadvantaged." *Future of Children* 15 (2): 117–137.

Farber, Henry S. 2008. "Short(er) Shrift: The Decline in Worker-Firm Attachment in the United States." In *Laid Off, Laid Low: Political and*

Economic Consequences of Economic Insecurity, ed. Katherine S. Newman, 10–37. New York: Columbia University Press.

Fernández-Villaverde, Jesús, and Dirk Krueger. 2007. "Consumption over the Life Cycle: Facts from Consumer Expenditure Survey Data." *Review of Economics and Statistics* 89 (3): 552–565.

Freeman, Richard B. 2004. "What, Me Vote?" In *Social Inequality,* ed. Kathryn M. Neckerman, 703–728. New York: Russell Sage Foundation.

———. 2007. *America Works: The Exceptional U.S. Labor Market.* New York: Russell Sage Foundation.

Friedman, Milton, and Rose Friedman. 1979. *Free to Choose.* New York: Harcourt, Brace, Jovanovich.

Fullerton, Andrew S., and Michael Wallace. 2007. "Traversing the Flexible Turn: U.S. Workers' Perceptions of Job Security, 1977–2002." *Social Science Research* 36 (1): 201–221.

García-Jimeno, Camilo, and James A. Robinson. 2011. "The Myth of the Frontier." In *Understanding Long-Run Economic Growth: Essays in Honor of Kenneth Sokoloff,* ed. Dora L. Costa and Naomi R. Lamoreaux. Chicago: University of Chicago Press.

Garrett, Thomas A. 2009. "War and Pestilence as Labor Market Shocks: U.S. Manufacturing Wage Growth, 1914–1919." *Economic Inquiry,* 47 (4): 711–725.

Glaeser, Edward L., Matthew G. Resseger, and Kristina Tobio. 2008. "Urban Inequality." NBER Working Paper 14419. Cambridge, MA: National Bureau of Economic Research.

Goldin, Claudia, and Lawrence F. Katz. 2008. *The Race between Education and Technology.* Cambridge, MA: Belknap Press of Harvard University Press.

Goldin, Claudia, and Robert A. Margo. 1992. "The Great Compression: The Wage Structure in the United States at Mid-Century." *Quarterly Journal of Economics* 107 (1): 1–34.

Gottschalk, Peter, and Sheldon Danziger. 2005. "Inequality of Wage Rates, Earnings, and Family Income in the United States, 1975–2002." *Review of Income and Wealth* 51 (2): 231–254.

Gottschalk, Peter, and Timothy M. Smeeding. 2000. "Empirical Evidence on Income Inequality in Industrialized Countries." In *Handbook of Income Distribution,* ed. A.B. Atkinson and F. Bourguignon, 1:261–307. Amsterdam: Elsevier.

Hacker, Jacob S., and Elisabeth Jacobs. 2008. "The Rising Instability of American Family Incomes, 1969–2004: Evidence from the Panel Study of Income Dynamics." EPI Briefing Paper no. 213. Washington, DC: Economic Policy Institute.

Haskins, Ron. 2005. Testimony to the District of Columbia Subcommittee of the Committee on Appropriations in the U.S. Senate. October 6, 2005. www.brookings.edu/~/media/Files/rc/testimonies/2005/1006childrenfamilies_haskins/20051006.pdf

Hearst, Norman, Thomas B. Newman, and Stephen B. Hulley. 1986. "Delayed Effects of the Military Draft on Mortality: A Randomized Natural Experiment." *New England Journal of Medicine* 314 (10): 640–624.

Heathcote, Jonathan, Fabrizio Perri, and Giovanni L. Violante. 2010. "Unequal We Stand: An Empirical Analysis of Economic Inequality in the United States, 1967–2006." *Review of Economic Dynamics* 13 (1): 15–51.

Heckman, James J., and Dimitriy V. Masterov. 2007. "The Productivity Argument for Investing in Young Children," *Review of Agricultural Economics* 29 (3): 446–493.

Heclo, Hugh. 1986. "The Political Foundations of Antipoverty Policy." In *Fighting Poverty: What Works and What Doesn't,* ed. Sheldon H. Danziger and Daniel H. Weinberg, 325–340. Cambridge, MA: Harvard University Press.

Jacobs, Elisabeth, and Katherine S. Newman. 2008. "Rising Angst? Change and Stability in Perceptions of Economic Insecurity." In *Laid Off, Laid Low: Political and Economic Consequences of Economic Insecurity,* ed. Katherine S. Newman, 74–101. New York: Columbia University Press.

Jäntti, Markus, Bernt Bratsberg, Knut Røed, Oddbjørn Raaum, Robin Naylor, Eva Österbacka, Anders Björklund, and Tor Eriksson. 2006. "American Exceptionalism in a New Light: A Comparison of International Earnings Mobility in the Nordic Countries, the United

Kingdom and the United States." IZA Discussion Paper 1938. Bonn, Germany: Institute for the Study of Labor (IZA).

Jensen, Shane T., and Stephen H. Shore. 2008. "Changes in the Distribution of Income Volatility." *arXiv*:0808.1090v1. Technical Report. http://arxiv.org/PS_cache/arxiv/pdf/0808/0808.1090v1.pdf.

Juhn, Chinhui. 1992. "Decline of Male Labor Market Participation: The Role of Declining Market Opportunities." *Quarterly Journal of Economics* 107 (1): 79–121.

Juhn, Chinhui, and Kevin M. Murphy. 1997. "Wage Inequality and Family Labor Supply." *Journal of Labor Economics* 15 (1): 72–97.

Karoly, Lynn A. 1996. "Anatomy of the US Income Distribution: Two Decades of Change." *Oxford Review of Economic Policy* 12 (1): 76–95.

Katz, Lawrence F., and David H. Autor. 1999. "Changes in the Wage Structure and Earnings Inequality." In *Handbook of Labor Economics*, ed. Orley C. Ashenfelter and David Card, 3A:1463–1555. Amsterdam: Elsevier.

Kenney, Catherine. 2003. "Hardship in Married and Cohabiting Parent Households: Do Cohabiting Parents Underinvest in Household Public Goods." Center for Research on Children and Wellbeing Working Paper no. 03–11-FF. Princeton, NJ: Princeton University. http://crcw.princeton.edu/workingpapers/WP03-11-FF-Kenney.pdf.

Kim, Kinam, and Peter J. Lambert. 2009. "Redistributive Effect of U.S. Taxes and Public Transfers, 1994–2004." *Public Finance Review* 37 (1): 3–26.

Krugman, Paul R. 2008. "Trade and Wages, Reconsidered." *Brookings Papers on Economic Activity* 2008 (1): 103–143.

Larrimore, Jeff, Richard V. Burkhauser, Shuaizhang Feng, and Laura Zayatz. 2008. "Consistent Cell Means for Topcoded Incomes in the Public Use March CPS (1976–2007)." *Journal of Economic and Social Measurement* 33 (2–3): 89–128.

Lee, Chulhee. 2005. "Wealth Accumulation and the Health of Union Army Veterans, 1860–1870." *Journal of Economic History* 65 (2): 352–385.

Leiserson, Greg, and Jeffrey Rohaly. 2008. "Distribution of the 2001–2006 Tax Cuts: Updated Projections, July 2008." Tax Policy Center Working Paper. Washington, DC: Urban Institute and Brookings

Institution. www.taxpolicycenter.org/UploadedPDF/411739_tax_cuts.pdf.

Lemieux, Thomas. 2008. "The Changing Nature of Wage Inequality." *Journal of Population Economics* 21 (1): 21–48.

———. 2010. "What Do We Really Know about Changes in Wage Inequality?" In *Labor in the New Economy,* ed. Katharine G. Abraham, James R. Spletzer, and Michael Harper, 17–59. Chicago: University of Chicago Press.

Lundberg, Mattias, and Lyn Squire. 2003. "The Simultaneous Evolution of Growth and Inequality." *Economic Journal* 113 (487): 326–344.

Luttmer, Erzo F.P. 2005. "Neighbors as Negatives: Relative Earnings and Well-Being." *Quarterly Journal of Economics* 120 (3): 963–1002.

Martin, Molly A. 2006. "Family Structure and Income Inequality in Families with Children, 1976 to 2000." *Demography* 43 (3): 421–445.

McIntyre, Robert S., Robert Denk, Norton Francis, Matthew Gardner, Will Gomaa, Fiona Hsu, and Richard Sims. 2003. *Who Pays? A Distributional Analysis of the Tax Systems in All 50 States,* 2nd ed. Washington, DC: Institute on Taxation and Economic Policy.

Munro, John. 2009. "Before and after the Black Death: Money, Prices, and Wages in Fourteenth-Century England." In *New Approaches to the History of Late Medieval and Early Modern Europe: Selected Proceedings of Two International Conferences at the Royal Danish Academy of Sciences and Letters in Copenhagen in 1997 and 1999,* ed. Troels Dahlerup and Per Ingesman, 335–364. Copenhagen: Royal Danish Academy of Sciences and Letters.

Nichols, Austin, and Seth Zimmerman. 2008. "Measuring Trends in Income Variability." Urban Institute Working Paper. Washington, DC: Urban Institute. www.urban.org/publications/411688.html.

Olsen, Mancur. 1982. *The Rise and Decline of Nations: Economic Growth, Stagflation, and Social Rigidities.* New Haven, CT: Yale University Press.

Oropesa, R.S., Nancy S. Landale, and Tanya Kenkre. 2003. "Income Allocation in Marital and Cohabiting Unions: The Case of Mainland Puerto Ricans." *Journal of Marriage and Family* 65 (4): 910–926.

Page, Benjamin I., and Lawrence R. Jacobs. 2009. *Class War? What Amer-*

icans Really Think about Economic Inequality. Chicago: University of Chicago Press.

Pencavel, John. 2006. "A Life Cycle Perspective on Changes in Earnings Inequality among Married Men and Women." *Review of Economics and Statistics* 88 (2): 232–242.

Pierce, Brooks. 2010. "Recent Trends in Compensation Inequality." In *Labor in the New Economy,* ed. Katharine G. Abraham, James R. Spletzer, and Michael Harper, 63–98. Chicago: University of Chicago Press.

Piketty, Thomas, and Emmanuel Saez. 2003. "Income Inequality in the United States, 1913–1998." *Quarterly Journal of Economics* 118 (1): 1–39.

———. 2007. "Income and Wage Inequality in the United States, 1913–2002." In *Top Incomes over the Twentieth Century: A Contrast between European and English Speaking Countries,* ed. A. B. Atkinson and Thomas Piketty, 141–225. Oxford: Oxford University Press.

Reed, Deborah, and Maria Cancian. 2001. "Sources of Inequality: Measuring the Contributions of Income Sources to Rising Family Inequality." *Review of Income and Wealth* 47 (3): 321–333.

Ruggles, Patricia. 1990. *Drawing the Line: Alternative Poverty Measures and Their Implications for Public Policy.* Washington, DC: Urban Institute Press.

Scholz, John Karl, Robert Moffitt, and Benjamin Cowan. 2009. "Trends in Income Support." In *Changing Poverty, Changing Policies,* ed. Maria Cancian and Sheldon Danziger. New York: Russell Sage Press.

Schultz, T. Paul. 2002. "Why Governments Should Invest More to Educate Girls." *World Development* 30 (2): 207–225.

Smeeding, Timothy M. 2006. "Poor People in Rich Nations: The United States in Comparative Perspective." *Journal of Economic Perspectives* 20 (1): 69–90.

Stevens, Ann Huff. 2008. "Not So Fast: Long-Term Employment in the United States, 1969–2004. In *Laid Off, Laid Low: Political and Economic Consequences of Economic Insecurity,* ed. Katherine S. Newman, 38–55. New York: Columbia University Press.

Stevenson, Betsey, and Justin Wolfers. 2008. "Happiness Inequality in the United States." *Journal of Legal Studies* 37 (S2): S33–S79.

Stewart, James I. 2006. "Migration to the Agricultural Frontier and Wealth Accumulation, 1860–1870." *Explorations in Economic History* 43 (4): 547–577.

Strudler, Michael, Tom Petska, and Ryan Petska. 2005. "Further Analysis of the Distribution of Income and Taxes, 1979–2002." Internal Revenue Service Working Paper. Washington, DC: IRS. www.irs .gov/pub/irs-soi/04asastr.pdf.

Thomas, Adam, and Isabel Sawhill. 2005. "For Love *and* Money? The Impact of Family Structure on Family Income." *Future of Children* 15 (2): 57–74.

Treas, Judith, and Esther De Ruijter. 2008. "Earnings and Expenditures on Household Services in Married and Cohabiting Unions." *Journal of Marriage and Family* 70 (4): 796–805.

Williamson, Jeffrey G., and Peter H. Lindert. 1980. *American Inequality: A Macroeconomic History.* New York: Academic Press.

Ziliak, James P. 2008. "Filling the Poverty Gap, Then and Now." In *Frontiers of Family Economics,* ed. Peter Rupert, 1:39–114. Bingley, UK: Emerald Publishing Group.Index

INDEX

opments and demand shifts in, 128–29, 130–31, 132; unemployment linked to lower, 125–26; wage declines and, 4, 27, 32, 40–41, 42–43*f*, 81, 101; wars' impact on, 123–26; welfare reform and, 74. *See also* education level

Social Security program: employer contributions to, 108; included in total per person income, 54–55, 59; income inequality impacted by, 135–36; taxes for, 106*See also* government income

social welfare: current and potential trends in, 159–60; economic shocks due to changes in, 135–37; increase in, to reduce income inequality, 153–56, 155*t*; limits of, 156; Medicaid program in, 59, 106, 199n5, 201–2n1; noncash government benefits of, 54, 59, 107–9; reforms of, 62, 198n9; Scandinavian model of, 6

Squire, Lyn, 193n3

Stevens, Ann Huff, 113–14

Stewart, James I., 134

Strudler, Michael, 199n4

Supplementary Nutrition Assistance Program (Food Stamps), 59, 107, 135

Supplementary Security Income program, 54, 59. *See also* government income; Social Security program

taxes: current and potential trends in, 159–61; income inequality impacted by, 106–7, 109, 135–36, 153, 199n4. *See also* Earned Income Tax Credit (EITC)

technological developments: cur-

rent and potential trends in, 158–59, 161–62; economic shocks from, 118, 129–31, 138–39; public policy's role in, 135; return for education level and, 41; skill-level demand shifts linked to, 128–29, 130–31, 132

Temporary Assistance to Needy Family, 54, 59. *See also* government income

terrorism, 121

top-coding, 20–21, 194nn9–10

total-income distribution, defined, 17

total per person income: changes in inequality for all persons, 62–63, 64–65*t*, 66–67*f*, 68–70, 174–75*f*; changes in inequality in married-couple family units, 75, 78–79*f*, 79–81, 82–83*f*, 84, 180–81*f*; changes in inequality in single-headed family units, 71, 74–75, 76–77*f*, 178–79*f*; changes in inequality in single individuals, 70–71, 72–73*f*, 176–77*f*; changes summarized, 86; definition of, 54; effects of earnings and other income distribution on level and distribution of, 96–101, 98–99*t*, 184–85; elderly members' income included in, 55, 194n7; factors in, summarized, 87–88; family size adjustments in, 23–25, 25*t*, 53–54, 195n12; family size and composition changes vs. changes in distribution of, 101–5, 103*t*, 185; by family size and number of each family type, 91–95, 93*t*, 183; increase overall in, 2, 8–9, 29, 30–31*t*, 32, 33, 51, 63, 64–65*t*, 70, 81, 84–85, 101, 103–5.149; measurements of,

total per person income *(continued)*
53–55; noncash government benefits in, 107–9; race and, 84–85;
sources of, 53, 58–59, 60–61*f,* 62;
taxes considered in, 106–7, 109,
199n4; well-being as measured
by, 109–12. *See also* family units;
family-unit size

unemployment: data adjustments
for, 21; economic insecurity
despite decline of, 113–14; economic recession and increased,
117, 124–26; possible attitudinal
changes on, 161. *See also* employment; social welfare

Valetta, Robert G., 195n12
Vietnam War, 123
Violante, Giovanni L., 18, 194n6,
196n8, 200n13
voting, inequality in rate of, 6

wages: current and potential
trends in, 159–60; different
paths of annual earnings and,
47–49, 50*t,* 51; disease epidemics' impact on, 126–28, 200n14;
economic recession's impact on,
124–26; equalizing changes in,
as income inequality reduction
measure, 145, 146*t,* 147–50; skill-
level change's effects on, 118–19;
well-being impacted by declining, 4. *See also* annual earnings;
hours per week; wages per hour;
weeks per year
wages per hour: changes in
inequality of, 33, 34–39*f,* 40–42,
42–43*f,* 112, 166–71*f;* components
linked to, 28–29; educational

level linked to, 40–41, 42–43*f;*
race and gender factors in,
45–46. *See also* hours per week;
weeks per year
Wallace, Sally, 199n4
war: diplomatic negotiations and,
121–22; economic recession
after, 125–26; income inequality impacted by, 122–24, 138,
199–200n2; production factors
impacted by, 118–20
weeks per year: changes in
inequality in, 30–31*t,* 44–45;
components linked to, 28–29.
See also hours per week; wages
per hour
well-being: concerns about, 4; economic security as measure of,
113–14; family income linked to,
53–54; family size adjustments
to income and, 24–25; happiness
as measure of, 6, 112–13; income
as measure of, 109–12; perceptions of, 69–70, 105
women. *See* female workers; gender; male workers; work effort,
female
Wennemo, Tom, 193n2
work effort: incentive to reduce,
201n4; increased annual earnings due to, 51–52, 110; simulations of, 48–49, 50*t,* 51, 164–65,
166–71*f. See also* hours per week;
labor (human capital); labor-
force participation; wages per
hour; weeks per year
work effort, female: education
level linked to increased, 80–81;
increased hours of work, 2–3, 27;
increased income (and inequality) due to, 68, 75, 78–79*f,* 79–80,

Text:	10.75/15 Janson
Display:	Janson MT Pro
Compositor:	BookMatters, Berkeley
Indexer:	Margie Towery
Printer and binder:	Maple-Vail Book Manufacturing Group